T0195752

A New York MAILMAN Corporate Conspiracy Story

ROMEO STAMPS DEVINE

Order this book online at www.trafford.com
or email orders@trafford.com

Most Trafford titles are also available at major online book retailers.

Printed in the United States of America.

ISBN: 978-1-4907-3128-5 (sc)
ISBN: 978-1-4907-3129-2 (hc)
ISBN: 978-1-4907-3130-8 (e)

Library of Congress Control Number: 2014905218

Trafford rev. 03/28/2014

 www.trafford.com

North America & international
toll-free: 1 888 232 4444 (USA & Canada)
fax: 812 355 4082

M y name is Romeo Devine, and I was born on August 4, 1969, and I am the son of Damian and Jahtayshia Devine.

My father, Damian Devine, financially supported our family by being employed by the New York City Bus Disability Transit Authority. His first position that he held with that company was of a maintenance cleaner and his responsibilities were to clean out all the passenger trash that was left on the train as he had held that position for five straight years. Then my father Damian Sr. set out to another department in the company to advance his second position with the company by becoming a bus driver. That position consisted of opening and closing the bus doors to let all the passenger on and off the train safely. And his third and final position that he held was of a maintainer helper to assist the department head maintainer to repair the trains' necessary needed parts such as the brake shoes and many other parts.

And as for my mother, Jahtayshia Devine, she was once employed by a company called TriState Healthcare Plus in Richmond Hill, New York, where she served the company well for ten years of service between

1970 through 1980. Her responsibilities were to computer key in all the companies information that consisted of the TriState Healthcare Plus. And when my mother was employed there, she worked many thirty-five hours weeks plus and multiple hours of overtime. And I remember when my mother used to work so many hours of overtime that she used to come home from work totally exhausted from working late hours in the office so much that she would be too tired to go into her place of employment to work her regular shift. So after that went on for a while her employers at TriState Healthcare Plus eventually terminated my mother's employment with that company. And my mother was so depressed and stressed out from working many long hours of work; then she eventually had a nervous breakdown that caused her to have my family admitting her to a mental institution in 1981.

When I was about seven years old, my parents explained to me that when I was about eighteen months old, they had both begun to take notice that my head had started to rapidly grow big in size. They had to immediately rush me to the hospital at New York City County Medical Center, located in Brooklyn, New York. And that was where I met my first neurological surgeon, Dr. Alfonso Kingsley. My parents were informed that the doctor that was going to perform my operation turned out to be the chief of staff, and he was ranked no. 1 in the United States of America. And the doctors had discovered that I had water on the brain and that I had to be immediately rushed to the operating room. In all my three operations, it had always turned out a total success with Dr. Alfonso Kingsley that he had performed the first three operations, and my parents then thanked him for all that he had done to save my life with his medical expertise.

Despite all my personal problems that were going on with my family household, I had still managed to continually to get very good marks in school as my grade average was at 77 percent. And I also managed to build good friendship as well with my old school classmates, Alvin Wonders, who was also a burn victim; Calvin Cooley; and my ex-girlfriend, Hazel Ruiz. And back then, Hazel and I had really had taken a liking to each other to the point that we would be making out with each other by kissing each other's lips in the back of the classroom every chance we got. And then our classmate friend Alvin Wonders would then tell my Hazel that he also had a romantic interest in her, and I didn't like that a bit that he was trying to come between me and my girlfriend.

Then Hazel said that she couldn't believe that she had two guys attracted to her at the same damn time, and she also paused for a minute and said that since we were all good friends she would accept both Alvin and me as her boyfriends. And when I heard what she had decided on, I could not believe what she had been telling us as I then felt at that particular time that Alvin should have never disrespected me by asking my pretty fine girlfriend, Hazel, to be his girlfriend as well because he had already had known that the girl was mine. But since that was the choice that she had made, and the very fact that at the tender age of twelve years old that I did not want to lose her in a relationship, I knew that she was giving me no other choice but to have me share her with our other classmate, Alvin Wonders. Alvin and I would sometimes get into arguments about who was going to be making out with Hazel first as we would then begin to push and shove at each other and then Hazel and the teacher Ms. Felicia Ambreas would sometime have to intervene and step in between the two of us.

And from there, our teacher Ms. Ambreas would begin to ask us all just what had happened between the three of us. And then Hazel would go on to tell our classroom teacher that Alvin and I had been fighting over who was going to have the first kiss from her because she was both our girlfriend. And from then, she said that Alvin and I had better separated from each other so very quickly before she's to have us both report ourselves to the principal's office. And we did just want she had commanded us to do as she had then have me seated at the back of the classroom while Alvin had to be seated in the front near the teacher's desk where she had said that she would kept a very close and watchful eye on him as well as myself.

On July 5, 1983, when my brother Damian Jr. had gotten into a big argument with our father, it had turned into a big physical fight that had gotten to be a bloody battle as well. My father had told my brother that he had better stop hanging out with his friends with him missing out of his workplace of the construction company that he was employed with Construction Industries in order for him to pay his fair share of the household expenses. And when my father told my brother Damian Jr. to leave our family home if he was going to continue to neglect his financial responsibility he had toward paying his monthly rent of $400. And my brother Damian Jr. had told my father that, no, he wasn't going anywhere and had refused to leave our family's house while he pushed his chest into our father's chest. And then our father then ran up the stairs to get a lead pipe, and he told my brother to leave our family home once again. My brother bumped his chest into our father's once again and then our dad proceeded to hit my big brother Damian Jr. in the head with a lead pipe as my brother Damian Jr. began to bleed from the top of his head. And my mother then came downstairs to our family basement to tell my father to come back upstairs and stop all of the violence between himself and Damian Jr. And then my brother Damian Jr. began to get disoriented as he fell on the basement still well. And my mother came to see about him as she saw Damian Jr. bleeding from his head, and I told her to please call the ambulance so that I may take Damian Jr. to the New York General Hospital. And when the EMTs finally arrived at our family home, I put my brother's arm around my neck to support his balance as we were walking toward the EMT's service van as he began to collapse again with me than needing the assistance to bring him into the ambulance as the EMT workers begin to help me bring him to their ambulance service. Than Damian Jr. ask me to bring his Stoneet to the hospital because he said that he was feeling rather cold and I did just that and we were on our way to have him treated by a doctor. And Damian Jr. had to receive several stitches for his head injury and after that I brought him back to our family home where he rested in our family home and once he got up the next morning, he then proceed to apologize to our father for being disrespectful to him.

On September 5, 1983, my father Damian Sr. once tried to use his lead pipe again and this time it was my mother Jahtayshia he intended to strike her in her head with that same lead pipe that he struck my big brother Damian Jr. with. My mother then began to argue with my father over his constant drinking again of his favorite beer beverage which was Colt 45 Malt Liquor beer and she told him that he sleeps in separate rooms until he silver up from being drunk. And I told my mother that even though she did not like my father's heavy drinking of any alcohol beverage that she should stop trying to pick an argument with her husband while he was under the influence of alcohol. As my mother refuse to listen to my reasoning to just leave my father alone so that he may silver up. My mother than continue to argue with my dad and he himself begin to get very angry with my mom after she knocked over his glass of a beer mug that he was still drinking from with it still being half full of his favorite alcohol beer beverage. My father then got so mad with my mom that he again went into the family living room closet to get that same lead pipe once again, as I at first just watched and listened to them both verbally arguing and then I watched my father grabbed my mother from behind and raised up his hand with the lead pipe in his right hand and then I immediately ran up behind him, snatched up the pipe out of his hand in order to stop him from striking my mother in the head. Then I pushed him back from me and then he went into the kitchen cabinet draw, and he had pulled out a small steak knife to me as if he was going to hurt me. Then in order to protect myself, I then struck him in his head and then he then dropped the knife and began bleeding from his head, and he was still angry that I had done that so much that he grabbed me by the throat, trying to choke me out, and then I got him off me and then began to slam his head underneath the kitchen cabinets. And after all that was over, I began to help my father by cleaning him up his head with paper towel and a wash cloth.

And later that same evening, I went to check on my mother to see just how she was doing after all that commotion that had happened between her and my father and seemed to be understandably quite shaken up by the whole ordeal, and I was just trying to make her as calm and comfortable as I possibly could.

In the summer of July of 1982, my father had gotten so depressed because of my mother's nervous breakdown that he started back drinking alcohol of a new beverage of red wine this time around.

My father said that he was really feeling depressed because of mom's nervous breakdown that caused her to lose her employment with the TriSate Healthcare Plus. And then that left him to be the sole provider for our family. My dad said that it was very difficult to financially support our family with only one parent being able to financially pay for our family monthly mortgage and household bills. My father often complained that he had no extra spending money for himself after he had paid all our family household bills to the point that he told my mom after she was fully recovered for her nervous breakdown that he was going to be in Brownville Brooklyn, New York, for just a few days. And my family and I waited to her back from my father after he was gone from the home about a week as my mother that call his cousin Louis house to see if he had seen my dad. And it turned out to be that my dad was in fact visiting our cousin Louis, and he complained to my mother that he was tired of having to be the only parent that was to be the only one to be financially responsible for our entire family and that his entire paycheck only went toward our family bills, leaving him with no pocket money for himself to spend as he pleases. He stayed away from our family home for the entire winter months, leaving us with no money to pay for the food a heating. My mother and brother and I were so cold that whenever we would talk or breathe, we could see our own breath as we talk as in making smoke signals. My mother then decided to take my father to family court for spousal and child support, and the judge awarded my mother 95 percent of my father's paycheck to be pulled from my his weekly income. After he found out from his employer at the New York City Bus Disability Transit Authority that through the family courts that 95 percent of his wages were going to be awarded directly to his wife and children for family support, he told me that he was in total shock how my mother did it once he arrived back home, but as I told him that he should have never abandoned his family in the first place as when he did.

In the very year of 1983, when my older brother Damian Devine Jr. was then just twenty years old, he then became a father by his then girlfriend who was named Dorthy Blessings as they were then both so very happy together for only about a few months' time in the years of 1983 after the very birth of my then infant nephew who was named Rashad Devine because of my big brother then consisted hanging out with his long-time male friend whose name is Tyrone Gracey as he used to always leaves his child mother, and their very own child in our then family household bedroom, which is located in the Astoria, Queens, New York area as it was then known to our very own family that my big brother was also a big drug user who had been so very paranoid of his then substance drug abuse that our own father Damian Devine Sr. told me that one day in the month of the mid-July season of 1983 when my big brother Damian

Devine Jr. had then came into our then family Astoria, Queens New York household as he had then been sweating a whole lot as our dad had then asked him just what happen to him to the point to where he had then ran his very own self home? And from there my big brother Damian Jr. and then said that he had then been thinking that someone had then been chasing him as he had then also said that he had then been running so very fast that the guy that he had then thought than had been chasing right after him just right out of his very own shoes and from there my dad Damian Sr. had then told me that he him very own self had then began to start to then laughing at him as his oldest son then being in the street just acting so very crazy. Then on January 10, of the same year of 1983 as it was then the very time when my very own older brother Damian Devine had then became a father to his son who was then name Rashad Devine by his daddy and his mother whose name is Dorthy Blessing as they were then both so very happy back in the good old days at least for a few month back then. And from there my brother Damian Jr. child mother Dorthy Blessing had then expected her baby daddy to then pay his then fair share of his part of his then weekly supportive child support payment on a voluntary bases as he had then refuse to then to then be doing so just as he had then been asked to then do as I had then heard about it when he had then told her to then go down to the New York City Public Assistant child welfare services program to then applied herself and there then baby boy who was then my nephew who was then name Rashad Devine. And then very shortly after that when the child welfare service had then started to then questioning my brother Damian Jr. child mother Dorthy Blessings about where were then the where about of her child father?

And from there, my then sister-in-law, whose name is Dorthy Blessings then finally told my brother that the child welfare system was then looking for him to pay his then weekly child support payment for there then young son Rashad Devine as they had then had to then attend a meeting with Public Assistant Administration as he had then told there office that he was only then working part-time for twenty hours a work week. And so then the Public Assistance Administration had begun docking his then weekly payment wages for his child support payments that was to be awarded to his child mother Dorthy Blessing weekly child support payment.

Growing up my parents never allowed me to learn how to ride a bicycle that was until I was fourteen years of age because they were too afraid of me to possibly have a hard fall on my head to hit the ground. They were very overly protective of me, trying their best not to let me damage my head by trying to avoid any type of head trauma because they thought that a heavy blow to my head might end my life because of my medical condition of me to have water on the brain. And because of that, I knew of my parents fear of me to possibly have a very bad fall I was kind of skeptical about attempting to even try to ride a bike. But eventually, soon after that I had finally mustered up enough courage to at least give it a good try. And I did with the assistants of my two neighborhood friends whose names are Corey Suthers and Alan Anderson who live across the street from my family home. As I was desperately trying to overcome my fear of falling by attempting several times to keep my balance, and I would wound up crashing into cars that were already park near the sidewalk as I had gotten really discourage to the point that I had decided not to even further pursue to try to learn how to ride a bike because I was so embrace at my age of fourteen years old to have a late start to try to learn how to ride a bike when the other kids on the block had already be taught when they were much younger in age.

In the spring of 1983, my older brother Damian Jr. had a serious drug abuse problem of using the illegal drugs of crack cocaine. And his drug addiction problems had gotten so bad that he used to steal from our family home whenever and whatever he could get his hands on to sell for a profit on the streets in order to support his drug addiction.

And as for myself, I had totally given up on how to ride a bicycle and had another opportunity to learn how to drive my first used car, which was given to me as a kind gift for my eighteenth birth in 1987 by my family's former next-door neighbor whose name was Jeffery Jacobs, who was also married to his wife, Lilian Jacobs, of five years. And soon after that I had decided to go down to the Department of Motor Vehicles to apply for a learner's permit, and I did just that and was able to pass my written test score of 80 percent average. And I had come back home to tell my family of my good news of me being able to pass my driver ed written test with a high grade score. That was good enough for me to finally be able to take actually on-road driver's test. And my family congratulated me on my success and wished me lots of good luck on my very next step, which was the driving test. My mother got so excited about me soon to be able to take my on-road driving test that she immediately informed her younger brother Solomon Gilbert who was my uncle that was ten years my senior to teach me how to drive my used car that I had received from next-door neighbors Jeffery and Lilian. But my used car needed a whole lot of expensive repairs to be put on the road. I may legally be able to drive it, but it only ended up to be able to sit in my family driveway for about an entire year. Than when the cold winter finally arrived that year that my brother Damian Jr. was still strung out on heavy drugs sleeping in his friend Tyrone Gracey's truck that was park on our family block of 212th Place. And then once day, he saw me in the street, and he asked me just whose car was that in our family's driveway, and I told him that it was my used car that was given to me as a gift from the neighbors Mr. and Mrs. Jeffery and Lilian Jacobs.

And from there since I had a used car to practice on the road, I was planning to get my license to learn how to drive my very first car ever. And my brother said that was great news for me. And Damian Jr. was not still decided that he wanted to quit his drug habit just yet as he still remained addicted to drugs while still sleeping in his different vehicles, which included my very own that I had parked in my family's driveway. That was only until our father found out what my brother was up to sleeping in my used car that my father said that he had a coworker friend that was looking for some car parts for his very own vehicle, and when he saw my old rusted car just sitting there, he then asked my dad if my car was for sell, and my father told him that it belonged to a son, which was me, and then he told him that he would ask me if I had wanted to sell the car instead of just to have it sit and rot. And I told my dad to tell his coworker friend whose name was Derick Chasey that he had a deal that I was in fact willing to sell my used car for a profitable fee of a $100. Then the following week he came by with a toll trunk to take the car away. And after that was all over, my father congratulated on my car sell with him also having to say that my brother Damian Jr. had to now find somewhere else to sleep instead of him sleeping in my car in the driveway. And soon after that, Damian Jr. finally decided to come in from the cold and prepare himself to go for a drug abuse rehabilitation program called "A Fresh Start in Life."

On July 31, 1987, as I had gotten place underneath punishment by my mother because I had come inside our family home thirty minutes late after my curfew of 12:00 AM, and she had also locked me out of the house until my father was to come home while I was riding around with my then high school friends whose names were Marcus and Tomas Benson, who had also had their brother inside their family car. I really lost track of the time as I also tried to call her from my friend's house, but she just kept on hanging up the phone on me as she knew it was me who had been calling the house for her to please let me inside our family's home. And when my dad finally arrived at our family's house, my mother finally decided to let me in the house to let both she and my dad handle my punishment for me being late to come in the house on time. And from there, I then tried to explain to my father the reason why I was late to come into the house by 12:00 AM. It was because I did not own a wristwatch to keep track of the time of my curfew so that I would know when it had reached the midnight hour for me to come inside for the evening. My mother said that was in fact a very poor excuse. That I should have told my friends that I had to be home at midnight, and I was told that I was only allowed to go back in forth to the grocery store whenever I was told to do so and to also be allowed to sit in our family's backyard deck area. And so the next morning, after we had all gotten up for breakfast, my mother then once again reminded me that I was on punishment to stay inside our family's home for an entire two weeks. And I had gotten so very rebelliously upset of my mother placing me underneath her punishment of me to stay in the house for weeks at a time that I had left the house anyway as I was not used to being stuck in the house for that long period of time in the summer months, And as I was walking in the streets at seventeen years old, I then met an older woman whose name was Montanique Haze.

And from there, we introduced ourselves to each other, and then she invited me on top of her apartment building's roof top to have an intimate sexual encounter with her, and I remember that I was so very excited because it was my very first time. It had been such a wonderful experience for me. And after that, we went inside her apartment. I also met her mother as I then had the privilege of meeting her mother, Ms. Anna May Haze. Then afterward, I knew that I had no other place to stay but my family's home with my parents and brother, so I then went back home. And when I arrived back into my family's house, my parents were sitting right there on our family's couch, just rightfully reprimanding me that I was living in their house, and that if I did not want to be shifted off to a border school for all boys where I would have to share everything, with the exception of food, drinks, and clothing with many of homeless children, then I'd better not disobey and run away ever again, trying to avoid my punishment that was to be placed on me.

And so from there, I still had to stay in the house for two whole weeks as well as to clean the entire house. When my big brother Damian Jr. had come in the house, he asked me just where the hell had I'd been for all those many hours having our family all worried about me. And then I explained to him that I realized that I was totally wrong for sneaking out of the house, with me trying to be disrespectful to our mother as I had felt so very sorry that I did such a terrible thing. And Damian Jr. asked me just where did I go to for all that long period of time as he said that he heard from our mom and dad that I didn't come home until 10:00 PM. And I then I told him that when I was just walking in our family's neighborhood of Astoria New York where I had met an older woman whose name was Montanique Haze. And from there, Damian Jr. then asked me just how old was this older woman. And I told him that she was thirty-seven years old, twenty years my senior, and he began laughing at me, saying that I knew that I was still a minor and that I had no business at all to leave the house disobeying our mother's punishment for me, and that it was time for me to go to bed as he said good-bye while still laughing at me.

And after my two-week punishment was finally over, I then found myself missing the good company of my newfound hometown friend Montanique Haze. I decided to give her a call. And when she picked up the phone, she said, "Hello, Romeo, where the heck have you been for the past couple of weeks?" I informed her that I had been put on punishment for two weeks because I had come in late past my curfew time that was given to me by my mother. And then Montanique said that was in fact was okay with her and that she had wanted to still have me come over her house to pay her a visit. I told her yes, and that I was on my way over, and she then said that she would be waiting up until I was to get there. And from there, as I was on my way to go see my friend Montanique, my uncle Solomon then asked me where exactly was I headed off to, and I told him that when I was underneath punishment from his older sister/ my mother. I then left the house without her giving me the permission to do so as I had been so wrongfully rebellious against her and had started walking outside around our family's neighborhood in Astoria, New York, where I then met my new friend, Montanique Haze. And then my uncle Solomon then asked me just what I know about my new friend. And I then proceeded to tell him that she was a friendly woman who also had a drug abuse problem, and then my uncle Solomon said that he had wanted to come along with me to meet my new friend. And when we both arrived there, I then introduced my friend, Montanique Haze, to my uncle Solomon as they said hello to each another. And from there, we all went back on the rooftop and then began to light up her drug of choice, which was Crack Cocaine. From there my uncle Solomon asked Montanique if could have some of her drugs, and she decided to share some with him. He also asked her for sex, and Montanique told him no. That she was not interested in him at all. And then shortly after that, my uncle and I then left to go back home. And once Uncle Solomon and I arrived back into my family's home, I then decided to give Montanique a call. When she answered her phone, she then informed me that she no longer wanted to see me again and that she had just wanted to stay with the good company of herself and her mother.

And once I finally graduated from Thomas Edison High School in Jamaica, New York, in June 18th of 1988, I then decided to look for employment, but I was not yet sure what type of job I would what to do. So then I decided to try to get a job in the fast-food industry at Queens, New York, Fried Chicken Restaurant. And so I went inside the company to fill out an application with the company's manager whose name was Steven Golden. And from there, he then interviewed me and said that he would possibly get back to me. And about a week later, I did in fact heard back from the Queens, New York, Fried Chicken Restaurant company, and the manager did in fact informed me that, yes, I had gotten the job. I remember that I was so very much happy to have my very first job.

So when I finally arrived at my then new job at the fast-food restaurant of Queen's Fried Chicken, my responsibilities were to place the uncooked chicken into the eleven herbs and spices of mild and spicy seasoning blend and then fry them all. And all the chicken had come out deliciously good as it had come out properly and completely cooked, and next, I was trying to learn just how to prepare the instant mashed potatoes mix. And I mistakenly added too much water into the company food mixer bowl as I also added not enough of the instant potatoes mix as it came out too soupy, and it had to be poured out in the sink to start over because I had not been paying attention to my instruction that were given to me as the QUEEN store manager hand to make a brand-new fresh batch of instant potatoes mix. And I became very discouraged with myself but kept trying to learn the company the way of properly preparing the food for the public. And when I was continuing to cook, I kept getting pop by the cooking oil grease while I was trying also to maintain my footing balance for the slippery floor. I became very annoyed with myself. And that job only lasted for two days until the restaurant manager Steven Golden spoke to me that he did not think that the fast-food business was the right type of job for me to be employed in and I totally agreed with him so my employment with the Queen's Friend Chicken company had been immediate terminated.

So after working at the fast-food restaurant industry of Queens Fried Chicken in September of the year 1988 that was located in Jamaica, New York, I was desperately trying to find a brand-new place of employment that would be more suitable for me than the last one. And my mother had known just how worried and concerned I was about wanting to find the right type of job for me. That was only until she found out about an employment agency that specialized in helping disable persons to find proper employment for themselves. And my mother Jahtayshia saw that there was in fact an employment agency that indeed specialized in finding employment for people with disabilities that went by the name the Employer of Institute. That was a job training and employment placement, and this particular job placement industry secured all three of my place of employment that I held.

In October 10, 1988, the employment agency then assigned me to be trained for a mailroom position at the Internal Resolution Service as a mail clerk trainee in Midtown Manhattan where my employment agency then counselor whose was Carla Smithers brought me in for an interview to meet the company mailroom supervisor whose name was Connie

Titus. And my interview went so very well that I had been very eager to begin my job training in the mailroom services. And my responsibilities was just to sort out all of the inter-office, in-coming and outgoing mail of the company, and making distribution mail runs to and from the post office and the internal company's offices as well. And I had done such a good job that the mailroom supervisor Connie informed my then job placement counselor Carla Smithers that I was now ready to be placed at a full-time position in another company.

And from there my then employment placement counselor Carla Smithers found me my first full-time employment position which was with a Corporate Law Firm who goes by the name of O'Connor Dash, Sapp & Marshall. And my counselor Carla brought me in for a job interview with the Mailroom Center Supervisor whose name was Jose Perez and he explain the job responsibilities that were required to be perform such as to do multiple mail deliveries of interoffice, post office and sorting of the mail as well. And then Jose ask me about how good do I think that I would be able to perform my responsibilities working in the Mailroom Center if I was to be hired for the full-time position, as I replied that I would be of great service to the company. And about a week later, my counselor Carla informed me that the company that I applied for a mail clerk position had accepted me as a new employee, and that I was to start right away the following day. And from there, I told her, "Thank you so very much for helping me to find a good full-time place of employment."

And in happier times in August of 1990, my parents decided to become foster parents of two little girls whose name are Fatima Devine, who came into the family when she was only seven months old, and Tameka Devine, who was only three years old when she also arrived in our family. And as for me, I was so very much delighted to have two brand-new foster little sisters. And when the adoption had been finally finalized, meaning that my two foster sisters, Tameka and Fatima Devine, were my official stepsisters who I adored them so very much as official new members of my family. And as I watched them grow up, I remember when my youngest stepsister Fatima graduated from her kindergarten school as my family and I attended her class ceremony of 1995. We were all so very proud of her accomplishments. And after the graduation of her ceremony was over the family, we then decided to stand outside to get a breath of fresh air. We had all also taken family photographs of the every special event as I had also been so very proud of my youngest sister Fatima's accomplishments so very much that I then decided to give her a hi-five slap on the hand, and I did just that as I then noticed that she bowed her head down to floor just like my parents Jahtayshia and Damian Sr. did within their own paranoia selves.

And then I had not started getting back involved with another woman until September 7 of the year 1990. I saw on a television that advertised a telephone chat line of a dating service called the Dating Personals, where I eventually got connected to a much older woman whose name she first said was Candy. We enjoyed multiple conversations we had together by phone. And then the woman who claimed her name to be Candy began talking all so very sexily and sweetly to me, and she was really making all so good impression of herself. And about a week later, we then decided to meet each other at her family's home. And when I arrived, I then rang Candy's door bell, and she answered it with a very lovely and sexy smile on her face and said hello as she grabbed me by my shirt and belt buckle to pull me inside her family's home to give me a very warm and huge hug and sweet and passionate kiss. She then introduced me to her young children whose name was Stacey Cuzack, her daughter, who was thirteen years old, and her son, who was seven years old whose name was Craige Cuzack. And then we first sat around the house just enjoying each other's company, watching television until shortly. After that, Candy and I went upstairs to her bedroom and closed the bedroom door for some privacy time, away from the kids so we could began to get much more better acquainted with each other. After an hour pass by, as her kids started saying that they were getting very much hungry and that they were ready to eat their dinner, she then made a very delicious dinner of spaghetti and meat balls.

Then after dinner was all over, I then took the liberty to wash the dishes and clean up the kitchen, with me wanting to show my appreciation of the wonderful meal that was prepared for all of us. And afterward, the kids wanted to get to know me a whole lot better as they asked me my full name. I told them that it was Romeo Devine, and then they asked me just how old I was, and I said that I was in fact twenty years old at the time. From there I complimented my then girlfriend Candy on just how well mannered her two children were as she replied that she takes a real good pride in raising them that way. And when her children kept on hearing me referring to their mother to keep calling her Candy, they then told me that wasn't their mother's real name. I couldn't believe what they were saying to me. So I then asked their mother, "Well there, Ms. Candy, just what is your real name I wonder. Hmmm?" And she finally told me the truth that her name was Stacey Cuzak, and I asked her just why she told me that her name was in fact Candy as she then explained that whenever she had been on the Quest chateline Personals she decided to use that name as her nickname. So from there I was just kidding around with Stacey when I shook her hand, saying that it was nice to meet the real you as she laughed, "Hahaha," and I really enjoyed us to spend so much time together in those days.

And when I got back home to my family, I immediately informed my mother and father that I was then involved with my then new lady friend whose name was Stacey Cuzak in Fort Green, Brooklyn, New York. My parents then became very much concerned with me having to traveling in any Brooklyn, New York, neighborhood as my father then told me that I better be very careful while I was to travel in that very dangerous area as he was fully aware of that fact he grew up there and he witnessed a lot of crime that took place there. From there, my mother then asked me just how old my new lady friend was, and I told her that she was thirty seven years old at that particular time as both my parents told me that lady was much too old for me to be involved with in an intimate sexual relationship. But I was a hardworking adult by that time, and even if my family did not approve of me dating a much older woman, I decided that I was going to still be involved with my lady friend Stacey Cuzak as much as I wanted to do so just as long as it pleases me no matter what anyone else thought about it. They still complained that the woman was much older than me, fourteen years my senior, way too much experience than me. They also went on saying that Stacey would probably try to con me out of my money, but I refused to listen to what they were saying to me.

On November 14, 1990, Stacey then told me that she was two months pregnant with my child, and at first, I was all so very much happy to hear that news as I sat with her all night as we were talking about our soon-to-be-born child. And I even offered to take Stacey to some of her prenatal care doctor's visits, but she then told me that her best friend Ella Griffin had a car and that the friend already offered to take her to all of her appointments. I then thought that was very strange that she did not want me to attend any of them with her, Stacey then told me that since she and I were to have a child of our very own together, she took it upon herself to try to find out just how much was my weekly net salary pay was that I was bringing home, and then she told me the exact money amount as she'd been totally correct having full knowledge of my take-home pay. I then told Stacey that she absolutely no right to go behind my back with her pretending to be some sort of a business person that was trying to get my financial situation information calling my place of employment, trying to find out my take-home pay after taxes. Stacey then began to argue with me over the phone that since we were to have a child together, she felt that she the preparental rights to personally investigate my weekly earning herself.

Then on December 15, 1990, Stacey then told me that she decided to get an abortion to terminate the pregnancy, and she asked me to finance the procedure as she then asked me for some money in the amount of $250. I told her that I would do that for her. I then offered to take her to the abortion clinic to help her take care of matters, and she refused me again, letting me know that her friend Ella who I never even met before was going to take her there. And then later that same evening, after I got back home from my workday, I immediately called Stacey to see if she in fact went through the abortion procedure, and she blatantly told me that, no, she did not go down to the clinic to finalize the abortion procedures. And from there, I asked her just what she did with the $250 that I gave her, and she said that she went shopping with my money. So I then said to her why did she even ask me to pay for the abortion procedure if she was going to go through with it and what did she do with my hard-earned money? Stacey told me that she went shopping with my money and that she didn't spend for our soon-to-be-born newborn baby, but she spent the money on herself.

After all of that what was going on with Stacey, I then ended our intimate relationship for at less until two months before the baby was due to be born in the world. I then decided to stay away from Stacey until it was getting close to see my child to be placed in my arms. On February fourteenth of 1991, I then decided to go back to Fort Green, Brooklyn, New York, to find out about what was going on with Stacey and our baby as I thought that she was still pregnant with my child. But when I rang her door bell, she then came to her window and saw that it was me, and she was totally surprised to see me that night. She asked me just where I'd been all of that long time that I decided to stay away. And I told her that I was home with my parents. I then asked her how she was feeling because it was almost time for our baby to be coming in this world. And then she then told me that she already gave birth to our baby as he was born premature at seven months old, and it was a boy, but that I came by at a very bad time because she met another man in her family's house and that I had to stop by the following week to meet our baby boy for the very first time. I said to her that it would be fine and that I would see her and our child next week. And when a week time passed by, I came back to Stacey's house to meet our baby boy as I felt so very proud to be holding our son for the very first time. As mother, father, and child were all sitting together, she told me that the baby's name was Mark Cuzack. And I asked her just why his last name was the same as her husband/her children's father? And she told me because I was not around for the child's actual birthdate that she then let her husband put on the childbirth's certificate, and I found that to be all so very much strange that she did that. Shortly after that, I told her that I would start to pay her child's support payment on a weekly basis.

So from there, I went back home to my family, and I told them the good news that my lady friend Stacey informed me that she gave birth to our baby boy and that his name was Mark Cuzack. And then my mom and dad asked me if I was sure that the baby was actually mine. And at that particular time, I believed that the baby was really mine, but my parents were so very suspicious of my situation. My mother then asked me, "Well, son, just when can Dad and I get to meet the little boy?" And I then told my mother and father that I had to check with little baby Mark's mother to see when it would be a good time for our whole family to meet my infant baby boy as I then told them that I would have to get back to them and let them know just what time would be good for Stacey to bring the baby boy to meet his grandparents for the very first time.

And from there, I Immediately went to my room to call Stacey back to tell her that I informed my parents about the good news concerning our baby being born as I also asked her just when did she think that she would be able to bring the little baby Mark by so that he could meet his family in Astoria, Queens, New York. And Stacey then asked me if I had any of family in the Brooklyn, New York, area where she would not have to travel so very far with the baby. And I told her, yes, that my grandmother also live in the nearby neighborhood area of Prospect Park Brooklyn New York as Stacey then agreed to bring the baby boy little Mark there to have him meet my side of my family. I then ask her to put our baby ear to the telephone so that he could hear his daddy voice as he just sounded so very cute as he was to try to call me dada. So after I then finish my conversation with us trying to make preparations when we could all finally me up with each other I went back to tell my parents that my child's mother Stacey did not want to have to travel so very far to bring the baby by to meet my family as she also had known as I told her that I also family in Brooklyn New York where my grandmother live in a nearby town in Prospect Park NEW YORK.

So my parents both agreed that in fact we all were on our way to the Brooklyn, New York, area to meet baby Mark Cuzack for the very first time as my parents were all so very much excited to finally meet the little boy. And then my parents and I then called a taxi cab company to pick us all up to head to my grandmother's house, and we were on our way. When we finally arrived to my grandmother's apartment, she herself was so very excited to finally have a great-grandson from me that she prepared a special family dinner for all of us to feast on. I then asked my grandmother whose name was Alicia Gilbert if I could use her telephone to call my child mother's Stacey, and she told me that of course that would be fine for me to do so, and then when I spoke to my child's mother, I told her that I finally arrived in Brooklyn at my other family's home so she could bring the child by my family, and she and I said that she would be over as soon as possible. I said that I would see them both when when they get there.

And when Stacey and baby Mark finally arrived, I introduced them both to my family as they all welcomed them with open arms for the very first time, trying to make them feel all right at home. So after everyone got comfortable, I wanted to then bond with my new family by having them to take some family portraits with me, but to my very much surprise, the woman that was claiming to be my son's mother refused to do show. And from there, my family got so very suspicious of Stacey, leaving us all to wonder why she did not want to take any pictures with me and the child that she claimed to be ours. I then took several pictures with baby Mark with my parents and Grandma as we all enjoyed a pretty discrete conversation and time with Stacey and little baby Mark as I also fed him a bottle of juice drink as well as having to change his pamper. And my grandmother then offered to fix Stacey a plate of food as little baby Mark just finished his baby bottle of milk. His mother then said that it was getting very late and that she was ready to go back to her family's home in Fort Green Brooklyn, New York. And I then told her that I would call her a taxi cab to take her and the baby home.

On November 1, through the fifteen in 1990, I was to be yet again hospitalized because I had another serious operation of having my new VP hunt plastic tubing vile replacement to be installed into my head that also ran all the way down to my abdomen by my second neurological surgeon, Doctor Roman Wheaters. My VP Shunt that to be implanted inside of me was to drain out the excess water that had always been building up in my head into my urine stream, as I had always have the urge to use the bathroom to release my urine more than the average person. And while I was in the hospital at Queens General, my then girlfriend Stacey paid me a visited to see just how I was recovering from my major surgery as she gave me a very warm huge and a kiss as she sat down with me and asked me just how was I feeling. And I told her that I felt so much better to have the excess water to be strained from my head into my urine steam with the doctors having to replace my VP Shunt tubing internally. And Stacey was so very happy that I survived from my very major operation, and from there, I then asked her just how our little baby boy Mark was doing, and she said that he was doing fine as she told me that she left him with her sister while she was visiting with me while I was in the hospital.

Shortly after that, my parents also came to visit me in the hospital while Stacey was still inside with me. My mother got so very disgusted with my then girlfriend about how she was desperately trying to trap me with a baby that she said was not even my very own child. And from there, the two of them had a standoff with me having to step in between the both of them to get them separated from each other as my father took a hold of my mother and I took a hold of Stacey as we had to separate the both of them in order to keep the peace between the two of them as it became a hostile moment. So my mother told Stacey that she should have the damn decency to excuse herself as she visited with her son. And Stacey agreed to what my mother wanted as she then waited until my parents was over as she told me that she was going to be in the kitchen cafeteria until they both left for the evening. I thanked her for being so very understanding of the unexpected situation as I had in no way of knowing that my mother would react in such a protective manner.

And while my parents were visiting, they asked me just how I was recovering for my major surgery. I told them that I was just trying to get plenty of rest. I also told my mom that she should not treat Stacey in a bad way, and my mother said that she did not want to see that much older woman trying to play me or our family like a damn fool with her wanting me to claim a baby that was probably not even my very own. And I totally understood how both my parents felt about my then situation as I begged my mother to please not to cause a scene in the hospital with Stacey and for the three of us to just enjoy. And then Stacey came back from the cafeteria when my parents were still in the room. They told me that they were on their way out to head back home and that they would call me the very next day to see just how I was doing, and I gave both my parents a big kiss and a hug as we said our good-byes for that time. And as my parents were on the way out of the door, my mother told Stacey not to visit with her son too much longer as it was very important that I got plenty of rest, and Stacey told my mother that she would be leaving from the hospital shortly. And at that time, I felt that my mother should have been much more civil toward Stacey at the very least while I was still in the hospital recovering from major surgery. And after my parents left, Stacey told me that she did not like my mother's negative attitude toward her as she also went on to say to me that as two grown women, my mother should treat her in a much more civilized manner. Then Stacey told me not to stress myself out about want just happened to herself and my mom and that I should just get plenty of rest so that I could build up my strength so we could get back into some serious lovemaking again. I said that I could hardly wait until the hospital release me so that I may intimately please her in every way possible.

When we finally returned back home in Astoria, Queens, New York, from my grandmother's apartment in Prospect Park in Brooklyn, New York, we were all so very much exhausted from our two-hour taxi cab ride. We all decided to just go to bed for the rest of the evening as my parents told me that we all would talk about myself and the baby the very next day in the afternoon after lunch as I said that I would be okay with that as I said to both of them to have a good night's rest. They responded that I should do the same thing. So once the very next afternoon arrived, both of my parents and I sat down to talk about my alleged son whose name was supposed to be name Mark Cuzack as they told me that the baby was so very cute and cuddly, but they still did not believe that a woman who was fourteen years older than me would have a baby by such a younger man like myself. They believe that my then girlfriend Stacey the baby whose name she was claiming to be my own the baby by another man and that the child might not be mine. Then my mother and father then said that Stacey was still legally married but separated from her husband whose name was Craige Cuzack, that it was a strong possibility that the child could be very much his baby boy rather than my very own. And my parents also said that the fact Stacey and her husband were legally separated from their still ongoing marriage, that whenever I was not around, they still could have been having sexually relations with each other without me knowing about it or that the child could even be a relative of hers and that she was so very desperate to claim me as little baby Mark Cuzack's father to try to get me to pay her child-support payments. She even went behind my back to call my employer at the corporate law O'Conner, Sapp, Dash & Marshall where I worked to find out my weekly wages.

And I thought that there was some truth to what my parents were saying about me not possibly being baby' Mark's father. I also decided that the only way for me to be certain whether or not Stacey was telling me the truth about the baby was to make a family court case of the matter to file for a paternity test to be performed on myself and the little baby boy whose name was claimed to be Mark Cuzack by his supposed mother Stacey. So once I received the family court summons to petition Stacey to appear in the family court, I went back home to inform my own family about what I was going to do concerning me wanting to have a paternity test done on myself and the little baby boy that Stacey brought into our family lives, claiming that I was the father. And my oldest uncle Ronald Gilbert was visiting my family home to see how everyone was doing as I explained that I wasn't doing all so well with the woman that I was involved with claiming that I fathered a child from her. And I asked my uncle Ronald if he would do me a very big favor to help me serve a family court summons to my now ex-girlfriend Stacey Cuzak along with us having to be companied by two New York City police officers.

And my uncle agreed that in fact he would help me with serving Stacey the summons for her to appear in the Queens Family Courts. From there my uncle and I arrived in Stacey's neighborhood present in Fort Green Brooklyn as we informed the officers that I had a family court summon to be served of a woman who was claiming that I fathered a child from her. And then my uncle Ronald and I were on our way to Stacey house to serve her the summons. And we got into the police officer's car to head to Stacey's family home, and when we got there, she answered her door bell as she saw me standing there with two cops along with my uncle to be the one who actually was serving her the summons. She began to curse us all out to ask the question what the hell did I bring these police officers around her family's house, for disturbing her for. She told me directly how I could send these cops to her house to serve her with those papers. She also told me that I could kiss her fat black ass. And when the two police officer witnessed everything that was going on right in front of their very own eyes to see the response that I was receiving from my ex-girlfriend, they began to laugh and said that I sure had a very wild woman to deal with. They also wished me good luck in finding out the truth about the paternity of the baby boy that was in question, and they also had driven us back to the Fort Green, New York, subway station so there wouldn't be any physical confrontation from me and her.

So as I was given a family court appointed attorney to represent me in my paternity case whose name was Ralph Chateman, I then spoke to him and told him my situation of my ex-girlfriend whose name was Stacey Cuzak claiming that I fathered a new born baby boy from her. She also had gone so far as to finding out from my then employer at O'Conner,

Sapp, Dash & Marshall, a corporate law firm just how much money I was bringing home after taxes. And the attorney informed me that I needed to find legal written documentation of proof of a birth in order to pursue my paternity case any further as he also said that he would also check my ex-girlfriend medical records as well. But he also had question me about just why I wanted to pursue the matter of paternity of a child that might not even be my own as he also claimed that must men wouldn't be bothered to do the same as myself. And I explained to him that I did not want a child that could possibly be mine out in the world without me knowing that we could be family to one other because I came from a family whose always there for their children to be a part of our family lives.

And from there, I was off to find out the real truth of the matter about the birth of little baby Mark Cuzack by visiting the hospital where Stacey said that she gave birth to him on April 1, 1991, in Brookdale Hospital in Brooklyn, New York. And when I finally arrived there, I asked a nurse if she could help me find the hospital medical records department, and she gladly pointed me in the right direction as she even introduced me to the supervisor to help me find whatever I needed. So I then spoke to the medical record supervisor whose name was Gladess Wittworth to help me get some information on my ex-girlfriend whose name was Stacey Cuzak, to see if there was any record of her giving birth of a baby boy on April 1, 1991. And as the medical record departmental supervisor was looking for any birth record of my ex-girlfriend Stacey to have given a birth in the year of 1991, she told me that there was no records of the woman in question to have any given any birth in that year. I then thanked the medical record supervisor for being so very much understanding of my family court issue of me trying to establish a birth record of a woman who claimed that I in fact fathered a child from her.

I then went back to my family home in Astoria, Queens, New York, to let my family know that I found out from the hospital where Stacey claimed that she gave birth to our alleged son that they had no written record of the birth in question. And after I informed my parents what I found out that Stacey wasn't being truthful about the birth of the little baby Mark as I also immediately had given her a call at her house shortly after I got home. And when I spoke to her, I then asked her just how could she lie to me about the birth of the baby as I told her that I went to visit the Brookdale Hospital in in the Brooklyn New York area, and I told her that I went to the medical record departmental supervisor to ask her if there was any record of a woman whose name was Stacey Cruzack to have given birth on April 1 in 1991. And I was told, no, that there wasn't any record at all of her to have given birth in that same year. And Stacey told me that she gave me that false information on purpose because she said that she knew that I was going to go to the hospital to actually see if that there was any record of little baby Mark birth, and from there, I got so disgusted with her that I slammed the telephone down on the receiver.

On our next family court appointed date, I went back to the Queen family Court to report back to the court-appointed attorney Ralph Chateman, and I went back to the hospital where my ex-girlfriend Stacey Cruzack claimed to give birth to a baby boy that she told me that she named him Mark Cuzack. I asked the hospital staff members if they could provide me with a record of birth of a woman who I had a sexual relationship with, and as the departmental supervisor were done in a complete research of the matter, she then informed me that there was no birth record of a baby being born of the woman in question of any kind in April 1, 1991. So then I had to appear before the family court judge along with my court-appointed attorney within the hour as I gave my uncle Ronald a call to please come and meet me at the family court's house. I saw Stacey brought a man inside with her with me having to feel somewhat fearful that after the case was over Stacey might try to have her male friend come and try to hurt me as he had been giving me a hard stare down of my eyes. And my uncle Ronald just happened to be in the area of the court house as he rushed inside to be with me just in case some harm might come my way by my former girlfriend. And then the judge to dismiss my case of me wanting to have a paternity test done to the little baby boy that was brought to me by Stacey as she had been claiming all along that I was the father of the child. And after the case ended, as my uncle Ronald and I was about to leave the family court house, Stacey then started shouting at me that I should have never taken her to court in the first place as she even had gone so far to lose her temper to slap me in the face right in front of the court officers as they then had placed her under arrest for assaulting me. And from there, I was told by the court officer to file a report with the court of Stacey Cruzack's violent outburst as I did just that, and after my uncle Ronald and I left the court house to head back at my family home in Astoria, New York. After all of that, I never heard from my ex-girlfriend Stacey Cuzak ever again.

I began working at the corporate law firm of O'Conner, Sapp, Dash & Marshall in the Mailroom Center, and as for my first day, I was greeted by the staff members with open arms and handshakes as I introduced myself to my new departmental coworkers. And at first, most of the mailroom staff seemed to be quite a good work environment for me with the exception of the younger immature guys who started making fun of my handy cap, according to my older and more mature coworkers such as Kathem Boon and Samatha Dorney. They started saying that the guys Hector Mason and his buddy Morace Conway were talking about me behind my back and that they had no business doing that. The guys started saying, "Hey, everybody, look at this guy Romeo's funny limp when he walks and his large-shaped head and an average-sized body" as I began to feel very embrace among the entire mailroom staff as I had no other choice but to continue on working that day. And those unpleasant commits were not appreciated by the rest of the staff at all that day as they were asked to stop the bad jokes.

So the following day the mailroom staff was still having a good time working and still cracking jokes at this time different coworkers every day while still performing their jobs well, even the mailroom coordinator whose name was Vincent Daily got in on the act as he himself started cracking jokes on the mail room staff members. But he himself got terminated from employment along with our mailroom head manager, whose name was Henry Hernandez, for adding false overtime billing hours on their time sheets that they did not work. As the entire mailman staff witnessed the company security escort our now former superiors out of the company's office as we all had been in total disbelief. But I was so very glad that I still was very much so very gainfully employment with a Fortune 500 company that I myself would never do anything dishonest to jeopardize my employment at the company.

On December 27, 1992, I found myself to be very much attracted to my now former head manager Henry Hernandez's secretary whose name was Gloria Knight as I then decided to ask her on a lunchdate, and she accepted my invitation to join me as I had been so very much delighted. And I found myself to be very much attracted to Gloria to the point as we were sitting together having lunch that I was treating her to. I then decided to ask her if in fact she was currently involved with someone? And she replied yes that she was in a relationship with a nice gentleman friend at that particular time as she went on to say that she wanted to see where her current relationship will go. So we continued finishing having our lunch as I recalled that although I tried not to show my disappointment of being let down easily I felt a kind of sadness in my heart. And when Gloria and I arrived back into the office, I had a surprise for her as I took the liberty to purchase one dozen of long steam of roses and then all of the lady's in the mailroom got so very much excited along with Gloria herself as she was trying to figure out just who sent her that wonderful gift as she then turned toward me realizing that I was the one who gave her the surprise as she then thank me for being such a sweet heart of a person.

So as the entire mailroom center witnessed me taking Gloria out to lunch along with me to have a surprise waiting for her when we got back into the office of a dozen of long-stemmed roses as she was so very delighted that I would care enough about her to give her such a wonderful gift. And from there, the jokes about me started once again with my former coworkers whose name was Stone Casey who began shouting out to another mailroom former coworker whose name was Craig O'Brien who also worked in the mailroom's copy center area just to take a good look at this guy Romeo. He really thought that he was really going to get somewhere with the former managers secretary Gloria with that big bouquet of roses as he had been trying so very hard to embarrass me in front of the entire mailroom center staff members. And I then turned around and took a good look at Stone with a very hard stare trying to figure out just why would he be at all concerned about me taking out to lunch the former manager's Henry Hernandez secretary Gloria Knight. Then Stone continued to say out loud to the mailroom staff members just to take a good look at this guy Romeo and his cold hard stare he looks like he could be part of an organized crime New York Mafia family. And when I heard him say that I had been in total shock as I could not believe that someone would be so crazy enough to say such a thing. And that conversation of a rumor whet on quite a while with some staff members still talking about they wondered if I could be a gangster criminal trying to assort money from the company.

So then shortly after that, I then decided to ask the mail center supervisor whose name was Noel Tomkins if he could then transferred me out of the mail center and into another mailroom workstation that was located on another floor where I could work alone like the other mail clerks on the other company floors. And he claimed that there were no other mail clerk workstations available other than the Copy Center Department. And I really did believe that the supervisor Noel Tomkins really did that for the sole purpose of him having full knowledge of the ridiculous rumor of me possibly having connections to a New York City Mafia crime family to have me closely watch by the Copy Center staff members. And as I was on my way to my new workstation that was directly inside the copy center, I overheard my former mailroom clerk coworker Stone Casey said directly to me that don't think for one second you are escaping us as some of us mail clerks still believe that in fact that I could be a mafia gangster and that the copy center were I had been newly reassigned to will be told to keep a close watchful eye on me.

And once I arrived at the fourth floor Copy Center, I quickly sensed a bad attitude problem with some members of the new department where I had been newly placed. And when I arrived in the department, I introduced myself to the department, and they did the same. And I noticed that the all-male department had been real close in friends with one another, and on some weekends, I would have talks of them joining together for a basketball game as I had never been invited by the group. Then one day I saw my departmental mailroom coworker Stone Casey walk up to the copy center customer service window as he also saw me working in the department keeping a written record log of all my copy center mail deliveries as I overheard him tell a copy center operator that the entire department better keep a close watchful eye of me because the mailroom believed that I could possibly have criminal connection to a New York Mafia family.

And then about a week later, as I had been at home with my family my parents asked me how things were going on my job, and I said that things still remained the same with my coworkers still having to talk about me possibly to have an organized crime connection to a New York Mafia family. And shortly after that, I started to notice a sudden change in my parents' behavior toward me with them becoming fearful of me whenever they were in my presents. And I took notice of whenever they came around me, they would have a very strange reaction around me of them to begin bowing their heads and turning their backs toward the wall completely away from me, and I could not believe that was actually happening in my very own family home that they began to think that in fact that maybe there could be some truth to the rumor that started at my place of my employment. And I couldn't believe that now my own parents where I was born and raised from started dotting me as well just like my coworkers at the law firm O'Conner, Sapp, Dash & Marshall had done with me, thinking that I wasn't still a good person. And I felt so very much betrayed by my very owned family members, but at the same time, I knew that I now had two stressful situations to deal with of my then employee, harassing me on a weekly basis and to try to figure out just how to deal with my parents' very strange behavior of me being rumor on my job as I had been desperately trying to bring everybody back to their normal behavior selves whenever they were in my presence with me trying to rid them of their paranoia of me possible being a New York City gangster.

And I felt so bad that my very own family would choose to treat me like a criminal mafia gangster just because I decided to confide in my family about the problems that started at my place of employment at the corporate midtown law firm of O'Connor, Sapp, Dash & Marshall. But at the same time, I decided not to worry myself about my family's now crazy belief in the own minds of me possibly being a New York City gangster as I knew that I still to go on living my life for me and no one else but me even though I will always have a caring heart for others. So I mostly tried to stay in the family's basement hoping to find a true love on several telephone dating chatlines. But myself along with my two little stepsisters Tameka and Fatima really did enjoy having so much fun playing doll house games along with them wanting to dress me up in makeup as they were very eager to put some on my face as I would say to them boys don't wear makeup girls as they would still try to put some on me as we would all be laughing and playing around with each other and I knew up until a point on at a young age that the brother and sister bond that all three of us shared would not be broken for a while as I knew a special proper way on how to care for children as I have done for so many years before baby sitting my little cousin Rena Avanti.

On January 11 of the year 1993 as I then approached by a copy center, then operator staff member whose name was Neil Harry who had then said to me that he heard from a very reliable source that the only reason that I was then in their department was to try to avoid some trouble that previous started in our employer corporate office of the O'Conner, Sapp, Dash & Marshall LLP second-floor mailroom center departmental staff member whose name just so happened to be Stone Casey as he then told everybody that they then said that they had reason to believe that I could be part of a member of a New York City-organized crime family that was then working undercover to then try to extort our employer money for some criminal capital gain of some very kind to then want to cause law firm a very serious financial problems for the job New York City office as he then also began to then push and shove at me right along with his departmental other male coworker friend whose name is Exodus Franklyne who was then nicknamed was then known to the department as to be Ex. And from there, the copy center daytime operator Exodus Franklyne said that our employer corporate midtown Manhattan of the Time Square Plaza section of the O'Conner, Sapp, Dash & Marshall LLP corporate law firm would spread the word to our entire place of all of our employment just how everybody should start to pay me some close extra attention as one of their mailroom clerks in order to be on a very good look out for me to have all of the company staff members to watch out for my ever single move that I was to make just in case I was trying to try something that was to be very unlawful just in case the proper authorities to be called in the New York City police department. And from there as I began to start back to remembered just how really awful I felt about all of the foolishness that was happening to me that I would start to become so very much stress out quite often to the very point that I would just sit myself across the company office hallway that was also the company mail distribution conveyer station belt system station that been newly built for the slightly heavier multiple documents of deliveries that were been under the weight of thirty-something pounds. And right alongside of me to occasionally give me some assistance was another good coworker friend whose name was Earl Finely as I do also remembered just how good it felt to just get away from the company copy center much bad attitude of certain people even if it was just for a very short while to try to rest my nerves a little bit.

And there was another time on January 13, 1993, as it would be time for me to start to go right back to work to make even more of my Copy Center documents deliveries as the day time supervisor of that very same department whose name is Carlton Circuit would began to asked me just why I was trying to avoid them all in the 4th floor copy center department? And the very answer that I have given to him as I explained that my reason was to as I felt at that very particular time that right across the very hallway of the company distribution mail conveyor station was a little more quieter the noisy copy center department as I also informed Carlton that I felt that I could be more in a relax mode just whenever there was absolutely no copy center documents to be delivered by me and from there he went on about his professional business of overseeing his very own staff members as he left me to just to rest my very self for a short little while just until it would be time to take my very own self to handle my inter-office mailman clerk responsibilities. But what I really actual been feeling at that very particular time and place was that I felt those guys that were in the copy of The O'Conner, Sapp, Dash & Marshall LLP that the copy center support staff members people constantly giving me harassment issues of me that I to endure on almost on a daily basis that I had thought was the very best temporary solution for me in order to keep my mental sanctity. And once that very same day came to a very end as I was so very much tired enough that I just felt like that I wanted to just go right straight to eating my dinner and to take myself right to my bedroom so that I may go right straight to sleep way back. And once I awaken my very own self from a very short time resting period at my family home in the Astoria Queen New York City as I thought it would be a very good enough ideal to confide in my two parents of Jahtayshia & Damian Devine Sr. about the trouble that I was having at my place of my now former employer that was of company The O'Conner, Sapp, Dash & Marshall LLP and so as I did in fact very much so informed them both just how a mentally insane that slanderous rumor been about me to possibly to be a part of a New York City mafia crime family of the New York City area as at first my mom and dad told me that they couldn't just believe what I just been telling the both of them. And I also continued to explained to the both of them just how the rumor actual originally started all because of I taken out for a lunch date my mailroom center manager whose name I explained was Henry Hernandez secretary whose name just so happen to be Gloria Knight as I found myself to be so very much so attracted to her way back as I also asked her out on a lunch date on December 27, 1992, if she would go out with me for a very nice pleasant lunch date? And from there she accept my invitation out for a nice afternoon out as I took my mailroom mailroom secretary whose name was Gloria Knight out for a very nice delicious lunch in a fine French restaurant that was simply called Frenchie. As I began to tell my mailroom department secretary who was Gloria Knight that I found myself to be very so much attracted to her as I asked her if she was at that current time was single? And from there my female coworker associate told me that she was in fact dating someone at that very particular time as she also continued to explain to me that she her very self wanted to see just where her current relationship was going to go from.

As from there as I also explained to parents of Jahtayshia & Damian Devine Sr. that my lunch invitation been accepted by my lady coworker associate as I also went on to also tell them both that I even taken the very kind liberty to order that very same lovely looking mailroom center secretary who was Gloria Knight a dozen of long stem red roses that was just all for her. And as my parents asked me well what just did happen the very next time at my job? And from there as I began to explain that there was my mailroom center mail coworker whose name I explained was Stone Casey as I went on to continue to just telling them both my situation of just how when that very same guy whose name was Stone Casey saw that just how much I was very much interested in the mailroom center manager Henry Hernandez secretary whose name is Gloria Knight as that very same jokester type of guy Stone been verbally teasing me right in front of all the entire second floor mailroom center staff members as he said that everyone should just take a real good look at this guy Romeo Devine as he continued to say that I really thought that I was going to be really getting somewhere with there mailroom secretarial manager Gloria Knight. And from there as I also explained to my parents of just because I given him a very hard some what of a very cold hearted stare of the eyes as that very same mailroom center jokester of a clown type of a guy told all of the 2nd floor of the mailroom distribution center that everyone should take a very good hard look at that the guy Romeo Devine as he also continued to say that I looked very mean enough that I looked like I can be apart a New York City mafia gangster family who just might been sent in the company of The O'Conner, Sapp, Dash & Marshall LLP corporate law firm to try to extort money from there company. And from there my very own parents also asked me the question of just how could someone be that so very dam stupid enough to start such a crazy enough rumerous and very slanderous rumor such as that one? And from there I said to my parents maybe that same departmental coworker of my employer of the corporate lawfirm that is called O'Conner, Sapp, Dash & Marshall LLP whose name is Stone Casey became jealous of me to be the very actual one to take out our mailroom manager secretary who was Gloria Knight instead of him to be the very one to accompany her.

And about a week later as I been at home with my family my parents ask me how things were going on my job and I said that things still remain the same with my coworkers still having to talk about me possible to have a organized crime connection to a New York Mafia family. And shortly after that I started to notice a sudden change in my parents behavior toward me with them becoming fearful of me whenever they were in my presents. And I taking notice of whenever they came around me they would have a very strange reaction around me of them to begin bowing there heads and turning there backs toward the wall completely away from me, and I could not believe that was actually happening in my very own family home that they began to think that in fact that maybe there could be some truth to the rumor that started at my place of my employment And I couldn't believe that now my own parents where I was born and raise from started dotting me as well just like my coworkers at the law firm O'Conner, Sapp, Dash & Marshall done with me thinking that I wasn't still a good person And I felt so very much betrayed by my very owned family members but at the same time I knew that I now two stressful situation to deal with of my employee harassing me on a weekly basis and to try to figure out just how to deal with my parents very strange behavior of me being rumor on my job as I been desperately trying to bring everybody back to there normal behavior selves whenever they were in my presence with me trying to rid them of there paranoia of me possible being a New York City gangster.

And I felt so bad that my very own family would choose to treat me like a criminal mafia gangster just because I decided to confide in my family about the problems that started at my place of employment at the corporate midtown law firm of O'Conner, Sapp, Dash & Marshall. But at the same time I decide not to worry myself about my family now crazy belief in the own minds of me possibly being a New York City gangster as I knew that I still to go on living my life for me and no one else but me even though I will always have a caring heart for others. So I mostly tried to stay in the family basement hoping to find a true love on several telephone dating chatelines personals. But myself along with my two little stepsisters Tameka and Fatima really did enjoy having so much fun playing doll house games along with them wanting to dress me up in makeup as they were very eager to put some on my face as I would say to them boys don't wear makeup girls as they would still try to put some on me as we would all be laughing and playing around with each other and I knew up until a point on there young age that the brother and sister bond that all three of us shared would not be broken for a while as I knew I a special proper way on how to care for children as I done for so many years before baby sitting my little cousin Rena Avanti.

My next relationship started on July 12, 1993, with a woman whose name was Erica Sticklev who lived in Shirley Long Island New York. Erica been my second adult relationship from the telephone chateline of Qwest Personals. Erica was a afro American female who was also a full figured in size who I found myself to be very much interested in seeing where a relationship could go between the two of us. And in the beginning things were going quite well as we been on a dinner and movie date as we both enjoyed each others company all so well. And I been running so very low on cash I decided to make a bank withdraw from a ATM cash machine as I did just that while Erica been standing beside me. So from there we went back to Erica's family home as she told me that she wanted to pay rent for her mother upstairs apartment and she ask me if I would become her boyfriend/roommate and live with her and her children who were triplets infants and I said yes that I would love to. Erica told me that would be great and that my share of the household expensive would be

$300 a month as I agreed to pay her what she been asking as she told me that she would also be paying the other half of her mother rent request of $300 from her public assistant monthly check.

So I told Erica that I to go back to my family home in Astoria Queens to inform my family that I was moving out to my girlfriend family house in Shirley Long Island New York. And my parents been very much skeptical about me just meeting a woman for the very first time with she and I wanting to move in with each other rather suddenly And I told my parents that I thought it would be a good idea because people do often put ads in the news paper or having the use of a realtor all the time and that the only difference was that I found a roommate by going out on a date with a woman who a idea that we should join together in having a intimate relationship while at the same time we would be living together, my parents ask me about how much was I to pay for my share of my new house hold expensive and I told them $300 a month as they agreed that sound like a fair amount. But my father wanted to talk to me about my sudden moving out of our family home as he explain to me I better be very careful about moving in with a young woman that I barely known as he began to teach me about certain trickeries of a woman as he told me that my new found girlfriend was wanting to move in with me all to quickly as my dad explain that I better watch out about my new girlfriend Erica might be trying to just use me to get money out of me as my dad also had told me that some women would try to steal money from men while they were having sex with the man by getting a man all sexually arouse and proceeding to help him to get undress while she herself would be pulling my paints off the lower part of my body with her desperately trying to get my money out of my own wallet. And I told my dad that I would definitely be keeping a watchful eye on my ATM bank card not to be stolen from my wallet as I also had thank my dad for what he was trying to teach me about women and I told him that I would be very careful. And from there I begin packing up my belongings to start to go to my new apartment home that I was sharing with ex-girlfriend Erica Sticklev and shortly after that I have kiss my mother and father good bye and told them that I would call them when I arrived in Shirley Long Island New York.

And when I finally arrived at Erica family home her family welcome me in quite well as I was quite please to be living with my new girlfriend and her family. And from there Erica's mother whose name was Debra Finley had offered me some food and red wine for me to eat and drink for dinner and I said that yes that I was very much so hungry and that I was ready to eat with the family. And dinner turn out to be so very delicious as I also offered to wash the dirty dishes and clean up the kitchen but Erica mother Ms. Debra Finely said that she would have her son Thomas to clean up everything. When Erica younger brother Thomas finished cleaning up the dishes he told his mother and sister that he was going to hang out with some of his friends in the neighborhood and Erica said to me that it would be a good ideal since I was living with her family that she thought that I should try to get to know her younger teenage brother much more better by hanging out with him and his guy friends as I agreed to do just as he ask me to do. So Thomas and I were off to have him introduce me to his neighborhood buddies and when we arrived at his friend house as we both went inside as I was introduce by Erica brother Thomas to his friend whose name was Jessus Styles and he greeted me with a friendly handshake and a smile as he told me to have a seat on his very comfortable reclidatable chair as I said thanks for his hospitality that I don't mind if I do.

once I made myself comfortable Erica brother Thomas ask his friend Jessus to step in the back room as he told him that he wanted to talk to him about something that was very important and off they went while leaving me to sit in the living room area. And once Thomas gotten his friend Jessus in his back room to talk with him I overheard Erica brother Thomas telling his friend Jessus about how I was now living with him and his big sister Erica inside the family home in there upstairs apartment and that she told him that I paid her 300 dollars for that month rent of July of 1993 from my ATM Debit Card and that they wanted to rob me of my money. And when Thomas friend Jessus heard what Erica brother wanted to do to me to rob me of my ATM Debit Card the friend told him that he and his sister was absolutely crazy to have me to move in with there family as I was supposed to be intimately involved with his sister only to have me to be sat up to be rob by them. And Thomas friend Jessus told him that wasn't his styles to do such a evil thing to a person and the friend went on to say don't you know that the robbery could be reported right back to the police and that since I was living with his sister and his family that if anything was to happen to me that officers would hold his

36

family totally responsible. from there Thomas friend Jessus told him to go home to his family and tell his sister that was the most stupidest ideal that he very heard of a woman trying to trick a man by making him think that he was in a intimate relationship with his woman only to be set up to rob by her family. So from there I also overheard Thomas friend Jessus tell him to get the hell out of his house as he also had said that he knew that I overheard our entire conversation and he said that if I any kind of common sense that I would leave Erica for good and never be involved with her in a intimate relationship ever again.

And shortly after that they both had come back into the living room as Thomas friend Jessus said that it was getting kind of late and he also went on to say that it was good to meet me and for me to stay safe out there in those streets and that I should keep a watchful eye on my friend Thomas as he began to laugh ha ha ha but I heard Thomas's and his sister Erica evil plot to try to set me up to steel my Debit Card. So once we gotten back to Erica family home she the nerve to ask me if her brother Thomas and I fun hanging out together with his friends? And I could not believe that whole situation that I gotten myself into but all the same while I just went on with everything as if every thing been normal. Erica put her infant triplets to bed for the evening in a separate room across the hall way where we were supposed to sleep together. And now that I known that Erica her brother Thomas to try to set me up to be rob me of my bank ATM him and his friend who turn out to be a very deceit gentleman I thought about what my father told me before I left my own family home about how I should really get to know a woman before I just up and move in with them.

Shortly after that Erica had come back into the room to tell me that she miss me a whole lot when I was hanging out with her brother Thomas and she told me that she was feeling very much sexually homey and that she wanted to please me right away as she made me all so arouse so much that I was totally ready to get some loving from her. Erica told me that she wanted to turn out the lights so that she could sexually please me. But I said to her that I like to make sweet and sexy love with the light on so that we may both see each naked as were to make love to each other. But Erica insisted that we make love only in totally darkness and as she begin to undress me by pulling my paints off of me as I remembered exactly what my father told me as she began sexually pleasing me until I reach my climax. And after all of the sexually pleasure ended Erica told me that she was tired and warn out from all of the sexual excitement of our love make that she was going to get ready to go to sleep in the kids room while I was to sleep in the other room across the hall way and I kiss and hug her good night and told her that I would see her in the morning. And when I went across Erica hallway apartment I immediately looked inside my wallet to see if she stolen my bank card and when I went to take a look to see if it been missing if was in fact been stolen for me by her. So Erica come back into the room to check on me to see just why I n't shut off the lights to just go right to sleep for the rest of the evening as she entered she saw me with my wallet in my hand as I told her that I notice that my bank debit cards been missing as I ask her did she herself know what the hell happen to it. Erica lied to me and told me that she know ideal what could happen to wallet. She told me to leave the room and to also leave everything in the room exactly where it was even my wallet that I been holding in my hand so that she could look around for my missing debit bank card. And once I step out of the room to go across the hall way I known that Erica been very much aware that I was on to her evil seems to once again to try to rob me of my ATM cash card like she planned to have her brother Thomas and his friend whose name was Jessus to do earlier that same night but the attempt failed them both just like the very first time. And Erica told me that it was know okay for me to come back into the room as she told me that she cleaned up the room and put everything back into its proper place and she told me to get a good night rest and that she would see me in the morning. So after Erica left the room to go across the hallway to go sleep with her triplet baby boys I check my wallet once again that Erica told me to leave behind in the room just the way thing was and when I looked back inside of it I saw my ATM Debit Bank Card been place back into it's proper place where I left it.

I guarded my wallet for the rest of that evening until day break arrived so that I could head back to my family home in Astoria, Queens New York and I did just that and call myself a Shirley New York taxi car service to pick me up from Erica address and while I been waiting for my ride to arrive I overheard Erica brother Thomas tell her that I been fully aware that they wanted to set me up to rob me of my debit bank card as she been half asleep saying that she didn't even care about what he was telling her and after fifteen minute pass my cab driver finally had arrived and I immediately grab my belongings and ran to get inside of the car service as I also had slam the Erica door shut as I was on my way to the Long Island Rail Road to head back home to my parents house. And once I arrived back home with my parents and big brother Damian Jr. they all asked me what happen with me living with my girl friend Erica Sticklev and her family? I told them that Erica tried to set me up to steal my debit card by having me to hang out with her younger teenage brother whose name was Thomas and his neighborhood friend whose name was Jessus but their plan failed them both. And I explained that once Erica brother Thomas hometown friend heard about what there plain were with them both wanting to get their greedy hands on my bank card his buddy said that he not wanted to have anything to do with what he and his sister was planning to do to take my money. And I started to think back what my father told me that I was moving way to fast to want to live with my girlfriend and her family apartment home and that he was right to warn me about certain type of woman who might try to just want to use me for my money.

Shortly after that my cellar phone ranged and to my surprise it was now my ex-girlfriend Erica on the line to ask me just want happen to me and why did I want to leave her family home in Shirley Long Island New York all the sudden without me having to say goodbye to her and her family as she also had asked me just why I stop calling her rather suddenly? And I told her the reason why I to leave her for good was because I found out that she and her younger brother Thomas was trying to set me up to rob me on my bank card but there foolish plan failed them both. I informed Erica that our relationship that was supposed to be all about us to be loving and caring toward each other to come to a end because I realized that she her brother Thomas was nothing more than no good for nothing money hungry thieves as I also told her that her family was very lucky that the police did not have to be called to her family home to have them both place underneath arrest by the Shirley Long Island New York police department. And thin she went on to denied the truth of what she was planning to do to me and afterwards she ask me just what I wanted to do with the rest of my things that I left behind at her family home? And I curse at her to say that I didn't give a dam what she did with whatever I left behind and I also told Erica to never call me again.

So after that very bad experience that I endured with my ex-girlfriend Erica Sticklev I decided to try to get right back into trying to find a good soulmate for myself and as I gotten back on the telephone chate line of the Qwest Personal I connected myself to a woman whose name was Armoney Gamesly who lived in Amityville Long Island New York. So Armoney and I decided to exchange each other telephone numbers with one another as we also had made plans to meet up with one each other at the LIRR Station in her neighborhood and when we finally had did so we went to rent a room at a motel call The Sleep Inn for the entire evening. And once Armoney and I entered our motel room I taking quite a liking to the mirror that was on the ceiling as I was thinking that It would be so very sexual freaky to watch ourselves while we were having a sexual encounter with each other. We decided that we were going to try to find a good movie on cable and in fact we did just that as the movie been entitled She's Gotta Have I

And Armoney said that she was very much thirsty and that she wanted me to get us some refreshments while we were both to enjoy the movie and I did just that. And the movie turn out to be very entertaining to the both of us. Shortly after the movie been over with Armoney and I started to feel very much aroused and we been ready to have our very sexual encounter as it was so very pleasurable for the both of us. afterward as it was getting late we decided that we were ready to go to sleep for the rest of the evening a I did just that.

And I woken up to use the bathroom and than I got back into the bed with Armoney and I decided to check my wallet to see if all my money was still there and when I did that I taken notice that $40 been stolen for my me. I realized that Armoney stolen my money right from underneath my noise while I been asleep but I began to wonder just why she didn't just take all the rest of my money that I as I $60 left over as I come to the motel with $100. I realized that Armoney Gamesly wanted to be paid for a sexual encounter like a prostituted. So I put my wallet inside my hotel pillow case until the next morning as we than had decided to go back to our separate ways. And I gotten so upset that I hope to never see that thief ever again.

On July 29, 1993, I met another woman from the chateline of The Qwest Personals telephone dating service whose name was Rena Rayes who live in the East Side Bronx area in New York City. And I found myself to be very much attracted to her as she been totally my preference as far as looks were concern as I thought that she a very beautiful and sexy looking shape as well as her to be a very pretty caramel light skin complexion woman who also smelled so very good with her perfume scent. Rena and I decided to meet up in the Manhattan area of Greenwich Village New York where we decided to go to a dance club that was called the Blue Star Club and party the entire night away and when we arrived inside we really enjoyed ourselves as we listen to a live musical band that was called the Tudore band as they given the crowd a very likable performance as we also had purchase two 12 oz. of red wine bottles with two orders of hot and spicy wings for some appetizers. And as Rena and I were sitting there watching the band performed as we been under the influence of alcohol we began to get very frisky with each other by kissing and cuddling quite frequently while we where still inside enjoying the music as it all felt so very good to me.

After we left the Blue Star Club Rena and I walked around the Geenwich Village New York neighborhood in Manhattan while we were holding each other hands just talking trying to get to know each other as I also tried to persuade here that the two of us should try to see if we could rent a hotel room in the area so that we may spend the rest of the evening together. So I told Rena that I was willing to pay half of the hotel fee of $100 if she was also willing to pay for the other half of the hotel cost of a additional $100. But Rena told me that she wasn't willing to sleep with me for a sex on our very first date. I became so very disappointed that she turn down my request for us to spent the rest of the night together that it giving me a very sad feeling in my heart to the point that I felt like I just had wanted to start to cry but I was in fact able to hold back my tears. So we continued to walk around the area and I was in totally shock when she walk us into a ally way where we saw a homeless man lying on the ground and I gotten kind of nervous that the homeless man might been totally out of his mind to the point that he might reacted crazy or violet toward Rena and myself as I change into my protective mode keeping my fist up ready to defend myself as well as my date. And once the homeless man saw my sudden reaction he shouted out please man don't hurt me and I assured him that I would not do him any harm as I felt so very bad for him that I decided that it would be a very godly thing for me to give

41

the man a five dollar bill and when I did that he said that he was so very thankful for me from the bottom of his heart for me to have been so very generous to help the less fortunate and I said to him that he was quite welcome as I also told him that he should really get himself off of the dirty streets and check himself into the nearest homeless shelter as he told me that he definitely would do so and my date for that evening Rena and I left out the ally way.

And I thought that it was totally senseless for Rena to have us both walk into a ally way like she us to do so and I decided to asked her do you always endanger yourself by walking into ally ways like that? Rena told me that yeah that she was not worried about anybody putting there hands on her because she plenty of boxing skills that she been taught my her older brothers. We proceed to continue to walk around town until 4:00 AM in the morning until I decided to walk her to the nearest subway station to make sure she gotten there safely and I told her that I would give her a call later in the afternoon but I never did. And when Rena did not hear back from me she called me back and asked me just why didn't I call her just like I promise her? I told her that I was looking to start a intimate sexual relationship with a woman as I also explain that how I was very disappointed that she would deny me of that Rena began to explain to me about her 6 months rule of having a male partner to wait until that time period was over to see if a man really had wanted to be with her in a serious committed relationship or if he just wanted her for sexual satisfaction and she ask me about us to have our second date together as she even told me that she would even pay half on our dinner date and I told her no that would not be good enough for me. And I informed her that I did not want to have to wait for an entire 6 months until she was ready to be sexual intimate with me because I explain that I a very high sex drive that always needed to be satisfy in the very beginning of a relationship.

My next relationship attempt was with another woman who I also meet thru the telephone chateline of The Qwest Personals Network whose name she told me was Mercedes Eastly. And that I told her that I thought that her name was a very fancy one as I explain to her that I never knew anyone with that very classy name before Mercedes than proceeded to want to learn more about me as in my employment status and I informed her that I was a mail clerk for the large corporate law firm that was called O'Conner, Sapp, Dash & Marshall and she herself was very much impress with me. And Mercedes told me that she's trying to become the latest rapper sensation in the music industry. And as we were trying to become much more better acquitted with each other while we both were still on the telephone chateline we decided that it was okay for us to exchange each others telephone numbers so that we may have more time to talk with one another without having to pay any other extra cost to the Qwest telephone dating service.

And after a full week of us talking the telephone Mercedes on May 21, 1993, invited me over to her apartment and as I finally arrived there and she and I sat down on her living room couch to try to get to know each other in every personal way as she has told me that she always dream to becoming a world famous musical rapper and that she was told by another up-incoming artist whose stage name was B-Nice that he thought that she a lot of Hip Hope music potential to reach the top of the rap charts. Mercedes told me that even though that she is not yet signed to any record label that she herself began writing her own rap lyrics down on a music sheet so if she was ever to be discovered by a Hip Hop record producer that she would have some music all ready for them to listen to that was already on a demo tape And as I taken notice of her bedroom wall it been filled up with plenty of music Hip Hop Legends from the '80s and '90s. So from there I than ask my up and coming potential Hip Hop friend Mercedes if she could rap me a few lyrics so that I could her just how he sound, and she did just that as she sounded all so very much professional as I been so very impress of her musical talent that I felt that when it would be her time to be discovered by someone in music business that she would be ready do give them a good sample of her Hip Hope lyrics. So after talking about Mercedes possible music career and I was trying to warm up to her by me attempting to embrace her with a warm intimate hug and with a possible loveable kiss of her soft lips but she turn me down flate leaving me just to sit with her while she refuse not to give me any foreplay.

And than I really tried not to really show Mercedes that I was so very disappointed in being rejected by her as I just sat there with a fake happy face look while continuing to listen to her about her possibly career in the Hip Hop. And the time that I spent with her without me having any physical intimate connection was quite difficult for me but I was able to get threw it even though she looked so very much beautiful that night as her hair was of a brunette color with blond high lights. So as the evening ended with Mercedes and I we shortly parted our separate ways for the evening and I told her that I would call her the very next evening. And once I arrived back to my family home in Astoria Queens at 3:00 AM I found myself to be totally exalted to the point that after I gotten myself out of my street clothes and into my pajamas and laid myself down to go to sleep. And when my parents yelled down the family basement where I lived they shout that I no business hanging out at some woman house during the work week while coming in after the mid night hour being to tired to get up the in the morning a 6:00 AM to get up so that I may make it in on time to go into my workplace. And so I knew what my Mom and Dad was telling me was so very right as I was kind of disappointed in myself but I realized that since I was not going into work that day I began thinking about my lady friend Mercedes as I just had wanted to her the sound of her voice as I called her telephone outgoing voice mail message service as she sounded as so very sweet to me. And when Mercedes finally had arrived back at her apartment she had given me a call and asked me just why did I kept on calling her answering machine while I known that she would be at her Job? And I explain to her that the reason was because I just miss hearing the sweet sound of her voice because she did not give me her cell phone # so that I may call her while she was on her lunch break.

During the corporate conspiracy situation that was against me there were several former coworker women within the corporate law firm of O'Conner, Sapp, Dash & Marshall that were constantly flirtatiously and sexually coming on to me while I was trying to perform a mail run within the company floors. The very first woman who flirted with me was Meshia Jamison who was one of the associate attorney's secretary who sexually harass me on the work week daily bases. As Meshia would see me coming around the corner she would asking me the question of how is it shaking sexy man as she would also get up from her secretarial desk and begin walking directly right in front of my mail cart and would also wink her eye and blow kisses at me and as she would also wiggle her hips as she wanted to perform a sexy walk for me and I would found myself to become quite arouse by here even though I did not normally find her to be attractive because she was not my type of woman that I would be interested in. She would also say out loud to her neighbor secretary lady friend whose name was Tempest Riley here comes my sexy boyfriend as I was making my inter-office mail run.

She might have been trying to sexually tease me but I was not sure. Meshia Jamison always kept herself looking so very beautiful looking as she usually kept her hair in multiple color long length braids styles along with her to where the most fashionable skin tight jeans and open tight fitted open blouse. Meshia would also ask me to approach her because she said the she wanted my very personal opinion on which perfume do I think smelled the best on her? And from there she sprayed a few frequencies on her neck and ask me just which one that I liked the best as she also had told up out of her set and grab me by my belt buckle to pull me closer to her neck as me the question which one did I prefer the White Diamond or the Henryo Armonty and which s of lip stick that I would like to see of a woman? And I told Meshia that I preferred the White Diamond fragrance and and the passion flavored lipstick for her. And she decided to give me a thank you gift she has bruise her buttocks up against my gentiles and I to get back to work as I could not believe what happen between the two of us.

So from there after all that flirting that I receive from my former co-worker Meshia Jamison I found myself to becoming very much attracted to her to the pointed to I wanted to see if just how much was she really attracted to me. So I come up with the ideal to buy Meshia a dozen of long steam roses with a card attach to them to say that I would love the good chance to romance you as long as you will allow me to. And I thought I would surprise her right after work but I did not see her so I became to wonder just want I was going to do with the roses since I did not see her pass by after work hours. And as some of my former coworkers saw me stand outside waiting for someone with me still holding a dozen long steam roses a lady whose name was Carole Holden out loud if you don't see the sexy lady your looking for at the law firm than be sure to put those lovely long steam red roses in the refrigerator until Than that following Monday February 14, 1993, Valentine Day I arrived into work a little early that morning and brought in Meshia Jamison long steam red roses from home and place them on her desk just hoping that she would be pleasantly surprise. And when I prepared myself do make my very first distribution mail run for that day as I arrive on the twenty-eighth floor were Meshia Jamison worked I than saw her and when she saw me she gotten up out of her chair and ran off somewhere with some documents in her hand. And I guest Meshia was so embarrass that she her coworker lady friend whose was Tempest Riley who sat right across from her to speak in her behalf to tell me that her friend was already intimately involved with another man that she been seeing for about a year now, and that Meshia said the flowers were a very sweet and thoughtful gift but that there would be no way possible she and I could have a romantic relationship only a professional one. And I told Tempest that I totally understood as I than delivered the two ladies mail and than preceded to continue delivering the rest of the company inter-office mail.

And when I finally had the chance to see Meshia on my next hourly mail run I guess Meshia felt very embarase because she eventually to face me because of I was one of the company's mail clerk as she tried to hide her face behind a few legal document as I place her and her associate attorney mail and her desk. And I guest that she was lost for word as I figure out the only reason that she was flirting with me was because on the rumor that spread around the whole law firm that I could be a New York Mobster trying to extort money from the company like a professional thief that went under cover from a crime family. And that situation that happen between Meshia Jamison and I kind of sadden me a little to the point that I just wanted to take a bathroom break to dry my eye out a little from sweeping tears of sadness. And from there I just wanted all of the company's harassment and sexual harassment to stop but at that time it never did so I just continue to work to the best of my abilities.

And back in the company 4th floor Copy Center department shortly after my former departmental coworker Stone Casey already informed them of the terrible belief of him believing that I could possibly be apart of a New York Mafia crime family and that everybody should what just about my every move that when a couple of peoples bad attitude started to kick into to gear. And the harassment began in my new assign department with two men of the company Copy Center Department whose name was Neil Harry and Exodus Franklyne constantly harass me on the daily bases making it a very hostile work environment, Monday morning and that I should have a good weekend.

The guys were a little older than me and hand a bit of a attitude problem with me because of the ridiculous rumor of me being a New York mafia gangster family member. There would be some occasions were the entire department would began cracking jokes on each other that would also at times include me as I would also get a good laugh out of it just trying to get the guys focus off of me for a while instead of them always always thinking of me as a criminal that was trying to extort money from the company. And from there the Copy Center operator Exodus Franklyne would making bi sexual lovers that were attractive to both men and women. I remember on July 31, 1993, it was a very busy and tiring day and I was not in the mood for any sexual harassment jokes what so ever. But later that very same day both Exodus Franklyne and Neil Harry started horsing around with me by sneaking up behind me and grabbing my hip bone on almost a daily bases.

And they actually really enjoyed sneaking up behind me watch how high I would jump up and by doing so it made me always feel like I almost a heart attack and having me to almost have the sudden urge to use the bathroom. And the copy center day time Supervisor whose name was Carlton Circuit his copy center operator Neil and Exodus call those two guys in his office with him leaving the office door open as I overheard him told his department guys to stop touching on me before we have major problem of some sort of harassment on there hands. And the sexual harassment stop for a short while but started back up again as they would all also have every support staff watch my ever move I made within the company especial the copy center operator Exodus Franklyne as I once overheard him say to his other department staff member that everyone should take a look at this guy Romeo walking around like I a attitude the New York mafia family was the most powerful force in the New York area and he added that he was going to have the job call the cops to have all arrested. And I could believe what I was hearing from him at first as I thought to myself that maybe he watch to many mafia gangster movies.

And after that Exoduswatching me bring in my lunch from home with him also asking me what did I bring in for my lunch? And I felt that in fact was very annoying but I decided to hummer him and tell him what I brought in which was a a chicken sandwich and a pasta salad that day as he just stood there and laugh at me with him having himself calling me by a nickname and saying that's good Rome. And when it been time for me to began taking my lunch break and when I look in the copy center department refrigerator where I always stored my lunch as I began looking I taken notice that my food been stolen right out of there. And it happen for a second time and I heard Exodusshout out load yea since the word in the company is that you could be apart of a New York family I should never bring in my lunch from home and that I should try to save money and that I would always buy my lunch outside and I was on my lunch.

And On November 23, 1993, when I arrived inside my very own departmental department of the mail room center I headed straight to the mailroom room manager Henry Hernandez office and ask him for a one on one meeting with me and he agreed that he would do so. And from there I began to tell him about the problem that I was having with the 4th Copy Center night time supervisor whose name was Jefferey Silverstone and how I was constantly be harassed by him. And I told Henry that Jefferey would sometime come in thirty minutes early before his shift actually officially would start as he would also would pick up a five to ten pound weighted copy center document up from my workstation desk and slam it down on the table and say to me that the document probably been sitting around for hours got dam it and that he constantly said to me if I don't get these documents out the copy center and deliver them to the proper persons that I was going to have a much major problem out of him. And from there Henry informed me that he would have a meeting with the copy center night time supervisor Jefferey Silverstone and tell him to stop harassing me and for him to instruct me on how to do my job sufficiently and from there I thank Henry for helping me for resolving my problem.

And when I arrived back into the copy center I heard the department telephone ring and Thomas answered and told Jefferey that the mailroom manager was requesting to have a meeting with him in his office in the mail center and from there he was on his way down to Henry's Hernandez office. So from there after Jefferey had him meeting with my

48

mailroom manager Henry Hernandez him seem like he calm himself down quit a bit and from there my work shirt ended for the work week and I was off about to enjoy my weekend. And once Monday once arrived again as 3PM arrived as that was Jefferey Silverstone time to start his work shift he once again came into the office with a very bad attitude as he bump into my shoulder as I said excuse me to him not wanting to show any disrespected and he said to me that I better watch out now before I get knock out now. And from there I could belief that that another harassment incident once again place again between he and I even after Henry once warn him once again.

So from that second incident I made the decision to filed a formal complaint to the company department of Human Resource and was I arrive in the office some directed me to one of there departmental Coordinator whose name was Clyd Montly. And was I informed him of all of the sexually unpleasant sexual harassment and harassment that I the displeasure of experience he ask me to please explain just what occurred the time I started working in the copy center from the year from 1993 through 1997. And I informed him that I indeed wanted to filed a official complaint against the two of the Copy Center operators Exodus Franklyne, Neil Harry and the evening Jefferey Silverstone. And from there he told me that he would call to a meeting all parties involved into a one on one meeting with him so that a complaint against them could possibly be filed against all parties involved and that he would call me back to the Human Resource upon further review my my incidences.

And I started thinking since it's seem that the entire support staff in the corporate law firm of O'Conner, Sapp, Dash & Marshall really did not want me to file any official complaint charges against any of their support staff members because of that insane rumor that originally had begin in the company Mail Room Center department by one of the mailroom clerk Stone Casey saying that I could possibly be connected to a mafia crime family that was really trying to get money out of the company some how by me beginning to taking official action against the company it might bring forth a possible law suit but after the shoulder bumping incident with the Copy Center night time Superviser Jefferey Silverstone, Neil Harry and Exodus Franklyne constanting sexual harassing me by grabbing me by the hips making me thinking that they were actually bi

49

sexual lover of sort I no other choice but to bring for charges on all parties involve as I always resented that fact I was just a common mail clerk trying to performed my proper duties just like any other employee. And so after I left the company Human Resource department I went back to the mail center to informed my mailroom manager Henry Henandez about my second incident that happen in the copy center of the constant of two of the copy cent operators Neil Harry and Exodus Franklyn grabbing me by the waist side and the night time supervisor Jefferey Silverstone he than ask me just why didn't I just come to him instead of me having to go to filed a complaint against the guys in the copy center? And I told him my reason for going over his head was because when I first complain to him about 3 of the copy centers department members even though I knew that he a face to face meeting with the night time supervisor Jefferey Silverstone the harassment still continued. And I told him that do to have already official filed harassment and sexual harassment charges on three copy center staff members that I was instructed by the Human Resource Coordinator Clyd Montly.

And I ask Henry did he hear by me official filing a complaint with the Personal department and he replied yes he did. So Henry to immediately transferred me out out he copy center department. And I ask him once again in order for me to try to avoid any more harassment problems from any other support staff member could I please be assign to a independent mail delivery station and again he told me no any that the only other available mail workstation that was available was the Telecopy/Fax Department so I said and of I went to my new workstation.

And on November 28, 1997, I arrived at my new distribution mail delivery station inside the company Telecopy/Fax center and began to join my other mail clerk coworkers whose name were Marco Applegate and John Porter. And I took the liberty of introducing myself to the forty-second floor Telecopy Copy /Fax Center Department crew as I said my hello's to the guy's whose name were Denise Hailey who Also used to work in the twenty-second floor mail distribution station right along beside me helping me to make all mail deliveries on the floor and as he also informed me that he was looking for a new company position were he could make more money so than he ask me just why don't I join his department as well? And I told him that I would indeed take his advisement under careful consideration. And I met the other coworkers whose name were Leon Abrames and Steven Watkins as greeted me with a friendly handshake. And the telecopy/fax center telephone rang and than Denise answered the call and said that the company personal department was calling for me to meet the Human Resource Coordinator Clyd Montly in his office, so I was on my way there.

And when I got to the human resource department and I immediately went inside to see Clyd Montly and when I arrived he ask me to please take a seat and he continued to say that upon further review of my complaint that I filed with the Human Resources department concerning all three parties involved that consisted of the copy center operators Neil Harry and Exodus Franklyn and there evening supervisor Jefferey Silverstone. And the H.R. Coordinator Clyd Montly showed me the written complaint that I filed against all three copy center support staff members as he also informed me that after he completed a full investigation of everyone involved in the incident in three separate meetings he told me that the copy center operators Neil and Exodus openly admitted that they did in fact sneak up from behind me and did grab me by my waistsides with them both to have me to jump up in the air and begging having there entire staff begin to laugh and make a mockery of me almost on the daily bases. But they claimed they thought that I knew that they were all just playing around with me. And the H.R. Coordinator Clyd Montly also informed me that the copy center evening supervisor Jefferey Silverstone blatantly denied the charges of him physically harassing me by bumping into my shoulder than making a verbal threat to me stating that he wanted to do some form of bodily harm toward me. And I ask him if in fact could I have a photo copy of my complaint and he he told me that it would be against company policy for him to do so, but he would in fact keep all written documents of my complaint in the department of the Human Resources files and from there I thank him.

And from there I went back to the Telecopycopy/fax center to perform my now telecopy/fax deliveries duties and when I arrived back inside Denise Haily began to asking me noisy questions about what happen inside the human resource department? And I first I told him that it was a private matter and that I didn't want to get into my personal detail, but he kept on pressuring me to answering his question so I than told him that when I was on the forth floor copy center department I endured a sexual harassment issues. And from there Leon Abrames also had began to began harass me saying to me, so what they here just playing around with you and that he wanted to know just why I felt that it was the best Ideal for me to report to the human resource department? And from there Leon begin to pull out his pocket knife and brandish me with it with the blade being still folded in a close down position while telling me that I was totally wrong for what I did to our fellow coworkers buy reporting them and that I should just asked my mailroom manger Henry Hernandez to transfer me to a different workstation.

And shortly after that Leon Abrames preceded to shake me up and spine me around as I was on my way to make some more hand deliveries of the telecopy/faxes documents and he bump himself into me as I was on my way out the department as he place his pocket knife into my lose backpocket without me knowing he did so and before I left the room he than stop me and said to me just wait a dam minute Romeo, and he ask me what is that hanging out of your back paint pocket? And when I taken a good look to see what he was talking about I saw his pocket knife hanging out of my own pocket. And from there he everyone in the telecopy department laughing and making fun of me as I just gotten a little upset and went on my way to make all of my telecopy/fax deliveries, as I also began to think that what if someone would seen me walking around with Leon Abrams pocket knife than perhaps than somebody would call the company security guards on me, but I guess the telecopy department better sense not to let their very crazy ideal of a joke go to far. Than after a while their Supervisor whose name was Patricia Helmsley walk into the department after I return back from my hand deliveries run and asked me just how did I like working in her department? And I told her that everything is just going just fine all the while thinking about how I better start writing down all of the many different incidents that would occurred to me while I was still working with the corporate law firm of O'Conner, Sapp, Dash & Marshall as my employer.

And from there on December 15, 1997, I decided to file a formal complaint with the New City Division of Human right regarding my sexual harassment issues that happen at my former employer at the corporate law firm of O'Conner, Sapp, Dash & Marshall. And once I arrive inside the building I been directed to the Divison of Human Rights Supervisor whose name was Sally Kendricks as I begin explain to her that I been a victim of sexual harassment concerning a copy center night time supervisor whose name was Jefferey Silverstone and two copy center operators whose name was Exodus Franklyne and Neil Harry she told me that she was going to allow me to file a written complaint with her secretary whose name was Kathern Champion in the from of a questionnaire. From there the supervisor told me that in order to file a civil lawsuit against all parties involved that I would need some form of discriminatory action against all of my harassment issues that I either to have some witnesses or a auto recording of each incident.

And after all of my New York Corporate Conspiracy situation I found myself so very stress out from my place of my employment I decided in order to keep some piece of mine that I should take out some time from work and go out on disability for at least three three months. And I just figured that because of my employers at O'Conner, Sapp, Dash & Marshall was putting me under some much emotional stress that my time off of work was well over due and well deserve. And when I confided in my parent Damian Sr. and Jahtayshia it really bothered me so very much so that they could possibly believe that there could be some actual truth to what my employers been saying about me to possibly have some sort of connection to a New York mafia crime family. So from there I decided since I so much stress free time from my the employer in the Manhattan law firm that I was just going to try to be social again by getting back on the Quest telephone chateline once again.

And so On November 29, 1997, as I was once again browsing on the chatline personals and I connected to a young lady whose name was Lacey Ward and after we talked on line for a few minutes we decided to exchange telephone numbers with each other as we than both got off of the telephone paid service and begin becoming much more better aquated with each other. So I began to ask Lacey just what exactly were her interest? And from there she told me that she was a mother of her six year old daughter whose name was Wonda Ward and that she was in the first grade and Lacey went on to say that she was really into rap music so much that she been trying to hook up a music career with a up and coming music producer who stage name she claimed was Super Sonic. And she began to ask me what about myself and what I did to make a living? And I informed her that I was a inter-office mail man working for a very large corporate Manhattan law firm and from there she said that she been very much express in what I did in order to make ends meet.

after a full week pass Lacey Ward and I decided that we have become better aquated with each other enough for us to want to meet each other for the very first time as we both been so very excited to do so. So from there Lacey ask me to come over to here family home to pay her a visit and from there I said that I would be there shortly in her home town of Deer Park in Long Island. And when finally had arrived at Lacey Warde door step after traveling on the Long Island Rail Road her father whose name was Mr. Derrick Ward answered and said hello to me as he also had told his daughter Lacey that her guest finally arrived as she come up from her family basement along with her mother whose name was Mrs. Tonya Ward as she greeted me with a friendly hello and smile as I also did the very same. Mr. and Mrs. Ward and Lacey me to join in there family living room so that I may get better aquated with there family.

So Lacey father ask me just how did I meet his daughter Lacey and how long did we know each other? And Lacey and I both told her parents that we both meet each other of the telephone chateline call The Dating Personals and after a half hour of speaking to one another we decided that we were ready to meet each other on a blind date and here we both are. And from there Lacey little six year old daughter come up from the family basement also and went to give here mommy a huge around her neck and proceed to ask mother and grandparents just who I was? And I introduce myself to my new girlfriend Lacey to her daughter whose name she told me was Abagail Ward and she went on to tell me that she was six years old.

Lacey parents asked me just what were my intentions with there daughter were? And I than explain to my actual intention were to begin to start to begin much more better aquated with each other and for us to have many of nights out of the town just to get to know each other in a personal way possible. And here Mother and giggle a little bite and said that sound like sweet idea as her father also agreed with his wife as they also add

54

that wished for us two to have plenty of safe fun as we both said that we intended to do just that and lot's of it. And Lacey, Abagail and I went downstairs in their family basement to play house and tea party with each other and we plenty of funtimes doing so.

I began to ask Lacey about her daughter Abagail father and she told me that he name was Colby Collins and that he was currently in jail on multiple drug charges and that he was going to be serving at least six month in a county correction facility. And she continued talking about her wanting to pursue her music career as a Hip Hop Rap Artist, and when I asked here to give me a sample of her rapping lyrics she denied me the great opportunity to her her supposite skills. And from there we decided to go out side for a breath of cool air and when we did so as we been only standing outside for about a minute or two when some guy friend of Lacey cruise by in a convertible with the top down whiling hooking his car horn asking the question of what's good with you sweet and sexy Lacey? And from there she told her friend/that she was doing good and that she was just hanging out with her new friend, and I develop some kind of a jealously attitude because I never like the ideal of a man being friends with a woman that I would be dating but I remain calm, cool and collected.

Shortly after that it started getting late and I was on my home to my family home in Astoria Queens New York. And when I arrive back home my parent been waiting up for me to see just how my date have went with my new lady friend. And I informed them both that everything gone smoothly between my new lady whose name was Lacey Ward and her mother whose name I told them was Tonya Ward and her father name was Derrick Ward. And I told my parent's that Lacey family really seem quite a decent family that I might want to become apart of.

after the following week arrived ask Lacey and I been stilling been of good terms to want to still be involved with each other, than was until I would continued to try to contact her by way of the telephone as when her parents would answered my calling of me wanting to speak to there daughter Lacey they told me than she was coming into and out of the house quit often, but they would give her the message that I called and from there I thank them both. And when Lacey finally the dam decency to pick up the telephone to give me a call back I gotten very upset with her shouting out loud where the hell you been and why didn't you call me back like you were suppose to? So from there Lacey told me that she begun going back into the studio to work on a album and as she claimed that was the sole reason why I den heard from hear. I so very exciting for her with her getting her music career on track and I than ask her if I could come along in the recording studio with her? And she told me that the guys and her were going to be to busy recording a album and that they could not afford in distraction of any kind as she explain to me time was money and that there was none to be wasted.

At the time of December 1, 1997, as I continued to talk to Lacey Ward over the telephone and plane to visit her mostly on the weekend as I started calling my girlfriend Lacey Ward brand-new cell phone number that I purchase for her as I gotten hardly no answered from her as the call went straight to her voice mail. And I began to wonder just why that kept on happening until I finally had gotten through to her, and I ask her just why did it take so long for her to pick up her cellur phone? And Lacey told me that she and her music producers been working very long hours and that she no time to chit chat with me. So I told her that I totally had understood her trying to work hard to making it in the Hip Hop industry.

I waited for two days before I called her back and when I did just that another woman pick up Lacey's mobile phone and to my very surprise another female pick up for her and when I realize that it was not who I thought it was and I ask the other woman just who was I speaking too? She said hello my name is Trickcey Dollars. And I ask the woman just who she was and why she was answering my girlfriend Lacey cellur phone? the young woman Trickcey told me that my girlfriend Lacey who is also her friend of 5 years visited her home in Deer Park in Long Island and left her cell phone at her house by mistake. So Trickcey begin questioning me about just how did I know her friend Lacey Ward? And I informed her that her friend and I meet through the telephone chateline of the Qwest Personals and that everything seem to go quit well between Lacey and I.

That was until Lacey friend Trickcey informed me that her friend was not being totally honesty and faithful toward me as I may always thought. And from there I asked Trickcey Just what every did she meant by that?

And Trickcey begin to explain that her friend Lacey confided in her and told her that while she was supposed to just be making musical rap music she was also having sexual threesome intercourse with two other guys in the studio when she was supposed to be working on a album. And I couldn't at believe what I was being told at first as I been in total shock of the matter.

So from there my girlfriend Lacey Ward friend whose name was Trickcey Dollars asked me since I now know the truth of the matter that I been cheated on by her friend she asked me if I would like to started having a new intimate relationship with her? And I told Trickcey that after the totally shock of me to being cheated on by her friend Lacey Ward that I would love to so. And afterward we decided to make plans to finally meet at my family house in Astoria Queens New York. And when Trickcey finally had arrived at my family home as she pulled up in a taxi cab as she gotten out of the vehicle I greeted her with open arms and multiple kisses on the cheek as we greeted each other on our way down to my family basement apartment. And I remember thinking that I was so very much glad that she seemed to be totally my type of a woman that I would love to be involved with her as I really had admired her hair braided hair style that she place in a hair weave fashion that black and gold hair coloring.

And once Trickcey and I finally had arrived inside my family home we headed to my family downstairs in the basement apartment and I took hold of Trickcey's two hands and took a step back so that I could get a even better look at her and it turn out that I was so very impress by her very sexy plus size curvy curves and she been totally my preference of what type of women that lam attracted to. And we decided to started to get to know one another so much better that also included sexually intimatically. So afterward as it was getting close to dinner time I asked Trickcey if she was getting hungry enough for dinning as of yet? And she said yes she certainly was ready for supper, and that she was also going to be the one to prepared our meal for the two of us. So she prepared a fabulous chicken parmesan dinner with a verity of vegetable and it was so very delicious.

So on December 15, 1997, I contacted my ex-girlfriend Lacey Ward by calling her and asking her if she been cheating on me while she was only supposed to be working on a recorded album, as I also informed her that when I called her cellur phone her friend who said her name was Trickcey Dollars answered and told me that her friend was being totally unfaithful toward me. So I asked Lacey was that story true was she cheating on me with one of her record producer by having a sexually relations with him while she was only supposed to be working? And from there she asked me just who told me that she been cheating on me and with whom? And I just to let her know that it's was her friend Trickcey Dollars. And Lacey been totally surprised that I told her that her friend Trickcey betrayed her by letting me know what her friend be doing behind my back as she totally exposed her secret that she was trying to hid from me.

So from there Lacey began to cry her eyes out and started saying to me that she felt so very sorry and ashamed of herself that she been cheating on me by having sexual relations with two other men while she was only supposed to be recording a album. And I told her that I in fact did suspected that she was cheating on me that why I asked her could I come into the studio to see just how she worked, as she denied me the privilege to do so. And Lacey had told me that the only reason that she a sexually relations with the record producers was that she was realing trying to get ahead of the music business. And she began to ask me just why did I cheat on her with her best friend Trickcey because she told me that was her best friend and that how could I done just a thing like that without me knowing that her friend could been lying to me about her friend cheating on me? And I told her because I been trying to reach her as my suppossitted faithful girlfriend for days at a time with me only being able to hear her voice message.

And I explain to her that the only reason I decided to be totally unfaithful to her by started a brand-new intimated sexual relationship with her friend Trickcey was because she was the one who told me what her my no good cheating girlfriend been up too. Lacey told me that even though that her friend Trickcey told me that I was being cheated on that I should have never cheated on her with her friend Trickcey who she grown up with ever since they were young teenagers. So I had shouted at her to say that she a lot of got dam nerve lying to me telling me that she was working on a rap album when she been cheating on me for about two whole months that why I decided to cheat on her with her friend because she decided to cheat on me first and that I known that I knew that by me having a intimate new sexual relation with her friend Trickcey that was a good emotional pay back from me to her as I knew that it would upset so very much so.

So from there Trickcey and I continued to having our very intimated relationship with Trickcey and she decided that that it was time that she introduced me to her family, so I once again was on my way back to Deer Park in Long Island. And when we arrived to Trickcey family home her I meet her father whose name was Floyed Dollars and her mother whose name was Betty Dollars as they both of them greeted me with a very friendly hug and a hello. And we all had sat down in the family living room so that I could begin becoming better aquated with them. As Trickcey father Mr. Dollars asked me just what did I did for a living to make ends meet? And I told him that I was a interoffice mail man that work for a very large law firm in midtown Manhattan. And from there both of Trickcey's parents seem to be very impress to the point to where they prepared a very nice dinner for all of us that also included Trickcey than six old daughter whose name was a Dolly Dollars as she asked me just who I and what I was doing with her mommy? And I told Trickcey Daughter Dolly that I was my friend and Trickcey said to dolly that right.

From there my former girlfriend Trickcey Dollars and I begin to get a little bored in the spring of April 1998 as we both decided that it would be a good ideal for us two to go on a Vacation together somewhere, and when I ask her just where she in mine that she wanted to visit to she told me that she n't seen her cousins whose name was Gushcey Dollars and her boyfriend whose name was Harry Stuckey in a long while and that she would like to visit them in Richmond Virginia. And from there we were on our way, so we decided to travel by the Greyhood buses and the actual ride been for a 5 hours ride from The New York City Port Authority Bus Terminal in Midtown Manhattan. And when Trickcey and I arrived to her cousins family home in Richmond Virginia they welcome us both with open arms. after all of the warm hello's and huges Trickcey family members asked her just who I was? Trickcey finally introduced me to her other family member that consisted of plenty of cousins.

So Trickcey family started questioning us about just how we first meet and what made us two want to come all the way down south? And we told the family that we just had wanted to take a vacation some where nice. So we asked Trickcey cousin Gusey and boyfriend Harry what's good to do in the state of Virginia? And they told us that the Amusement Park King Demenia was the best entertainment attraction in the state. So we were on our way there and when we finally had arrived at the amusement park when it was time to pay for the admission to get inside Trickcey cousin Gushcey and her boyfriend Harry said that no money.

And I remembered thinking that I couldn't believe that Trickcey cousin and her boyfriend agreed with her to come along with us to the King Demenia Amusement Park and absolutely no money of there very own, so I to pay there way in as well as Trickcey's and my very own. And I been thinking to myself that what a bunch of broke ass people in that family. But after that very stressful financial burden of Trickcey's cousin Gushcey and her boyfriend Harry being totally broke I just knew that I to get over the upset way I was feeling and just go on right ahead and began having a good time anyway. And it turn out that we all wound up having a good time anyway as we gotten on multiple rides. And afterwards I the urge to want to buy some silvernairs for myself and Trickcey as well than Trickcey cousins Gushcey and her boyfriend Harry the got dam nerve to ask for silvernairs as well and I told them only a few items that was all that I could afford. And from there we left the Amusement and was back on our way to Trickcey cousin Gushcey family house.

And when we all arrived back at my ex-girlfriend Trickcey's family cousins house in Richmond Virginia all of us were so very much escorted as the family asked us well just how was the King Deminiona Amusement Park? And we told Trickcey's family that we all a very fun and exciting good time to the point to where we all screamed so very loud that we made jokes to each other that the entire park probably could hear our big mouths. And Trickcey's family just had laugh at us as they all said that they were so very much glad that we all a very wonderful good time together. So after we settled back in Trickcey's Cousins family home they asked all four of us if we were very hungry? And we laugh and giggled and said you bet we are plenty of hungry after that long trip and Trickcey and her Cousin Gushcey said family let get our food on the family table so we could all begin eating.

And the food was so very delicious so much that it would almost make me lick my plate totally clean, and we also plenty of fun and laughter as well. And Trickcey family asked her and I just what were our attentions were for each other? And we told everyone that we were just having a good time just enjoying each others company and that we decided that we were going to take things slow in our new founded relationship, and Trickcey family agreed on our very wise decision to see where things go between the two of us. Trickcey's family and I just sat around watching her family's home movies of themselves.

the next morning Trickcey said that if I could afford to rent a rental car so we can all curse around the Richmond Virginia area? And I said yes that it would be okay to do so just as long that the car rental wasn't to expensive. And when we went to the car rental dealership called Avis in the Richmond Virginia area we found out that it only had costed $35 per day and I rented a vehicle for s three day special that the company offer me. So after I paid for the car rental and Trickcey to show her driver license to the car dealer the car was all ours for a few days and Trickcey and I stroved off to pick up her cousins Guschey and her boyfriend Harry to go to some of the clubs that they in town as we all a very good time until the dance club called Gallacy closed down for the evening.

And when we all arrived back at Trickcey cousin family Gushcey home it gotten quit late as we were all so very tired from hanging out together we all retired for the evening to get a good night rest so I thought that was until a knock come to the door and it was Trickcey cousin whose name was Carlos whispering to her saying that he wanted to borrow my car rental and if it was okay? And I was a half asleep and the next morning arrived and when Trickcey and I finally had awaken up the next morning she said that it was time for us to get up and out of the bed and for us to take a shower. And she said the most sexiest thing to me that we should save lots of time and hot water by having us to take our shower together as one, and I said yes that I totally agreed with her very sexy idea. But when some of her family members saw us both go inside of their bathroom together they begin to laugh and question us about where were we both going? Trickcey and I explained that we the idea that we would save lots of time if we taken our showers together instead of separately. And Trickcey female family members joked around with her and said you go girl you just keep your good man very close to you and don't let no one else around here have him.

So after Trickcey and I taken our morning shower together and a very family hearty breakfast that consisted of pancakes and beef sausages along with some freshly squeeze orange juice she told me that she wanted us take a trip to the corner grocery store so we did just that. But before we left out the door we made sure that we thank the family for that very wonderful meal that been prepared for the both of us. And we told the family that we were both headed out and did anybody want us to bring them something back from the store? And they all had said that they were all good and that they did not need anything at all, so we were on our way out the door. And as we were on our way out the door I told Trickcey that her Richmond Virginia family really had seem very nice and that I just knew how happy she was to see them and see thank me for bringing her all the way there so I would have the good chance to meet the other side of her family and I said to her that she was quite welcome.

But when we gotten to my Honda Accord car rental I quickly taken notice of a sudden small dent on the driver side of the door and I had asked Trickcey I wondering what happen to the car rental? And Trickcey told me that her cousin Carlos come into the room and asked her if he could borrow the Honda Accord car to take it to the store? And Trickcey told me that she told her cousin Carlos that it was okay for him to do so. And I gotten so very upset that she did not contribution any money for the trip but the guil to len out my rental car that I pay my hard earn money for. And Trickcey told me that it was a very small dent and when we were to take the car back to the car rental dealer that I would not be charge any extra money, and I that I taught I hope that she was right.

as we were about to get into the car her cousin Carlos would come outside and he asked where were we going? And Trickcey told him just to the store. Trickcey cousins Carlos asked her did she want him to drive? And at first told her cousin no and that he did enough damage to the car and that she was going to be the one to drive us to the store, but when she started up the car she intentionally had stop the car short pretending that she hit her head on the steering wheel. And when her cousin Carlos saw that he again asked her if she wanted to drive us all to the corner grocery store? And she said yes it was okay. And from there I just known that she was just faking a steering wheel head bump just to let her cousin drive the car. And I was quite angry with the both of them for her to have the nerve to be so very giving of the rental car as she did not have any money to pay for anything, so off we went to the store and back.

So after a few days it finally been time for Trickcey and I to start to head back to our family homes in the New York City area, as she informed her family members as they were all to sad to have to see us leave them so suddenly. And Trickcey and I to return the car rental back to the dealership and afterwards we took a taxi cab car service back to Trickcey's Cousin house to pick up our personal belongings and we said our goodbyes to Trickcey family members as they all gave us both very warm hugs and as for myself a very firm handshake. And from there the family called a taxi cab service for Trickcey and I, and as it arrived we were finally on our way back home. And as we been traveling back home to the New York on the Greyhood bus Terminal Trickcey ask me just how I enjoyed the trip to meet her other family members? And I just told her that I a greet time meeting her extended family members very much so.

And once we both arrived back into the New York area we hand headed back to Trickcey family home in Deer Park in Long Island and Trickcey rang her family door bell and her parents Mr. & Mrs. Dollar let met Trickcey and myself inside and ask well just how was the trip to visit there family in Richmond Virginia? And we told them that we a nice time staying with the family we were hanging out in the dance club and having the best time every at the King Deminya Amusement Park. And Trickcey's Daughter Dolly came into the her family kitchen area and said mommy, mommy I really did miss you so very much so as she also preceded to give her mother multiple kisses and hugs as she also had said hello to me as well to also say that she was also very glad that we both made it back to there home safe and sound. And Trickcey's daughter dolly grab both of our hands and told us to come down to their family basement to play a doll house game with her and we were once again on our way downstairs to there family basement to play house.

after about a half and hour past Mrs. Dollar ask us all if we were getting hungry as of yet? And the three of us said yes and that were very much so hungry that we all felt that we could eat a cow as we been laughing with each other in a very jokey matter and shortly after that we began to enjoy yet another delicious meal from Trickcey family. And as it gotten late and we both had put Trickcey's daughter Dolly to bed the both of us gotten into a very romantic mood to have foreplay by Trickcey lighting a little candle and just watching it drip by drip pour on my body chest hairs and I did the very same to her as I really had enjoyed seeing the wax drip on her very large nipples as we also had been ready to have very passionate sex as it turn out so pleasantly satisfying to us both. And once we awaken up the next morning it was time for me to go back to my parents home in Astoria New York as I said my goodbyes to Trickcey and her family and I told her that I would call to let her know that when I made it home, and she said that I better make sure that I do call her just as soon as I get back to my family home.

on April 15, 1998, Trickcey said that she was in fact bored and that she thought that it would be a good ideal for us to go to her neighborhood shopping mall that was called The Galexcy Shopping Mall to just window shop and I said Okay let's be on our way out there. And as we were supposed to only be hanging out just looking around as we been just been passing by we wounded up at one of the malls jewelry store that was called the Barkley Diamonds as we been looking at some diamond rings as I asked Trickcey just what ring that she thought was the prettiest diamond of the them all? And she said that she liked the ring that the 1 Karat in the center setting with the two sided triple diamonds. And the store manager ask if we were interested in making a purchase of any jewelry?, and at first we told him no and that we were just looking around and that was until a diamond ring really had interested Trickcey and she said to me that since we were already dating each other she asked the question why don't we just get engage to be married someday in the very near future? And I said yes to her proposal of marriage as I decided to let her pick out the diamond ring that she wanted and worked out a monthly payment plain with the store manager and after Trickcey propose to me asking me to please be her husband and I said yes I do accept and than began to place the Diamond ring on her hand and we were off to break the good news to our two families.

And when we arrived back at Trickcey family home to her parents house we broke the good news of Trickcey and mine brand-new engagement to Trickcey's parents Mr.& Mrs. Dollars they both congratulation us and welcome me to there family and told me that I better take very good care of there daughter Trickcey and grand daughter Dolly as I ensured them both that I would do just that and that I was so very glad to finally fine a very special lady to share me life with. And Trickcey mom and dad welcome me to there family with open arms and a firm handshake from the father Mr Dollars. And it started getting kind of late and I told Trickcey that I was going to start heading back home to my own family house and break the good news to them. And Trickcey said to me okay future hubby that she would let me go for now but I better make double sure that when I finally do get home and settle myself in for me to be sure that I was to give here a call so that she would know that I was at home safe and sound and I told her I will do just that after I break our good news to my own family.

When I finally had arrived back at my family home in Astoria NYS and I immediately had said my hello's to my mom Jahtayshia and my dad Damian Sr. as I began to let my parents know about my good news on my brand-new engagement to my new fiance whose name was Trickcey Dollars and they been in totally shock of what I was tell them. And they congratulation of the matter. Than my mother began to ask me just how long have we been dating each other? and I told her only about 2 weeks and my mom and dad ask me where did we meet? and I told them both the telephone personal of Qwest chateline and the told me that they both had thought that we was both moving way to fast in a relationship and that we should slow thing down a little bit and just date each other for a long while until we both really gotten to know each other better. And my dad told me with that my young lady Trickcey having a last name like Dollars that what she might want to use me for is my money and that I better be careful of that new fiance wanting to try to rush me in a marriage just so she could try to use me for some money. And I said that I would be very carful not to let that happen, mom hand asked me just when do she and my father get the chance to meet my girlfriend Trickcey Dollars? And I told that I would to get back to them to let them know just when she would be able to meet with our family.

And after a short while later as we still engaged to one another as Trickcey realized after I was able to make a big purchase of her 1 carat

Diamond ring that she must had figured out that at that particular time I a very good credit standing so she asked me if I wanted to increase my credit limit? And I asked her just why she was asking me? Trickcey went on and begin explaining to me that her father known several different ways on just how you could expand your credit limit so we both could have more chances to shop for herself, and her daughter dolly as well as myself. And I said that yes it was in fact okay for her Dad Mr. Dollars to go ahead and see if he could in fact increase my credit limit as she told me that she would get right on it and pass the message to her dad so that he could get things started for the three of us. And about two weeks later I had started to receive multiple credit cards in the mail than short after t Trickcey asked me did they arrived as of yet? And I informed her that yes they did.

Trickcey told me that she would be right over so we could begin do some more shopping near my own neighborhood malls. And when she finally had arrived to my family home as she come through the front door to meet my family that consist of my mother Jahtayshia, my father Damian Sr. and Damian Jr. and my two younger sisters whose name are Tameka who was 8 years old at the time and Fatima Devine who was six years old at that particular time. And my entire family said there hellos as my mom and my two little sisters all sat down with Trickcey to have a little girl talk with her. And my mother asked Trickcey about her parents and just how they were doing? And Trickcey proceed to say that her mom and dad were doing quit well as she also had thank her for asking about them. Trickcey went on to say that she a six year old daughter whose name Dolly and that she was a only child and that she would love to bring her by so that she could play with my two little sisters Tameka and Fatima and we said that would be great for her to meet the girls. And little Fatima and Tameka Kept on getting so very much exciting to meet Trickcey little daughter Dolly and they were both hugging on her asking Trickcey does she really promise to bring her daughter dolly by so they could all play together? And Trickcey assured them that she would defiantly bring little dolly by.

And a short while after that it started to get very late as we all said that we were going to retire for the evening to get a good night rest and from there we said our good nights to each other and that we would she each other in the morning and from there Trickcey and I were headed downstairs to my family basement. So from there Trickcey ask me how about those credit cards that she her dad arranged for me to get as there been two that recently had come in the mail? And when I showed her she gotten so very exciting she begin unfastening my belt buckle to undress me as she the climb on top of me to sexually ride me like a pony as it felt like the best sex ever. And as I known that Trickcey was going to be eventually coming over for a visit as I took the liberty to buying some whip cream for a very special sexually occasion like that one. And I brought it into the bedroom as I began to spray it on Trickcey's every sexual body parts as she did the very same thing as we just started licking and sucking all over each body and it felt so very good as we reached our climb max point.

And as we awaken up the very next morning on of April 23, 1998, Trickcey gotten up first with her being so very exciting about us going shopping that day that when she said good morning my darling future husband as she also gave me a big sweet kiss on my lips and said that she was going to be so very happy to make us some breakfast that morning so we could have enough energy to do some shopping for us. And I told Trickcey that before we would start eating our morning breakfast that I was going to take me a hot shower to clens myself, and Trickcey said that wound be okay just as long as I didn't take to long because the food would take only about ten minutes to prepare, and I said okay I'll be right there. And from there Trickcey set the table as a candle lite breakfast simply because it was still dark outside and she told me that we should get a early start and beat the crowd. And our very romantic breakfast been so very good that time around I wanted a second serving of the meal, so she made a little more for me.

shortly after that my mom and dad gotten my two sisters Tameka and Fatima up for there schooling day that same morning as they said there good mornings to us both and also had asked us just how we were both feeling that day? And we said that everything was going and that we were going to be doing some shopping that day as my mom said okay and for us not to stay out to late out there and we answered her and said okay we won't. And we were on our way there and Trickcey quit a shopping spree off my credit cards that my future father in law Mr. Dollars arranged for me to get a large amount of line of credit. And she picked out a few dresses for herself and a few outfits for her daughter Dolly and she said that she saved just enough on the credit cards so that I could get something for myself and I said that was fine. So from there I pick out a few outfits that I preferred to have for myself as when I also went inside to try on several outfits Trickcey said that they all looked good on me, as she went on to asked me if I was also done shopping for myself as she was? And I told her yes and that I was more than ready to go to leaving out the Midtown Manhattan mall and from there we where on our way back to my family home.

We than went to The Lobsters Seafood Restaurant to enjoy some fine dinning out as we ordered two ultimate seafood platters and it turn out that was my No. 1 favorite type of dish that I always enjoyed as Trickcey said her to. And from there we dranked some alcohol beverages of sex on the beach as it been so very tasteful to the both of us. So after we sat around and laugh and giggle with each other for a short while it began to get kind of late so we headed back to my family home in the Astoria Queens area. So I called for a Astoria New York taxi cab service to pick us both up to take us both back home with me until the very next afternoon.

And once we arrived back at my family home as I reached out to open my side door entrance screen door I noticed that the door been locked, so Trickcey and I to go to my family front door and ring the door bell in order to get into the house and so I did just that. And my mother come down stares to answer the door bell and from there Trickcey and I said our hellos to my mother. And I asked my mother just why the side door be locked? And my mom said that my father to take out the garbage from the side door entrance as he always does and he must locked the door by mistake and I said oh okay mom. my mother said hello to Trickcey as she also had went on to asked her that she see that we a little shopping spree as we were both out ha? And she hand told my mother yea just a little one Mrs. Devine

So we took all of the shopping bags downstairs to the family basement apartment as we been so very exsorsted from all of those hours of shopping in the mall and from there my mother began to question us by asking just what did we buy while we were out for all those many hours? And Trickcey shown my mother all that we brought from the shopping mall and my mom said that everything was so very beautiful and that she hope that we didn't over spend on what we brought from the department stores. And Trickcey said to my mother that oh no she wouldn't do that at all. And after that we taken everything back downstairs to my living couch. And we watch a good dance movie that was playing on cable television that was called Crush Groove.

And we watched television until we fallen asleep until the next early morning than Trickcey told me that after a few days away from her family that she better start to head back to her family home in Deer Park New York Long Island and she given me multiple goodbye kiss and hugs and said that she would call me much later when she gotten home and I told her that would be fine and that I would wait to her back from her and she told me to be sure to wait up for her call. And later that very same day my parents called me from the basement and said that they wanted to talk to me about something and I told them that I'll be write upstairs in just a few minutes. And my mom and dad began to say to me that they see that my girlfriend Trickcey and I went on quit of a shopping spree. And they asked me just who paid for all of everything? And I told them that I did so, and when they heard that they asked me just how I could afford all of the things that I brought from the department stores? And I told them that Trickcey father arrange to expanded my credit limit so that we could buy the finer things in life because I was engaged to his daughter Trickcey. my father went on to asked me didn't I tell you that Trickcey was just trying to use you for money and that was her excuse for her to tell you to buy that very experience diamond ring and now clothes? And my father also went on to say that my girlfriend Trickcey Dollars was just trying to use me for dollars as he began to laugh at me along with my mom as they both had warn me that I should take very good notice when my credit card would run out of credit Trickcey would run out of my life and that I should just wait and see just what will happen between us two as he began to laugh at me.

So on April 30, 1998, Trickcey called me that afternoon and tolded me that she missed me so very much so that she a sexual dream of us to making love on a waterbed just like the one in her parents bedroom along with some lovely rose pedals on top. And I told her that I thought that was one of the most romantic dreams that I ever heard of. And from there I asked her just when was I going to get the good chance to she her again? And Trickcey told me that she was going to be visiting me that very same day and that she was going to also be bringing her little daughter Dolly by to also visit my two little sisters Tameka and Fatima so they all could play together and I said that would be great for all of us to be together so we could have the best of good times that we could share together. Trickcey told me that she to go and begin to grease and braid little Dolly hair into a nice hair style of some kind so that she may make a very good first impression for all my family and I to see and I said that sounded great and that I would see the two of them when they were to arrived at my family home.

And when Trickcey and Dolly finally arrived at our family home we all welcome them both into our family home with warm family hugs and a kisses as my two younger sisters Tameka, Fatima and Trickcey daughter Dolly been so very excited to play together as they also wanted to play doll house together right away and so they all gotten right to it. And my mother Jahtayshia giggled with Trickcey and went on to say that she thought that was a very sweet name for her little girl as she whet on to also say that she even looks like a precious doll baby. from there Trickcey thank my mother for that very special commit. the girls asked Trickcey and I to come down to the floor and play with them all and we gotten a big laugh at what they been asking of us as we eventually played right along with them playing tea house party.

my mom and dad prepared a very wonderful steak and potatoes with gravy and a biscuit meals that turn out so very tasteful along with my mother baking having to bake a sweet potatoes pie that we all also enjoyed. And after dinner my mother decided to play a children movie of Beauty in the Best so that the three girls could be entertain. And they all laugh and giggled all through there movie as we adults also did so just by watching them all enjoying there show. And shortly after that we all decided that it was getting late and that it was time to prepared ourselves for bedtime and from there we all wish each other to have a good night rest and that we would see each other all in the morning time. And Trickcey, Dolly and myself all went downstairs to my family basement apartment. And Trickcey and Dolly changed into there pajamases and we all sat down to watch another movie that was called Sleepen Beauty until the girl fell asleep. And from there I picked up and carried little Dolly to my bed so she could On May 8, 1998, on mother day Trickcey than informed me that there was going to be a Caribbean Day Parade in the Prospect Park Brooklyn New York area and she said that she wanted the two of us to attend all of the wonderful festivities that was going on that day and I said to her that sounded like a very wonderful thing to do for that very special day and from there we left her daughter with my parents so that my little two younger sisters Tameka and Fatima and Trickcey daughter Dolly could spend even more time together while we were both out for the day as mom told me that it was okay for her to baby sit one extra child and from there we were on our way. We decided to take the New York City Mass Transit Authority train to the Prospect Park area as it been very much so crowded as we suspected that once we gotten on the train to the Brooklyn New York area that mostly everyone was also headed in the very same direction that we were going as we taken noticed that a lot of other passengers gotten off the very same stop that Trickcey and myself gotten off of and was headed in the very same direction as we both were. And when we finally had arrived at the park we really had begin enjoying ourselves quit a bit as we than enjoyed lots of good food and music along with the parade performers putting a good show for the audience. And we even saw a few sports athletes legendes and boxing promoters that bend riding on top on the multiple floats as I also brought my camera along with me so that I may take plenty of pictures to savory the memories of that very special day that Trickcey and I both shared together just between the two of us.

And after the parade been over with I treated Trickcey to a few gifts to pick out some silvernares for her as well as myself. And from there we were both headed back to my family home in the Astoria Queens area as we also had check in with my parents to see how everything was going with all of the girls, and my mother told us that things were going just great as Trickcey's daughter Dolly asked to speak to her mommy and as Trickcey been talking with her she asked her just when she was coming home? Trickcey asked her daughter was she okay? Dolly told her that yes she was doing just find with here mommy boyfriend Romeo's two little sister Tameka and Fatima playing the dolly game but she also added that she wanted her mom to come back and take her home to her grandma and grandpa's house.

And Trickcey told me that we better head back home to my family house because her daughter Dolly was starting to get very irritable wining for her mommy a bit and from there we were on our way back to my family house. But by the time we gotten back there the kids were all asleep. And Trickcey asked my mother just how her daughter behaved with her? And my mother told Trickcey that her daughter behave quit well just tiring herself out quit a bit just like her very own two daughters. And Trickcey began to laugh a little bit what with my mom was saying and we both thank her for taking so good care of her little one and my mom told her that she was quite welcome as we both said good night to my mother as I also giving my mother a good night kiss as we also said that we would see each other in the A M hours.

A the very next morning when the three of us than awaken up from our very restful night sleep Trickcey told me that after a little while later we were to have breakfast that she was going to have to start heading back home to her folks house because she hand said that her daughter Dolly was starting to get a little home sick, and I told her that I totally had understood that she to get back home to her own people. And shortly after we enjoyed yet another delicious meal Trickcey, Dolly and I went back upstairs from the family basement to say our good mornings to my family as well as the two very special ladies that were in my life to give my mother and two younger sisters Tameka and Fatima a very warm good bye huge and kisses as they were about to leave for Long Island. And from there we all told Trickcey and Dolly to be absolutely sure that she was to give me a call shortly after she gotten the two of them home safely. And Trickcey told me that she would be sure to do just that as soon as they were to get settle in.

And when they finally did arrived Trickcey taking the liberty to give me a call to let me know that she and Dolly were in fact okay and made it in the house safe and sound. And I told them that was good that there travels turn out okay because as it was getting kind of late I began to getting some what worrisome that I started thinking about calling her parents to check to see if you hand came home yet. And Trickcey assured me that she and Dolly were very safe and sound. So from there Trickcey told me that some of her extended family members come by and that she to leave me and get off of the telephone to began socializing with her family and that she would also be giving me a call much later and I said that would be fine and that I would talk to me.

So afterward my two younger sisters Tameka and Fatima told me that they really a very fun time with my girlfriend Trickcey's daughter Dolly as they kepted on asking me when they both were going to be coming back over to our family house? And I told them that they would probably be right back over sometime next week and my sisters Tameka and Fatima told me that they so much fun while Trickcey and I was out to the park parade as they also told me that our mommy let them play plenty of fun games such as pin the tail on the dunky and penyanta game that been filled with lots of delicious candys that was all so good to eat. And I had a good laugh at what the girls were telling me as they also offered me a few pieces of candy from there busted wide open penyanya. And the girls covered my eyes with there blind fold and placed there dunkey tale pin in my hand so I could play pin the tale on the dunkey right along with them as we all had a good laugh at playing the game while also eating very tasty snacks.

On July 14, 1998, Trickcey called me and said that she missed me a whole lot and that she was on her way over to come pay me another visit and I told her that I couldn't hardly wait to see her as well and that I would be awaiting for her arrival. And when Trickcey finally had arrived at my family house she come straight downstairs to my basement apartment and said her hello to me she asked me what was up with my credit cards that her father gotten for me? And when I told her that they were all max out over the credit limit Trickcey than asked me dam is that it is all the good credit use up already? And I told her yeah that about it as far as all of that shopping goes for us for a while. And Trickcey went on to asked me if I wanted to break off our engagement? And I told her yes if that is what she wanted and she precede to give me back the diamond ring that I originally had made the purchase for our engagement to each other and she said her finally goodbye to me as she left out of my family home.

And after all of that I couldn't believe what just had happen to me of just as soon as those credit cards reached there credit limit my Finance broken off our engagement of only a few months of us being together as I realized that what my father told me that my girlfriend/fiance whose name was Trickcey Dollars was just using me for my credit cards that was equal to my own dollars. And I just knew I to let my mother and father know what just happen with me and Trickcey breaking off our engagement so I was on my way back up the family basement stairwell to break the shocking news to them both. And when I saw them I told them that I just broke up with my now ex-fiance Trickcey Dollars who my dad worn me that woman was just trying to used me for my own dollars or my credit limit that her own Daddy arranged for me to get. As he also said that he warn me that was going to happen as he again told me that she was nothing but a hoggy mama type of woman trying to play me like a fool for my money and didn't even have a job of here very own.

my mother went on to say that was a dam shame that Trickcey set out to use me for my hard earn money for her own selfish gain by having me to going out and do all of her shopping for her and her daughter Dolly. And I to shamefully admit that they were both been totally right as I also had told them that I realized that Trickcey and her parents Mr. and Mrs. Dollars were nothing but a bunch of money hungry players and my parents both agreed right along with me. And from there I to explain to my adorable little sisters Tameka and Fatima that little Dolly would not be coming to visit anymore because she broken off our relationship that we together. And my sister said that was to bad for me and them as well because they all really a very fun sleep over slumber that they all enjoyed.

And the very next day after Trickcey Dollars broken off our engagement to be married someday as I been laying around in my bedroom my telephone rang and when I answered it turn out to be a female teller marketer that was trying to sell me a news paper. And the lady teller marketer began giving me her sale pitch for me to sale her employer company news paper, but I was not interested making a purchase of what she been trying to convince me to buy. But since I just recently broken up with my now ex-fiance Trickcey Dollars I decided to show some romantic interest in the female teller marketer by telling that I was really interested in buy her employer company new paper but instead I told her that I was very much more interested in knowing what was her name was and she giggled and she told me that her name was Elite Windgate. And I proceeded to asked her if she was in fact single at the time?

And Elite told me yes that she was in fact still single looking for a very nice guy. So from there I invited her to come over a pay me a visit, and she asked me if it was safe for her to come over to my house? And I reassured her that yes it was absolutely safe for her to come over and visit me as well as my family and that she told me that she would be right over the very next day to visit me and my family. So on November 27, 1998, when Elite first pulled up in a taxi cab service care she call me on her cellur phone to come meet her outside so that she could come inside to meet my family and I did just that. And when I first laid eyes on the lovely Elite Windgate been so very much pleased to finally have the good chance to meet her that I gave her a big juicy kiss on her left cheek as we said our very first hellos in person and from there we headed back downstairs to my family basement. And when we both gotten ourselves inside the house we just sat around as we began to just start to get to know each other quit well.

after a little time pass by I told Elite that I wanted her to meet my family that was living upstairs and she said that is was ready to start to get to know them so much better. And we were on our way upstairs and I said hello there family it's me Romeo and my new lady friend whose name is Elite Windgate. And when my mother Jahtayshia first saw Elite she hand began to smile at her and say hello to her as she also given her a warm welcome huge hug and a kiss of her right cheek as my two sisters Tameka and Fatima been so very excited that they did the very same thing. And when my father Damian Sr. and big brother Damian Jr. come inside the house from there work day they hand also greeted my new girlfriend Elite quite pleasantly as they also had said there hello's. my family asked Elite about her own family and just how they were all doing? And my new girlfriend Elite told my mother that her family was doing quite well as she also went on to say that her mother name is Wonda Windgate and that she also had a few siblings that consisted of her older brother whose name is Mason Wingate and her younger brother whose name is Epico and her younger sister whose name is Epiphany Windgate and that her family all live in the Long Island City Queens New York area.

my two younger sisters Tameka and Fatima asked Elite just how old was her little sister in age? And Elite went on to tell the girls that her little sister whose name is Epiphany was just a little bit older than they were themselves at the tender preteen age of twelve years old. Fatima and Tameka asked Elite just when they would have the good chance to meet her family? And Elite told them she probably would bring the family by for a visit sometime next weekend when she was off from work, and the girls said that sounded great and that they would be very glad to finally be able to meet them all especially Epiphany.

So on the December 4, 1998, my new lovely ladyfriend Elite Windgate called me up on the telephone to first asked me just how did I sleep that night after we finally meet for the very first time in person? And I said to her that I felt really happy when I finally had awaken up that morning as I been thinking only of her at that time and she said that all sounded so very good to her and that she also missed me a whole lot to the point that she said that she and her mother invited wanted me to come over for a nice dinning out to a fancy restaurant that was called Clansey. And I begin become quite thrilled of Elite family wanted to make a very good first impression of themselves to me as I accepted my invitation out to meet her family for the very first time. From there I was on my way over to meet her family and when I finally arrived by the New York City Transfit Mass Transit subway system to Elite's Long Island City Queens New York apartment building I called Elite on my mobile phone to let her know that I finally had arrived to see her and the family.

And she told me that she and her family was on the way out the door to finally have the good chance to meet me and when when they did Elite mother Ms. Wonda Windgate greeteded me with a very warm embrace and a friendly hello as I also had said my hellos to her two teenage son Epico and teenage daughter Epiphany as we were on our way to dine out. And we all gotten Into Ms. Windgate family car as we were all on our way to have a lovely night dinner out, and when we all finally arrived I been very much impressed with the family good taste of choosing such a very fine Classy restaurant to take me to so that I may start to become much more better aquated with Elite immediate family members. And as we all been enjoying our meals Elite mother wanted to learn more about me and what I did to make a living for myself? And I begin telling her that I was employed with a very large corporate law firm that was called O'Conner, Sapp, Dash & Marshall as a inter-office mailman clerk of five years of service with the company. And Ms. Wonda Windgate said that she been so very much impress of her daughter Elite to have such a nice man who is very hard working and I said thank you.

On about December 20, 1998, Elite informed me when she and I was on a date together about her father who was also a Vietnam veteran whose name was Faarooq Cultler who was a captain in the United States Marines Core where he service his country for twenty years very proudly I might add. And Elite began to explain that she really started to really miss her father and her aunt whose name was Victoria and her uncle whose name was Tyson Fonzelrelly quit a bit to the point that she and her family members with the exception of her half brother Mason was planning to take a road trip to visit her dad family in Memphis Tennessee, and she went on to asked me if I would like the good chance to meet them all and I said yes I absolutely would be honored to meet the other side of her family for the holidays seasons. But I told my new girlfriend Elite that I to tell my parents about the good news about me going to finally meet your Father's family and she said that would be fine to do so. And after spending a half of the day together as it started to getting very late a night as we just had said our good nite farewells to each other along with us leaving each other with a big fat juicy wet kiss until the next time we would see each other.

And when I finally had arrived back in my family house I told them the good news to my mom and dad about my new relationship with my new girlfriend whose name was Elite Windgate and about how she wanted me to meet her father whose name was Faarooq Culter and that he was a veteran of the U. S. Marine Core and how she informed me that he was living in Memphis Tennessee with his sister whose name was Victoria and her husband Tyson Fonzelrelly. And my mom and dad said that they were so very much happy for me to finally found a good woman who really seems to come from a very good family instead of that hoochy mama ex-girlfriend whose name was Trickcey Dollars and I told them that you got that right family. And they both asked me just when we were supposed to be leaving from the New York City area? And I told them that my girlfriend Elite and her family and I would all be leaving in a matter of days and that I would also have them come inside to meet them both when they were to pick me up.

When Elite, and her mother Ms. Wonda Windgate, youngest brother Epico and younger sister Epiphany finally arrived at my family home by car I asked them all to come inside so our two families could finally have the good chance to meet each other in person for the very first time so they may become much more better aquated with each other. And when they all gotten inside our family home my mother welcomed them all with a very lovely warm tender hugs and kisses as she said her hellos to Elite's mom and her two adorable teenage children Epico and Epiphany to come inside for a little while so that we may all become much more better aquated with each other. And my two little sisters Tameka and Fatima wanted to say theire hello's to Elite pre teen sister Epiphany and ask her all sorts of question such as what school did she attend to and how did she like going there? And Epiphany told them both that she attended the Long Island City Elementary School and that she like going there very much so. And they began to asked Elite brother Epico the very same questions and he told them I. S. 231 that was in there neighborhood school of hard knocks as he been laughing and just joking around with my sisters. And shortly after that Elite family members and I were on our way to pay Elite father family a visit in Memphis Tennessee.

And when my girlfriend Elite Windgate family and I was finally on the road to go and pay her Dad Mr. Faarooq Cultler, aunt Victoria and Uncle Tyson Fonzelrelly a lovely family visit as Epiphany and her brother Epico started getting so very much bored with very little to do while there mother Wonda and big sister Elite been doing all of the driving headed down south the kids hand started singing old folk songs like old Mc Donald a farm E i E i O and I'll be there in the early morning A.M. I thought they been very entertaining in order to pass the time. So as Elite been taking a break from driving I asked Elite to asked her mother if we could stop by my aunt Shellby and Uncle Gunnar family home in Knockville Tennessee? And when she did finally the good chance to asked her mom Ms. Windgate said yes in deed Romeo I would love very much so to meet your extended family members and that it would be her pleasure. And I thanked Elite mother Ms. Wonda Windgate for agreeing to that me this since our two extended family live in the same southern state of Tennessee.

So when we all arrived in the Memphis Tennessee area at the Fonzelrelly household Elite family welcomed us all inside with a very warm embrace from Elite aunt Victoria and her Uncle Tyson and last but certainly not lease former Captain Faarooq Cultler as he welcomed me to there family and said that he hoped that I have been taking very good care of his loving daughter and I said yes sir Captain Faarooq Cultler sir I most certainly am just giving him that much respect as a former member of the United States Marine Core. And once the Windgate family and I settled in Elite aunt Victoria asked us all if we were all very much so hungry from our long trip from New York City? And Elite and her mom and the kids said yes that we certainly are ready for dinner so much that that we feel that we could eat a whole cow. And as we were very much enjoying a very delicious country meal Elite's father family wanted to know more about me and how long we been a romantic couple?

And Elite told her father, Aunt and Uncle that we only had been dating for about months time but that even though we only known each other only for a very short while that I was still willing to make a true committee to her right in front of her family by pulling out the diamond ring from a previous engagement to my ex-fiance Trickcey Dollars and proposed to Elite and as I asked her will she do me the honor of being my wife and she said yes absolutely I do. And when Elite's family witness what did just happen they been so very much happy about them to actually see me make a proposal right in the presents of there very own family they started applaussings and cheering us and saying that the way to do it young man. So from there Elite father Mr. Faarooq Cultler brought out a vintage bottle of fine white wine that he said that he been saving for a very special occasion such as to see his daughter finally finding a good hard working man to take good care of his daughter Elite.

So after all of the big celebration of me finally having the courage to make the most wonderful marriage proposal that I ever made before to my brand-new fiance Elite Windgate right in front of her father Faarooq, Aunt Victoria and Uncle Tyson we all decided to turn on there family digital stereo system and began dancing and singing the entire night away. And on December 25, 1998, Christmas Day after having our very first family breakfast together Elite told her father Faarooq that she a wonderful Christmas gift that she has been wanting to give him for a while and that gift was a brand-new gold watch that she brought from A GiftShopStore in the Valley Stream New York. And when Elite father received his lovely present from his daughter Elite he was so very much happy that he given his lovely daughter a big hug and a wet kiss and said to her thank you my sweet child and may good bless your heart in every possible way. And from there his other two children Epico and Epiphany also giving him a very wonderful gift of some ceramics gifts that they made for him in there school work shop.

And Elite's dad showed his family some of his many medals of honor that he been awarded in the Vietnam War such as in the Silver Star that he earned while saving a few other soldiers of war by helping bringing them all to safety. And after telling that very courages war story all three of his children said that they was in fact so very much proud of there dad. Elite began to get very emotional and starting to cry her eyes out and as for myself I thank her dad for serving our United States great Nation so very honorably and proudly and he replied your quite welcome son. So from there the family started looking through some of there family photos albums as they all been remembering all of there good family moments they used to have as they all just sat around laughing and crying about there good old times they used to have with each other. And I said that I was so very proud to be among such a good family that I really hope and pray that it's lastes us a entire lifetime and the ladies replied that was such a very sweet thing for me to say and that they all hope that Elite and I last for many years to come.

as it started to get very late when we said our good nights and sleep tight to each other we all went to to sleep and Elite slepted in the room with her mother Wonda while her brother Epico and sister Epiphany slepted in the family spare room that was available for family spending the night over and I to sleep on there family pulled out couch. So when we has arisen up the very next morning shortly after brauch Elite's mother Wonda told her childrens family members that we to make yet another stop to meet her daughter Elite new fiance Romeo's family members in Knoxville Tennessee to visit his Aunt Shellby and Uncle Gunnars family as well and that we better start to get on the road to start driving before it was to begin to get to dark outside for driving. And from there everyone giving there goodbyes handshakes and hugs as we said that we would call them all later to let them know that we all made it in safety. Ann as we were all headed on our way to the Knoxville Tennessee area to finally pay my Aunt whose Is name is Shellby, and her husband Uncle Gunnar Sr. who was also a Major in the United States Marine core who is now a Veteran, and his son Gunnar Jr. and two daughters whose name are Eva and Kharma Ruckust.

And as we finally arrived at my aunt Shellby and uncle Gunnar family home as I rang there door bell as they open up their door and arms up to me and my new family members with my new fiance Elite, here mother Wonda, youngest brother Epico and younger sister whose name is Epiphany Windgate. And my Aunt and her family welcomed the ladies of my new family in with a big warm embrace from the cold winter weather. So after I introduced Elite family members to my Aunt and uncle family everyone was getting to become much more better aquated with each other as we all sat around a warm and cozy fire that my uncle Gunnar Sr. and cousin Gunnar Jr. build as we all roasted marshmallows on a open fire and begin to eat them while also sipping of some red wine that they said they saved for a very special occasion like the holiday season. my cousins Eva and her younger sister Kharma taken Elite sister Epiphany and brother Epico to there back bedroom and started to teached them how to play the piano.

So Elite and I broken the good news of our new engagement to each other as my aunt Shellby and uncle Gunnar Sr. also congratulated us both of the matter. And my Aunt Shellby asked Elite and I when was the actual wedding day was going to be taking place? And we just told them that Elite and I haven't yet decided as of yet but as soon as we were to figure when and where the wedding was going to be taking place that we will be letting the entire family know, my uncle Gunnar started to tell about his old Desert Storm war stories and he serve very proudly as a United States Marine Military Police as a Major rank for seventeen years of service.

He started to tell us how he and the other solders to battle themselves to safety and how he himself shield his Colonel commander officer to safety single handedly and that made him a Green Beray war hero Soldier among the ranks of the military Marine Core. And my uncle Gunnar showed Elite and I his medal of honor of his Purple Heart Meadal that been giving to him by his commander and chief officer. And after hearing that very brave story of my Aunt Shellby husband uncle Gunnar telling his very heroic story of how he fought through the war to help secure our United States of America national security I sauted my veteran relative and took the proud liberty shaking his hand and than saluting him for his good and hard work and dedication to our great nation. And from there my aunt Shellby asked everyone to come and prepare to eat a real good and hearty meals for us all to enjoy together and from there we all feasted all the food that she prepared so very much deliciously for us all.

on December 27, 1998, my aunt Shellby and her husband uncle Gunnar Sr. told us that he some tickets to go see the Tennessee Tittans play against The Tampabay Buccaneers and he asked the whole family if we all wanted to go see the game live and in person, and we all shouted out hell yea you betcha we want to be there I And when we all finally had arrived at the football stadium it been a good but close in scoring of the game that ultimately the home town team of the Tennessee Tittans won in double overtime as my entire family cheered there team to sweet victory as it began to snow fall. And from there we all thank my uncle Gunnar Sr. and aunt Shellby for inviting us all to see a very exciting football that took the Tennessee Tittans all the way to the first around playoff season. So afterwards Elite and my family all went out to a lovely restaurant that was called Champions Grill House and as we been dining out there was some good music that been playing that we eventually had hoe dancing to as we all became to move to the rythem of the music that was playing by a live music band.

And shortly after that on December 31, 1998, when New Years Eve finally had arrived my aunt Shellby said as she and her husband uncle Gunnar Sr. brought out two bottles of champain that been already chilled to it's perfection as they made a very wonderful toast to say that she and her husband both wish our entire family to have good health and prosperity throughout the year and life itself. And after we finish yet another wonder dinner we all started to prepare ourselves to celebrate bringing in the New Year of January 1, 1999, as the clock struck 12:00 PM as we all shouted out Happy New Years to each other as we the hug, handshake and kiss each other as we popped open yet another bottle of bubbly champain. So from there twenty of my uncle Gunnar veterans Marine friends stop by the house to help he and my aunt Shellby celebrate the New Year by making a party of all of his buddy's to come and hand out with us all. And all of my aunt Shellby husband Gunnar Sr. colleads started to tell old army combat stories about how they won many battles overseas as Elite family and I all been all so very proud to her that our family troopers always seem to make it through there battles that ultimately by the grace of god always brought them all.

after the New Years come and gone my uncle Gunnar's Marine Core veterans soldier buddy's left out of there family home as they all slap each other a high five hand slap as the were saying there good byes to our family members. So shortly after that it been time for Elite's mother Wonda, brother Epico and sister Epiphany and I to started to head back to our homes in the Queens New York area as we said our goodbyes to my aunt family member and my cousin Gunnar Jr. informed my new family that he would be joining the United State National Gaurds in just a few months and after hearing just how courages he was just like he's father Gunnar Sr. was. I went to give him a good bye hug, handshake and a salute to our family newest soldier and from there Elite and I along with her mother, brother and sister said our goodbyes to my family. From there after Elite and her mother driven me back to my own family home as my mother Jahtayshia answered the door bell she be so very happy to see that we all made it back home very safely from her sister Shellby and husband Gunnar Sr. house and their family home in Knoxville Tennessee. And we told my mother and even my father Damian Sr. and Damian Jr. that we a good time at the foot ball game and how it was quite an honor to meet some of uncle Gunnar Sr. U.S. Marine veteran buddy's who he once served with in the war in order to protect and serve our great U. S. nation.

So as Elite and my relationship was still doing quit so well while I was still on long term disability for all of my job related stress problems that happen at my place of employment at the corporate law firm of O'Conner, Sapp, Dash & Marshall where I endured multiple harassment issues all because of a very ridiculous rummer that started with a fellow mailroom coworker whose name is Stone Casey saying that I could be a New York Mafia gangster that was trying to extort money from the company and I just knew that I eventually had to go back into my workplace hoping that the support staff members would probably forgotten about the lies that been said about me. So on March 30, 1999, I I'd eventually did to return back to my employers law firm were I worked as I taken noticed to my disappointment that the support staff did not forget a got dam thing as my harassment issues still very much continued concerning my same problematic issues. On April 1, 1999, as I went to continue to do my job of hand delivering of the multiple large stack of Telecopy/Fax documents and when I returned back to the department as I began to talked to another fellow department mailroom coworker whose name was Andy Rayes as Denise Hailey came over with a big attitude problem of me having to take way to long making my hand deliveries to the other floors as he complain that the guys in his department been looking on the forty-second floor where we were on station at but he said that they could not find me anywhere, and he asked me where the hell have I been all of that dam time? So from there I informed him while still keeping a very professional attitude despite his very bad unprofessional one that do to I over twenty something documents of telecopy/ fax hand deliveries documents that it taken me a little more time to hand them off to their proper multiple destinations. Denise went on to say well let me tell you something that the word in the law firm is that everyone is watching you Mr. Mailman very closely and that he known that I was a lier that according to him I would be never up to no good and that next time for me not take so very long in the future mail runs and he also went on to say about how he did not trust me at all just being one of there company mailman as he falsely accused of me being a New York crime organize gangster that was trying to take money from the company.

And from there I asked him now where did you hear of such a crazy rummerous lie such as that? And Denise Hailey and said to me that he heard that from several reliable different sources in the company and everybody is watching me in the law firm. And that kind of made me feel very uncomfortable at first and uneasy to know that the entire staff was basically watching my every move and some times the forty-second telecopy department coworker Denise Haily notice when I would even go into the bathroom stall as I would be sitting on the toilet with him to say that he would sometimes hear me trying two even move my bowls as he claimed that I would make a loud enough straining noise to release all of the food out of my system as the street lingo called it taking a shit in private. And after hearing him say that I should try not to be so loud while doing so and even his own departmental coworkers told Denise now that is way to much information about him to take notice whenever I was to be using the bathroom facilities and I told him to back up off of me and his own telecopy departmental coworkers laugh at him with them saying to him now that is to dam nasty for anybody to hear as they all been laughing at him making fun of him at that time. Than from there I made a joke of Denise and I asked him could he let a man have some privacy without him to be so very much to dam noisy? And them his own telecopy departmental friend been laughing at him instead of always have them to focus on me as I even to laugh at him myself. And from there the work day ended and I laugh my way straight out of the telecopy/fax center and headed straight the company doors without evening to say good night fellows have a good weekend as I just headed straight o home.

And I went to my family home in Astoria, Queens New York area and I told my parents Jahtayshia and Damian Sr. about how my non departmental coworker whose name was Denise Haily said that he taken noticed whenever I would be using the bathroom to move my bowels and how he would go on and continue to say that I would be making a loud enough grunting noise that he would take notice of me and that even his very own coworkers Steven Wattely would say that he should get off of my case and the rest of the staff just started laughing at that dam foolish of a man. And when I finally had gotten home father said what I and that he couldn't believe it that my coworker Denise would be that much foolish to try to embarrass me but wound up embarrassing himself being that stupid. And my parents again asked me just why my employer keep on harassing me like that? And I once again told them of the crazy ridiculous rumor of the mail room coworker of mine whose name was lack Casey spreaded a rumor around the entire law firm that I was apart of a New York mafia gangster family trying to extort money from their corporation. And from their they begin to once again to become very paranoid amongst the two of them of thinking that I could actually be some of truth to the rumor that was being said about me that started from my employer as they started back acting very much strangely again as they once gain bowed there heads to me as they also turn there faces around in the opposite direction and I thought that if my own parents were still thinking that there could be some possible truth to the corporate rumor of me being a New York mafia gangster than let them because I been so very much worn out from another hard working stressful harassment day and I was way to tired to care as I told them both good night and that I was going to see them in the morning time and that I was going to be calling my fiance Elite and see how she and her family was doing and from there I went downstairs to our family basement apartment do just that.

And as the weekend finally had arrived on April 9, 1999, my fiance Elite Windgate called me and asked me just how I was feeling and I said that I was feeling so very good enough that I wanted her to come over to pay me a visit and she said yes she would be at my place in the afternoon time and I said I'd would see her here when she would get here. So when Elite arrived by her mother Ms. Wonda Windgate driven her to my home as I also went out to greet them both to especially say my hello's to her mother as she did the very same as she driven off. And I took hold of her little weekend suit case and brought it inside the house and once we were both inside Elite been very cranky as she explained that she a very bad day at the office as she said to me and if I was to be wanting to get on her very bad side today that she was going to have someone to beat me up very badly from her neighborhood in Long Island City. So from there I been in totally shock that my fiance Elite Windgate just threaten to have someone to do me bodily harm to my person. So from there I grabbed her and thrown her on my bed and shaken her quite a bit as I told her that I was going to make her threat a very real reality to do her some real bodily harm to her now was as I been making only a idol threat to her without her knowing so as I would never want to do any bodily harm to any women.

So I asked Elite just who the hell that she think that she is sleeping with while having sexually relations with me? And from there as I was still holding her down to keep her calm she apologized to me and said she was very sorry to me. And I told her if ever she felt that crazy enough to want to have someone beat me down to the ground than by all means please just leave me the hell alone and stay out of my life, as Elite said that she was so very sorry and that it would never happen again and I said well okay. From there I calmed myself down and begin to prepare to make our dinning for the evening. And I just acted normal toward Elite as I brought her dinner into bed. And after that we watched a adult porno movie and sexual enter course all not long until we both reached our climaxes. And afterwards she fallen sleep as I was still awaken I started thinking what type of unstable frame of mine that my fiance Elite Windgate really did have and was she actually dangerous as I just figured that I guest time will tell everything I will need to know.

the next morning came in and I made Elite and myself some brauch while I was in the downstairs kitchen basement as I given her food on a silver platter as she thanked me as she also went on to say that she really appreciated such a wonder meal I made, as I asked her if she really been thankfully enough in how I wanted to take good care of her and that she is to never try to in danger me in anyway possible and from there she said okay Romeo and that she understood me. And I asked her just why she acts like that? And she told me that she was just used to acting that way because she live in a drug infested neighborhood as she grew up with a whole lot of drug dealers that would do her that type of favor. And from there I couldn't believe what she was saying to me thinking that she was kind of crazy in the head in someway. And my two little sisters Tameka and Fatima came downstairs just to see how Elite and I was doing as the girls both ran right straight toward the both of us to give us a big huge hug as they said there hellos to us. And my two sister was so very happy to see us that they wanted us to come outside to play in the snow to build a snowman and the four of us did just that as we a mighty good time do so after getting my parents permission.

And on April 21 of the year of 1999 as I meet a woman who worked on my now former employer that is called The O'Conner, Sapp, Dash & Marshall LLP midtown Manhattan corporate law firm in the Time Square area in the department of the telecopy/fax center/Word Processing Center which was located of the company forty-second floor whose name she told me was Tracey Whittley and as I started taking quit a good notice of her as she been also kind of flirty with me by pulling on my shirt as she said hello to me. And there would be also many of times when I would be just going out on the company forty-second telecopy/fax and Word processing floors to make multiple hand deliveries when that very same woman Tracey Whittley made her very own self seem so very muchs so very sweet and sexy toward me as she would sometimes be also grabbing my hand whenever we were sometime talking to each other even though she was not really the type of woman that I would normally be attracted to as the type of woman that I will always prefer to have a intimate relationship with would be of a plus size type of woman. And once the guys in the Telecopy/Fax Center saw Tracey Whittley be some what flirtatious toward me in a very romantic interest of a way my harassment issues started right back up again and this time it been directed toward the both of us. And my now former coworker Denise Hailey and his other departmental coworker who was Leon Abrames came over to her to say Tracey that she better watch her self hanging out with that guy Romeo Devine as they also went on to tell her that I was nothing but a trouble for the whole entire company of The O'Conner, Sapp, Dash & Marshall LLP corporate law firm as they also said that there was alot of the support staff members who there own reasons to believe that guy Romeo Devine could very much be apart of a New York City organize crime family gangster members who was sent out to do them all some criminal unlawfulness act of some very kind as it also been said back that it could not be proven in the eyes of law enforcement as of yet. And the company Word Processor Tracey Whittley said that probably wasn't even true at all of what those guy been saying about me as she was been warned it she value her place of her employment as it was demand that she still better stay the hell away from me.

Tracey even though I was engage to my woman Elite back in the Long Island City New York Queens area. And I realized I better stop all of my wishful thinking and that I just better try to focus on my work and my engagement in my personal life because I knew that the company meant me no good at all. And I even had felt so very said about how I was somewhat attracted to Tracey that I just to go into the bathroom stall and started to sweep some crying wet tears quit a bit.

The next time when I saw the Word Processor Tracey Whittley at 12:00 PM lunch time I for some very strange reason asked her if she was currently single at that time? And Tracey informed me that she was in fact already romantically involved with another man in a long term committed relationship. And she asked me how about myself and I told Tracey yes that I was in fact currently also romantically involved with another woman who was actually my fiance. And as we been on our lunch break outside of the office as I seen her in a fast-food restaurant I also went on to tell her for some strange reason of some kind I begin to develop some feeling for her as well and I asked Tracey since it always seemed that she and I some sought of physical attraction to one another how would she feel if we both two time our other two relationships that we with our significant others by becoming a romantic couple ourselves?

And Tracey told me that even though that she been flirting with me while still on our employers law firm of O'Conner, Sapp, Dash & Marshall company time that she wasn't really attracted to me at all that much as she said since the company was saying such bad things about me to possibly being a New York mafia gangster of a organize crime family that she the idea to flirt with me to actually emotionally teas me quit a bit for a funny laugh as we all to work inside the office in order to keep me in a very calm state of mine and manners just in case the telecopy guys were to make me very angry at times as she than laugh at me again herself saying ha ha ha. And I told Tracey well from here on out at our employment at the corporate law firm O'Conner, Sapp, Dash & Marshall that I told her that she could just keep all of her very flirtatious ways to her got dam self because I did not appreciate the fact how she been constantly flirting with me as I told her that she should never tried to infatuate me for any reason at all. And for some other strange reason as I told her that I really did think that she should get the hell out of my face and go on about her own business. And from there she began to act very strangely by grabbing me to kiss me on my right facial cheek bone and began to sit herself on my lap as she began to sit on my lap and bounce her booty up and down on me like some sought of cowgirl riding a pony and I push her the hell off of me and from there she given me a very soft playful slap on my face and walked away from me as she also sStoneed herself on her own buttocks checks area and said that she just knew that I liked that very firm booty of hers even though I couldn't never get any from her and than she just walked herself away from me with her to say just be sure to keep cool Mr. New York mafia gangster man with the company.

So after all of that what went on with Tracey Whittley and me I myself begin to fell quit broken hearted of my whole employer situation that

I as I been finished eating my lunch that I just spent the rest of my lunch breaktime break time just crying my eyes out from all of the emotional heart ache that I was going through with some of my female coworker as I known that I just to keep on doing the very best job that I could possibly do as one of the company corporate law firm mail men. So from there Tracey kept herself clear away from me as her days of sexual harassing me finally had been over with. shortly after that I was told by one of the telecopy/fax operator Denise Hailey that the Word Processor operator Tracey Whittely left out of the law firm company as her internship been completed with she completed her internship with O'Conner, Sapp, Dash & Marshall LLP law firm. And it really begin to bother me that the support staff member kept on trying to infatuated me just because of a very ridiculous rumor that started by a fellow departmental coworker whose name was Stone Casey all because of him wanting to play around like some kind of mailroom center class clown at my very own expense all because he gotten kind of jealous of me being the one to take our mailroom manager Henry Hernandez secretary Gloria Knight out for a lunch date instead of him to do so.

on June 30, 1999, my mother Jahtayshia and my father Damian Sr. have thrown a cook out party in our family backyard as they invited a few family members that consisted of our cousins Antonio Sr. Antonio Jr. and his his two daughter Ava and Arleana and a few other our my dad's side of the family members. And from there I invited over my fiance Elite Windgate and her family members over to join me and the family for a family back yard barbecue family get together and she told me that she was going to have her mother bring her by my family home and I said that I would see them when they would arrived. And when Elite finally had gotten at my family home in the Astoria Queens area along with her mother as I also had said my hellos to them both as I told Elite and her mother Ms. Wonda Windgate that my family was throwing a family barbecue cook out and that the family would love it if they could both join the family festivities? And Elite said yes that what she is definally her for and that she also a very wonderful surprise for me and my whole family that she wanted to tell us all. And Ms Windgate told me that she could not join us at that time because she another previous engagement of her very own and that she to get back as soon as she could possibly could.

So from there Elite said her farewell to her mother as she told her that she would call her much later that very same night and she said okay Elite my dear sweet daughter as told us to take real good care of each other as she driven off on her way somewhere. From there I taken Elite duffle bag that she brought over to spend a few nights over with me and my family. And as we went downstairs to my family basement home Elite asked me to take a set on my living room couch and as I did so she placed my two hands on her stomach and told me to began to give her a belly a genital rub down. And when I asked Elite if she had a upset stomach ache she said no sir poppa bear but that we were going to be two very proud parent together.

And when I first had heard her say those very sweet words of Elite was going to have our baby I embraced her so very gentally as I given her a very wet and sloppy kiss that she would probably never forget they day when she informed me that we were going to finally have a life long common bond that we were going to honner for the rest of our lives. And I wanted to go upstairs to tell my family members that been at our family barbecue the good news and when I finally had made my big announcement to them all of Elite and myself are expecting to have a baby of our very own they all started applauding for the both of us as we both received multiple handshakes, hugs and kisses and my parents made a toast to say here here thank you heavenly father the good God almighty to bless us with a new edition to our two familys. So as the music continued to play after my family heard the wonderful news of Elite and I were about to have a brand-new baby they all suggested that she and I should take the backward dance floor and have our very first dance as a brand-new expected parents to be and we did just that as we also did it so very gracefully. And from there all of the question started in from my family members such as my mother and father with them to begin to question Elite about when there brand-new baby grand child was about due to come in this very beautiful world of ours. And Elite told us that our baby according to what the doctors told her that the due date for her to be given birth was on May 8, 2000, on Mother Day and my parents along with my other family members that been at the back yard party said that was very wonderful news for them to all hear on this very wonder family day of ours.

So after my family barbecue cook out finally had to ended as we all had come inside from after all of that back yard partying ended my two sisters been so very excited for us both as she asked us both the question of if we were going to be brand-new mommy and daddy to our new baby what would that make the two of them to our little baby that was about to be born? And I explained to my two little sisters Tameka and Fatima with a little help from my fiance Elite that they would become our little baby aunts because they were my two adorable little sisters who I love so very much so and that we were going to need there help in taking good care of the baby that was on way to our two families and they both said that they would love to help our new baby of our family. And my two little sisters Tameka and Fatima asked Elite could they feel the baby kicking as of yet? And Elite said oh yes of course you can as she placed there two sets of hands on her pregnant stomach as they also put there little ears to hear the baby in Elite stomach as well as they said that they could her the baby just trying to get out of her belly so the child could come out and play with his two aunts.

And Elite and I all began to laugh as we thought that my to sisters Tameka and Fatima sounded so very cute and sweet in what they been telling us. So as Elite been over to my family home I the good pleasure of to begin to really started taking very proper good care of her as I cuddled up with her all through the night until the early morning hours. And this time when we awaken up the very next morning I began to wait on her hand and foot in order to keep her comfortable in every way possible. And I served Elite breakfast in bed all weekend long as she really did enjoy all of the pampering attention that I was giving her as I also had to massage her neck and back side as well as her feet as they began to get somewhat big from her water gain from the pregnancy.

And my mother Jahtayshia shouted out downstairs to say her good mornings to the both of us as we also did the same toward my mom and my sisters Tameka and Fatima also said there hello's and come mornings to Elite and I and asked if it was okay if they could both come downstairs to see just how we both were doing? And we said yes girls absolutely please come downstairs and keep us some good company. And from there they were own there way down to see Elite and myself. And Tameka and Fatima begin to asked Elite just how she was felling with the baby still in her stomach? And Elite just told them both that the baby was still warm in her belly just waiting to be born for all of our family members to see and the girls said to us both that was a very good thing for them to know.

So shortly after hearing the good news of Elite and I were soon to be very proud parents to our little baby to be I than asked her if she wanted me to accompany her to some of her prenatal doctor appointments and she told me yes that she would in deed enjoy all of the moral support that she could possibly get from me and even my very own family members. So from there I asked her when was her very next prenatal doctor appointment for us to attend to? And she told me that her next one was on the 4th of July of 1999 and I comfitted her to know that I would be right there with her by her waist side to hold her up very strong. And from there Elite said thank you sweety to me and that she really appreciated all of the tender loving care that I was giving her as I told her that she was quit welcome mommy to be.

Elite and my family and I all sat at the family dinner table to enjoy some nice ordering of our neighborhood Chinese restaurant that was called Chinese Best Restaurant that was just around the corner from my family home in the Astoria, Queens New York area. And my big brother Damian Jr. asked Elite and I just how we both felt about us to about to become proud parents? And Elite and I said that we felt so very excited that we was going to give our two families a brand-new miracle baby that is absolutely a gift from our god the heavenly father. And after our family dinner was over with Elite and myself my family members they began to asked us both what did we prefer the baby to be a boy or a girl? And Elite told my family that she wanted to have a girl so that she could dress the baby up in the newest and cutest up to date fashions and my mother Jahtayshia, sisters Tameka and Fatima told Elite that they would help her pick out some good clothes for her if the baby turn out to be a girl and from there my fiance Elite thank them all as she also giving them a glowing smile as she been so very happy to also have my family love and support for our baby that was on the way to be born.

So a few weeks pasted by as my harassment and sexual harassment issues had stop for a little while as I told the telecopy/fax operator company coworker that my fiance was expecting with my child. And everybody in the department congratulated me on me to soon to be a father to be. And the telecopy operator whose name was Denise Hailey begin to verbally tease me quit a bit as he said now that I was about to be a new baby daddy that I should start to have a whole lot of motervasion to make my deliveries much more faster as he begin to make everyone in the department to laugh at that very funny joke as I also had find him to be quit humorous myself at that particular time. And from there I felt very much relieved that some of the company pressure been taken off of me.

when it finally had been time for me to take Elite to her July 4, 1999, prenatal care doctor appointment I went over to Elite's family home in the Long Island City of the Queens New York area as she had been already ready to leave out of her family apartment home as she told me that she called us a taxi cab service so that we could be on our way out to see the doctor at his office. And when we finally had arrived at Elite's doctor office his nurse told us to step right in and the doctor would see us now. And once we were inside Elite's doctor office whose name was Dr. Cleo Morey and he asked her just how she was feeling with our soon to be new born baby? And from there my fiance Elite told her doctor that she been feeling very much so very tired as of late but she just knew with the help of her baby father which is me and the both sides of our two families to always to be there for the both of us that we were going to make the very best of a already beautiful blessing situation from God. So Dr. Cleo Morey said that was a very wondering thing that we both a very strong and supportive family to help us through all of the good times as well as the bad ones. he asked more about just how she been feeling with the baby still waiting to be born into the world very soon?

Elite told her physician that she felt sometime very tired and more hungry than she every been before. And her doctor told her that was to be expected of mostly all pregnant women as he also had informed us both that he wanted to give her a thero examination of the baby and we said that great news because that what we were both her for. So the doctor asked Elite to lay herself down on the doctor office bed so that he may examine our baby by giving her a sonogram just to see how our baby was doing while inside of her. And once he finish the examination of the fetish he said that everything seemed quit find with our baby.

Elite's Dr. Cleo Morey asked us both if in fact we wanted to know the sex of our baby to be? And Elite and I both looked right at each other as we smiled toward one another and turn to her doctor and told him yes we would very much so liked to know the sex of our unborn child to be. And from there he told us that we were soon to be the proud parents of a beautiful baby boy. So from there Elite and I was so very happy that we finally had known that we were going to have a son of our very own to the point when we thank the doctor I my given him a handshake and a hug and Elite kiss him on the right cheek and also given him a huge hug of her very own as we both thank him so very much for taking such good care of her and our baby boy as we left the doctor office and said that we would see him again very soon as we had said our good byes for now as he did the very same.

And after only a few months later on September 15, 1999, I met a new employee whose name was Afreaka Braithwaite as I to introduce myself to her as one of the company mailman that would be making multiple mail runs on the thirtieth floor where she been station. And at first Ms. Afreaka Braithwait treated me just like a regular employee coworker until a few days later already past by as she also had a attitude toward me totally changing her professionalism demeanor toward me because she began to started having quite a sexy attitude with me because I suspected that some of the other support staff members must have informed her that I previous filed serval sexually harassment complaint charges against two of support staff members whose name was Neil Harry, Exodus Franklyn and there departmental night time supervisor whose name was Jefferey Silverstone to the company Human Resource Department. And as I kept on making my mail run deliveries the associate secretary Afreaka Braithwaite started making sexually advances herself directly toward me as she would began to blow kisses at me as she would also take the liberty to bend her body over so that I may take notice of her buttocks area right in front of me just as she was to been tying up her shoe laces as she also push her dairy air body part into my grind genital area with her to began to rub herself into me as she had said by her doing that to me that should kept me very much calm, cool and collected just so no harmed may come to the law firm of O'Conner, Sapp, Dash & Marshall and as for me I almost reached my climax all over myself but I back myself away just in time in order to avoid myself any embarrassment of any kind. And after that sexual harassment occurred with me I realized that secretary whose name was Afreaka Braithwait was going to be another company in fact a waiter that I just to put up with while I was still on the job of me being the company mailman.

the very next day when I once again been delivering my employer mail at the law firm of O'Conner, Sapp, Dash & Marshall I again saw the associate secretary Afreaka Braithwait at the company water cooler area where she again made yet another sexual advancement toward me by slapping her hips as I been standing right in front of her with the company mail parcels right in my hands as she said hello to me as she also splashed some water in my face as she said her hello to me. And I begin thinking to myself maybe I should consider to asked Afreaka out on a date for a night out dancing and for us to go out for some fine dinning out and when I did just that Afreaka told me no and that she was always to busy to being hanging out with the likes of someone like me because she told me that she heard a lot of very negative things about me possible to be some kind of New York mafia gangster family member that was trying to steal from our company corporate law firm of O'Conner, Sapp, Dash & Marshall and I said that what she heard about me just wasn't true and I begin to asked here just why in the hell she been flirting with me? And Afreaka told me that she just wanted me to find her to be very much attracted to her just like those other women in the support staff department. And after all of that I told the associate secretary Afreaka Braitwaite that she better stop her sexual advance toward me because I was engaged to be getting married to my fiance who is expecting to have my baby.

And I had asked her a smart alec question if she would want to have a baby of our very own together with me? And Afreaka told me hell no and as she also went on to asked me didn't I tell you that I was just sexually teasing you to keep you very calmed down with our employer corporate of O'Conner, Sapp, Dash & Marshall? And I replied yes and if that is the be the case between the two of us than the best thing for us to do is to keep everything between the two of us strictly professional ya heard me Ms. Afreaka Braithwaite? And she said I heard you and for me to just go on and make my little dog on mail hand deliveries while she told me that she was just going to be finishing up her work load for the day. And I said okay as I been on my way just trying to do my job as one of the company inter-office mailman.

Things remained quite normal at my place of employment at the corporate law firm of O'Conner, Sapp, Dash & Marshall LLP that was until December 18, 1999, when I came into my workplace to only do my job when the telecopy/fax operator whose name was Leon Abrames came into his departmental work area and started the day off with cracking jokes about me with him also begin to questioning me like so Romeo tell us guys just why he heard from a very reliable source that I filed official charges on the those guys in the copy center department? And I told Leon along with the rest of his departmental coworkers that my issues of that matter was rather personal and that I did not care to discuss the matter with them at all. Leon just kept on pressing the issue of the matter as did his other departmental coworker whose name was Denise Hailey been pressuring me for me to give them all a direct answer. So from there I told them all that I gotten rather tired of those copy center guys whose name was Neil Harry and Exodus Franklyn sneaking up to me from behind and grabbing me by my waist sides in order to trying to scare me as I also informed the telecopy departmental guys that the copy center guys even bump into me with their gentialya parts.

once those telecopy/fax operator heard what I been through with the copy center department the guys at first said dam that was a very mess up situation that I was in with those other guys. But Leon went on to say yea but that was all to bad that you to go through all of that very bad situation that I to go through but that still doesn't give you the very right to bring official charges on some of our company people and the telecopy operator Denise Hailey had decided to join in with him to at that time of me to being harass as he said hell no that wasn't the right thing to do toward anybody whose worked for the law firm of O'Conner, Sapp, Dash & Marshall LLP. Leon begin to pushed me around quite a bit that was until he decided to grabbed a hold of me by sneaking up behind me with him also saying get him Denise and than I thrown Leon to the floor with very heavy force. And as some of the company corporate associate lawyers been looking at what just happen they called in the company security team to the telecopy/fax center to see about the very disturbing matter that was going on in the company.

when the company security team arrived into the telecopy/fax center they asked what happen between the two of us I told the armed guards that I myself was just minding my very own business when I been question by the telecopy/fax departmental guy whose name were first Leon Abrames and his coworking friend Denise Hailey by them to began to asking me just what happen in the copy center department when I used to work there? And from there I told the company security officers that Leon began to grabbed a hold of me with him asking for some assistance from his departmental friend whose name was Denise Hailey. And from there the company security team hand asked the people did anybody see anything happen between the two us guys and even the two associates attorneys didn't say a word of the matter even though they both witness the whole incident what happen between Leon Abrames and myself as they both just walked away from the incident not wanting to get involved with the matter that was at hand in there very own corporate law firm. And the company of O'Conner, Sapp, Dash & Marshall security team took us both to the company Human Resource department as we both been called into the Human Resources Department to discuss what just happen between Leon Abrames and myself. And I once again told the Human Resource Coordinator whose name was Clifford Montely. And I explained that how when the telecopy copy guy Leon Abrames been questing me about why did I in fact brought pervious charges on member of the 4th floor copy center guys? And after he and another of his departmental coworker began to pressured me to give them a trueful direct answer of me to being sexual harass by the two copy center copy operators Neil Harrys and Exodus Franklyn Leon himself began attracting me from behind as I thorn him to the floor to get him off of my backside. And from there Leon denied what happen and he was official warned by the Human Resources Coordinator Clifford Montley that he better back up off me and just only continuing to do his job to the best of his professional abilities and he said yes sir okay and proceeded to leave the Human Resource department. And I myself said my thank you's and began to go and continue to making my telecopy/fax mail deliveries.

On December 20, 1999, just five days before the Christmas holiday season began as I was making yet another mail run of the company telecopy/fax documents I meet yet another female associate secretary whose name she said was Metta Morehouse as I taken the liberty of introducing myself to her as one of the company mail man as she herself also replied back to me with a very friendly hello and that also said that she was very pleased to meet my acquaintance. And to my very own surprise the associate secretary whose name was Afreaka Braithwait showed up sitting right next to her now new neighbor secretary Metta Morehouse as they both explained to me that the two of them were long time friends of each other going all the way back from high school and I said that sounded so very nice to here, but I really didn't care very much that they were both friends because of the previous problem I had with Afreaka Braithwait herself. And after I hand delivered those two associate secretary their telecopy/fax documents along with some multiple pieces of mail I just walked off quietly continued to making the rest of my hand deliveries throughout the corporate law firm. And after I left Afreaka associate secretary desk I started to thinking that she would informed her neighbor secretary whose name was Metta Morehouse what the rest of the corporate law firm of O'Conner, Sapp, Dash & Marshall LLP been saying about me about me being rumored to possibly have criminal connections to a New York mafia family but no one was ever for certain of the true facts.

So on December 23, 1999, as I was riding on the employer of the corporate law firm of O'Conner, Sapp, Dash & Marshall building elevator were I saw the two associate secretaries whose name were Afreaka Braithwait and her long time friend whose name was Metta Morehouse get right on with me. As it been only the three of us on the elevator when Afreaka Braithwait and her secretarial long time neighboring lady friend whose name was Metta Morehouse attacked me as they intentually press the emergency button to stop the elevator from reaching it normal multiple floor stations as we were all three stuck inside the elevator shaft. And from there the two associate secretaries Metta Morehouse and Afreaka Breathwait asked me is it absolutely true what the corporate law firm of O'Conner, Sapp, Dash & Marshall LLP been saying about you that you were a New York mafia gangster man? And as they both thrown me up against the elevator wall bar as I said hell no ladles please believe me.

And they both said that they heard that I a fight with one of the guys in the telecopy/fax department and I told them that wasn't my falt at all. And the associated secretary Metta Morehouse and her long term friend Afreaka Braitwait asked me didn't some of the other secretary told warned you that they all wanted me to always to remained calmed so no bodly harmed wouldn't come to anybody in the workplace? And I answered yes ladies yes. the two associate secretary Metta Morehouse and Afreaka Braithwait said that they know of a sure way to keep me very calmed down as they grabbed me and held on to me as tight as they possibly could as they unzippered my pants down as they also grab on to my private man part and forced a cherry flavored condom on my penis part as they both taken there turns to perform oral sex on me until I reached my climax moment. And when I final had reached my climax point they both decided to release there strong hold that they both on me. And Afreaka Braithwaite and her long time friend whose name was Metta Morehouse told me that they better not hear anything about of what just happen between the three of us all you hear me Romeo just be cool in the company because they both had said that it was their very sexy pleasure to service the company favorite mailman okay and I said okay there ladies and that I would never report those two ladies simply because that was my very first oral threesome that I ever had. And they helped me fix up my clothes nice and neatly as they started back the elevator to it's proper working order so we could all get back to our work day and as we were on our way out of the elevator as they both said to me that they both hoped that I very much so enjoyed my early Christmas present and I said to the both of them that yes that I defiantly had enjoyed myself very much so as I thanked them both and the both had said your quite welcome Mr. Romeo mailman sir as I to just give them both a happy smile.

So I left from my place of employment of the corporate law firm O'Conner, Sapp, Dash & Marshall to prepare myself to than to start to enjoy the Christmas and Happy New Year season just as I went to my family home were I still lived at that particular time and came inside with me being totally exulted from a very hard working day that also including me to be sexual harass by my female coworker in the best way possible. And once I gotten myself totally settle in and comfortable from a very stressful work week my mother Jahtayshia and my father Damian Sr. asked me just how my day went? And I told them both that I gotten into a big fight with one of my fellow coworker whose name was Leon Abrames and that even the employer at the law firm of O'Conner, Sapp,

Dash & Marshall LLP company security team even to be called into break up the fight. And when my mom and dad heard that very bad news of me getting into a very bad scuffle fight they asked me did I get myself hurt into the fight?

And I told them no absolutely not and in fact that I gotten the upper on the guy whose name was Leon Abrames who was a day time telecopy/fax operator as I told my mother Jahtayshia and and father Damian Sr. that I tripped him onto the company floor. my mother and father at first couldn't believe what I was telling them both as they also began to start laughing a whole lot about what I was been telling them both. And my father Damian Sr. made a joke that it was a very good thing that I tripped that coworker guy down to the floor as he also went on to say that he bet me that guy would never want to pick a fight with me ever again and I said yes your probably right dad only time will tell. And my big brother Damian Jr. came in from his very hard working day of him to be a maintenance man for another large corporate company of his own where he was employed called Mr. Cleans maintenance services.

And as my father been laughing at what to the guy coworking who I worked with me on the job he told me to tell my story to my big brother Damian Jr. and when I did once again explained what happen with me as I flipped my male coworker to the floor just because he decided to want to pick a fight with me than Damian Jr. himself began to start to laugh a whole hell of a lot himself. And from there my big brother Damian Jr. said that he was so very glad that I to flipped that coworker guy on his backside as he also said that was good for that man to experience a minor defeat such as that and that I shouldn't have to many problems out of that coworker no time soon as I than told my big brother that I hope that he was right about that. And from there I saw my two little sisters adorable sisters Tameka and Fatima as they said that they also had overheard about what happen with me while I was all at my place of employment as they both asked me if I was okay and did I get hurt in the fight that I on the job? And I told the girls no that I wasn't the one who gotten hurt and that it been the other guy who happen to be my coworker who was the one who gotten himself hurt in the fight for wanting to pick a fight with me.

So as I taken the entire week of off of work for the Christmas thru New Years holiday season of 1999 I started to miss my fiance/baby mother to be quite a bit when I decided that I was going to give her a call to see just how she was feeling while her to be still pregnant with our son to be. And when I finally gotten around to doing so I was so very happy to here my fiance who was soon to be my child mother Ms. Elite Windgate and when I spoken to her she said that she a graving for something very sweet and tasty and she also went on to say oh yea Romeo Devine and she also said that she miss me a whole lot and that she was going to take a taxi cab to my family home in Astoria, Queens New York and come a pay me and my family a nice visit for the holiday's. And from there as she was on her way over I told her that I was going to than run to the neighborhood supermarket which was called Shop Foods to bring back something sweet and delicious for her to eat and snack on until dinner was to be served just before is was to come over. And when Elite's taxi cab ride finally arrived at my family home I once again welcomed Elite with a very warm hug and multiple kisses on both of her facial cheeks as well as her lips as I said hello there baby momma to be.

And once my fiance/baby momma Elite Windgate and I gotten into my family home we went straight upstairs so my family could also sit and visit with her and our than unborn baby boy as well as myself. And when they did both of my two parents Damian Sr. and Jahtayshia said there hellos to Elite as well as my to younger little sisters Tameka, Fatima and even my big brother Damian Jr. And everyone in my family household really then made Elite felt so very much at home and we informed them all that we founded out just what the sex of our baby was going to be and that we were going to be the proud parents of a little baby boy. And when they all heard of Elite and my good news they were all so very happy for the both of us as well as themselves as we were about to have a new edition to our two families hers and mines.

my family told us that since the baby was almost due to be born into the world that we better start to get the proper things that our baby boy might need. And Elite and I told my family that we totally understood what they been telling Elite and myself. And we went on to informed them that since we now know what the sex of our baby was going to be a baby boy that we were going to start to do some of the shopping for the baby over the Christmas holiday season. And my family said that was a very good idea for us to go ahead and get a head start on our shopping for the baby but that we should do our shopping a little while after the Christmas holiday season in order to avoid the big crowd of the other shoppers that would be in the stores right along with us and we said okay and that we were going to do just that in order to beat the crowd.

So on December 27, 1999, as my fiance Elite Windgate along with myself awaken up that next morning with us still being so very much excited about the two of us were about to than get up and prepare ourselves to shop for our soon to be born infant baby boy. So I prepared my baby mother to be Elite a very healthy breakfast of pancakes and sausages along with a one medium glass of milk and orange juice. And from there I given a big fat juicy wet kiss to Elite as she thanked me so very kindly for me to been treating her so very right and I told her that I would do just about anything for my future baby mama. And we prepared ourselves to begin our soon-to-be busy day by us to take our showers together with me cleansing Elite from her front to her backside and she did the very same thing for me as well as we also had made out in the showers just kissing and caressing all over each other body.

I have taken the liberty of helping my fiance/ future baby mama Elite Windgate to help her get herself dress up so we may begin to start to do some shopping for our baby boy. But before we left out of my family home in the Astoria, Queens New York area we taken the liberty to stop upstairs to see my family before we were to head out of the house to start our day just shopping for a soon to be new born baby boy. And when we finally had did just that as we said our good mornings to my family members as they all did the very same as my mother Jahtayshia Devine had asked Elite just how she and her future baby grand son was feeling today? Elite told my mom and the rest of my immediate family that she was feeling rather strong enough to go out to do some shopping for our little new edition of a baby boy of our family and from there my mother and and two little sisters Tameka and Fatima Devine given there future common law sister in-law Elite Windgate a big hug and a kiss on her right cheek to say there good bye as they said to us both that they will all see us latter after we were to do our big shopping for their little nephew to be, and we said okay everybody we would see you all when we were to return back to the house as we also had said our goodbyes for now to my family and they did the very same thing and from there Elite along with myself were on my way to the Left Frack City Shopping Center mall in the Queens New York Area.

And my fiance Elite Windgate and I arrived at the Left Frack City shopping Center mall when seen a store that was called Toddlers 'R' US and once we saw the store very large selection of baby accessories my fiance Elite and I really felt more in love with the ideal with us to becoming soon to be very proud parents to be for our baby boy. But it turned out that Elite did not like anything in the baby store because she said that everything was to very much expensive for our family budget and that she also went on to say that she known of another infant baby store that was much less expensive than the baby 'R' Store. so from there she asked me if I would give here there money to buy our baby boy crib in a much less expensive store that she would asked her mother Ms Wonda Windgate to take her so that they may do some shopping for our baby with them to also to have a day to also bond together as a future mother and grandmother to be? And from there I said to Elite yes that would be fine for she and her mom to do so as I given her the money for the baby crib and from there she called her mom to pick us both up from the shopping mall and when Ms. Wonda Windgate finally had did arrived to pick us up Elite said to me that she was going to have her mother drive me home to my family house so that the next day she and her mother would go out to began to some shopping for our soon to been baby boy and I said that would be fine for her to do so and we were there we all been on our way to my own family home. And once we arrived at my parents home Elite and her mother Ms. Wonda Windgate came inside my family home to say a quick hello to my family members as all of the ladies in my family given each other all multiple warm embraces of hugs as well as for the two new ladies that were than in my life also said there to my father Damian Sr. and older brother Damian Jr. and did the very same thing.

So on December 28, 1999, my fiance Elite Windgate informed me that she and her mother Ms. Wonda Windgate brought our soon to be infant baby boy a much more affordable crib for him to sleep in and be very comfortable. And once I heard that good news and I said that I wanted to come right over to see the baby crib for myself but Elite and her mother Ms. Wonda Windgate kept on making many excuses for me not to come inside there town house such as to tell me her mom has been getting very sick a whole lot with some symptoms of the flu and that the family did want me to catch her cold germs. So I just said that was okay and that I totally understood. Elite hand told me that her good next door neighbor friend whose name is Ally Martin was going to give her a baby shower for our little boy and I said that sounded like a very sweet ideal.

So when I asked Elite when and where the baby shower was going to be taken place? Elite told me that her neighbor lady friend Ally Martin was going to be giving us the party at her own town house and I said that sounded like a great news for us both. And I said that I really did think that my mother Mrs. Devine as Elite always referred to her would defiantly like to join the family festivities as well and she said why of course that would be okay for me to also invite my mother and even my two little sisters Tameka and Fatima to come along to join us all. And when I finally had broken the good news to my mother Jahtayshia and my two little much younger sisters Tameka and Fatima that my fiance Elite's neighboring friend whose name is Ally Martin was about to give her a baby shower for our baby my mother said that sounded like a very wonderful ideal and that she and sisters girls would defiantly be there to join us all and I said that it was all good thin and that I would let our family know just when the baby shower was to be taking place. about a day later my fiance Elite Windgate informed me that the baby shower was going to be given to her on December 31 on New Year's Eve of 1999 and she said that we would have the celebration of our baby shower for our baby boy and we will all be parting the New Years in at the same bless it time.

Elite called me and told me to tell my mother Mrs. Devine and my two little sister Tameka and Fatima that the baby shower was going to be giving for us on New Years Eve of 1999 at 8:00 PM and I told her that we would all be there in honor of our baby boy just as soon as we possible could. So shortly afterward helping my mom to get my two sisters girls Tameka and Fatima ready for the baby shower I called the nearest neighborhood taxi cab service company to come pick us all up so that we may make it to the baby shower on time and when the car service came we were all on our way the Long Island City to Elite neighborhood.

And when we all arrived at my fiance Elite's lady friend Ally Martin townhouse home the baby shower already had started as I introduced my mother who was to be preferred to other as Mrs. Devine and my two adorable little two sisters Tameka and Fatima and all of the ladies greeted my family with a gentle kiss on the side of each other facial cheek. And as we were all been socializing with each other it been time to to started to open up the presents for our baby and when Elite and I finally had did she as well as myself were very pleased of all the love and support that was being shown for our soon to be born baby boy to the point we both had began to shed tears of joy as we thanked everyone that was there for showing our new family so much love and every one said that we were both so very welcome and that it been the pleasure to celebrate our baby soon to be birth right along with us both. And shortly after it been time for the clock to strike 12:00 AM as we all been watching the countdown until the New Year of 2000 come in and when it finally had did we all shouted out Happy New Years in the New Minullium in 2000. And we all began making multiple toastings as Elite and I only been drinking only apple sidders beverages instead of any alcohol simply because it would been very bad for our baby boy for his mother to consume that in the mother system while she was still pregnant at that particular time.

So after celebrating bringing in the New Years of 2000 and my fiance Elite Windgate baby shower for our soon to be born baby boy we were than given a multitude of gifts for our baby that consisted of little baby shoes, toys, and clothes. And from there Elite and I thanked all of her neighborhood lady friends for than caring enough about us and our baby boy to throw such a wonderful baby shower in our future child honor as all of the ladies saw Ahhh and that we were quite welcome. And even my mother Jahtayshia and two little sisters Tameka and Fatima a very nice gift for Elite and my baby boy to be a very large assortment of multi colored of baby bottles as we both thanked them all for them to be so very sweet to do such a wonderful thing such as that. And from there Elite lady friend Ally Martin started to served dinning for everyone as my family all did really love the fact that all of her lady friends really did care so very much to give us a wonderful baby shower such as they did.

And shortly after that Elite's baby shower ended at 2:00 AM on New Year's day as everyone began to than gather their very own personal belongings as they were leaving out of Elite's friend Ally Martin apartment when everyone that been there shouted out Happy New Years everybody as they were making noises with their blow horns. And after all of Elite and Ally's lady friends left from the baby shower my two little sisters Tameka and Fatima fallen to sleep and than my mother Jahtayshia thanked us both as she also went on to say that since my two sisters fallen to sleep that it was about time that our own family has started to head back to our own family home. So I said okay there mom and that I would be ready to leave with her, Tameka and Fatima just as soon as I was to help Elite bring all of our baby shower gifts to Elite's family townhouse home and my mom said that she would wait for me to return. And my mother and I helped Elite up out of her chair so that she and I could started to go to take all of the baby presents to her own apartment town house and when we finally had gotten their as I been helping caring most of the gifts for our baby she stopped me at her family door and said that the reason that I did not see her very mother at the baby shower was because she was still feeling rather sickly and that she did not still want any company to come over as of yet.

So I once again said that was okay Elite and that I still totally had understood that her family still wanted to remain private. And Elite taken the gifts for our baby inside her family townhouse home as she came back out of her family place to go back to her neighboring lady friend Ally Martin townhouse so that I may go get my mother Jahtayshia and my two younger sisters Tameka and Fatima for me to bring them all back to my own family home. And from there when Elite and along with myself gotten back into Elite's lady friend Ally Martin townhouse my mother Jahtayshia had asked Elite if she could called a taxi cab car service for our own family to start to go back home to the Astoria, Queens New York area. And Elite did just that and when it did finally arrived we all given each other a quick kiss on the cheeks as we had said our good byes for now family and once we gotten into the taxi cab service car we were on our way back to our family home.

So once the New Years finally had came in 2000 my harassment/ sexual harassment issues still continued on January 8, 2000, the associated secretary whose name was Metta Morehouse was still trying to than seduce me because of all of the company employees been still spreading a terrible rummer of me to be possibly involved with a New York Mafia crime family members that was out by a unknown gang of gangster thieves to still try to extorted money from my employers law firm at O'Conner, Sapp, Dash & Marshall as that was the way that I would sometimes overhear my coworkers talk about me on a daily bases of the 5 day work week. And when I used to her my former employees at the company of O'Conner, Sapp, Dash & Marshall said those very awful lies about me it made me feel quite uncomfortable for me to always her all of the negative things that were always being said about me but I realized that as long as those foolishes coworkers insisted on believing that insane ridiculous rumor that would never be the real truth of me to be some kind of New York Mafia gangster that I might as well play a tough guy role with me to have a bad attitude to than pretend to be one just like they to do in the movies. that very next day I came into my workplace inside the midtown corporate law firm where I worned a all black suit with a white tie along with a very lengthy white scarf and all of the employees really did started talking about me even more so than ever before saying everyone should continue to keep a close watchful eye on me just in case I was to back in sudden moves that may be something out of the ordinary. And on January 9, 2000, as I was once again getting on the building company elevator I once again saw that associate secretary whose name Metta Morehouse as she gotten on as it been at it's full compacidy as she been standing right in back of me as she also been whispering in my ear that I looked very good and sexy enough to suck on again as she called me by my nickname and said to that she really liked that new look that you Romeo Devine as she also made a sexual harassment advancement to grabbed me by my buttocks area as she also told me that she really did think that my suit looked rather dapper on me just like a New York crime family gangster member as she said to me to please do hurt no dam body in the corporate law firm of O'Conner, Sapp, Dash & Marshall Mr. New York Mailman Sir. And I told the company associate secretary whose name was Metta Morehouse to stop trying to turn me on sexual because I already another beautiful women that was in my life that was about to be soon to be having my baby as she and I were already engage to each other.

And from there I asked Ms Metta Morehouse if she heard me what I been saying to her? And the company associate secretary told me yes she defiantly heard me very loud and clear. And I told her that I wanted her and even her other associated secretary friend who, name was Afreaka Braithwait to also stop her sexual harassment as well simply because I been fully aware of all of you female coworkers been sexual harassing and even violating me for much to long know. And from there Mette Morehouse agreed to stop harassing me in any way.

And than I shaken Mette Morehouse left hand and continued to say it's should be all good between us now and that I also wish for her to have a very easy going day and I hope that she would than allow me to have the very same as I was to continue to be making my multiple mail runs hand deliveries of the company mail services. And Metta Morehouse went on about her own business as she had walked off away from me. And from there I was so very glad to feel some relief from some very sexual unwanted attention while I was still at the law firm at least for the time being. So from there things seemed to cool down just a bit as everyone back the hell of of me and hand allowed me to just do my job to the best of my abilities. So from there I just been trying to focus on doing my job as one of the company mailman.

And about a couple of weeks later even though I a major problems in the 4th floor Copy Center department were at one time found myself to to be physical and sexual harass by two of the company copy center departmental operators whose name was Neil Harry, Exodus Franklyn and there evening time supervisor whose name was Jefferey Silverstone. On about February 5, 2000, the copy center operator whose name is Neil Harry been making jokes about there goes that guy Romeo Devine with his slick looking self just trying to get some of us guys in some serious trouble with the company Human Resources department by going ahead to back to filed a official report on the 4th floor Copy Center Crew members as he told his friends in that department. And Neil Harry began to laugh and began to make jokes of how they the guys from there department put the good word out in the corporate company O'Conner, Sapp, Dash & Marshall LLP to have a few of the female support staff members to began to infatuated me a whole of a hell lot in order to try to break my tender heart as he was still to hand deliver the company mail. the copy center other operators began to laugh and trying to humiliated me by saying that the very first set of two women that they sent out to try to keep me feel very foolishly in love by way of me to be infatuated with Tracey Whittely who was the company Intern Word Processor operator who decided to leave the law firm and that associated secretary whose name was Meshia Jamison who was still with the firm as they all continue to laugh at me with them to say that I felt so in love with Meshia Jamison that I was so very foolish to go out and buy her some long stem red roses and they also began to to start to verbally teas me by chanting La La La La and that I could never have her. And the copy center operator Neil Harry went on to say that they so many support staff members watching just about almost my every single move to the point that everyone would hear about whenever I would go inside the company bathroom stall to than to start to weeping crying wet tears of saddens from those company infacuator women.

And after all of that crazy non sense still been going on in my employer corporate law of O'Conner, Sapp, Dash & Marshall LLP I still been acting like they weren't trying to give me a emotional problem of some of the female support staff members to always seem to come on to me in a very sexual harassment matter on almost a daily bases as I just knew that I to try to really focus on my fiance Elite Windgate and I were about to bring a brand-new infant baby into this very beautiful world of ours that was the greatest gift from God all might himself. So I realized that I to have a sit discussion with my day Coordinator whose name was Russell Wright to talk about that my fiance was going about to be having my baby and that I really had wanted to be there for her and our soon to be born infant baby boy. And my day time Coordinator than congratulate me on me about to becoming a father and I thank him so very kindly by shaking his hand. And I explained that since I was soon going to be a father that I wanted to be right there for my fiance and our very soon to be expected boy baby so that I may assist my soon enough baby mother to be to also help her to deliver our baby in this very world of ours. And from there my mailroom center day time coordinator whose name was Russell Wright hand told me that everything was going to be all right and good for me to be there whenever my baby mama was to be needing me in the hospital so that I may give her all of the moral support that she might definitely need in order for her to have a very healthy baby delivery of our very own as he also went on to say that the only thing that I to do was to give him a telephone call into my workplace so that he could give me some time off of my workplace of my employer of The corporate law firm of The O'Conner, Sapp, Dash & Marshall LLP. And from there I thank my employer mailroom center day time coordinator who was Russell Wright for doing so very much so right by me and my very own little family of mines as he himself told me that I was quit so very much so welcome way back. And soon after having that very one meeting with my day time mailroom center coordinator Russell Wright as I left the company 2nd mailroom center to continue working back into the company copy center department for only for a short time. And from there my fiance whose name was Elite Windgate called me while I was working in the Copy Center for only a very short while back as the day time supervisor whose name is Carlton Circuit picked up his department telephone at the front desk area to answer the call as my fiance Elite Windgate been asking to speak to me. And from there the daytime copy center supervisor whose name was Carlton Circuit asked my soon to be my baby mother Elite Windgate just who was calling for Mr. Romeo Devine ? And from there as the telephone volume been turned up rather so very loudly as I would overhear my fiance who was Elite Windgate asked to speak with me because she said that she thought that she was might a emergency as she told my employer of the corporate law firm that is called The O'Conner, Sapp, Dash & Marshall law firm daytime supervisor Carlton Circuit that she was pregnant with my child as he just did so as she also said that she just said to the employer of The Corporate Law of the O'Conner, Sapp, Dash & Marshall LLP corporate law firm whose name was Carlton Circuit that she thought it was time to being having our baby back. all of a very sudden straight out of no where the day time employer company supervisor said to us both that he was so very excited for the very both of us as he also went on to tell my soon to be baby mother Elite Windgate and I that how he considered for me to be like a good son to him. And once my fiance and I heard my employer coworker copy center supvisor speak in such a way as we both also began to giggle and laugh right along with him. When all of the very sudden he asked both my very soon to be my baby mother Elite Windgate and I if we would both do him the very surpurve honor to make him apart of our very own family as our child God Father? And from there we once again started back laughing with him as well as we just start to hummer the company of my employer of The O'Conner, Sapp, Dash & Marshall LLP day time supervisor Carlton Circuit as we just made up a very untruthful excuse as we just explained to him back that we would have to think about a little as we also told him that we would have to get back to him on that very same matter sometime in the very near future. And from there Carlton agreed with us both as he also said that was a good enough answered for him right as my soon to be baby mother Elite Windgate and I asked okay there Mr. Carlton Circuit. And from there the company copy center day time Supervisor Carlton Circuit even asked if we would bring our little baby by the office someday soon? And from there we said sure maybe so if we both were not to be so very much busy with our child, and soon after that I just went back to do my actual job as one of the company of The O'Conner, Sapp, Dash & Marshall LLP corporate law firm New York City Mailman.

So on February 14, 2000, on the beloved Valentine Day at 8:00 AM when I received a telephone call in the early morning as I picked up to hear just who was been calling me at that particular time as it turned out to be my fiance Elite Windgate's mother Ms. Wonda Windgate telling me that her daughter water just broken and that it was time for her to be giving birth to our child. And I was told by Elite's mother that I should meet them both at the hospital in the Long Island City New York area that was simply called L. I. C. Hospital and I assured Ms. Wonda Windgate that I would definitely be there just as soon as I possibly could as she said to me that they would both see me when I was to be arriving there. So right after I gotten off of the telephone with my fiance Elite's mom I immediately called my employer at the corporate law firm of O'Conner, Sapp, Dash & Marshall LLP 4th floor mailroom center day time coordinator whose name was Russell Wright just to informed him that it been time for my fiance to about to being giving birth to my son. And when Gus had heard again of my good news of me to about to become a father he congratulated me once again as he also wished me to have many blessing with the baby as I told him that I needed sometime off of work for at least a five day work week period to take care of my baby mother and child.

And my day time coordinator whose name was Russell Wright said that yes it been okay for me to do so and I thanked him ever so kindly. And from there after hanging up from that call I awaken up my parents Jahtayshia and Damian Sr. and told them both that Elite's water broken according to what her mother told me as I just received her called and as I told her that I would be right there in the hospital just as soon as I possibly could. And from there my mom and dad told me that once the baby was to be born into the world that they both wanted me to be absolutely sure to pick up the telephone to call them both to let my side of the family know just how Elite and our baby was doing. And from there I assured my mother Jahtayshia and father Damian Sr. that I would definitely do just that as what they asked of me. And from there after I taken a very quick shower to clens myself I quickly called myself a taxi cab service company from my neighborhood town of the Astoria, Queens New York and as when it han arrived I grabbed my house keys and went outside to rush inside the taxi cab car service and from there I was on my way to see the birth of my fiance Elite Windgate and my child.

When I finally arrived at the the Long Island City Queens New York Hospital I franticly started looking for my pregnant fiance Elite and her mother Ms. Wonda Windgate and when I found my soon to be my common law mother in law she told me that her daughter was in the delivery room as we been speaking and than she said that Elite been asking for me to come into the delivery room so that I may help assist and witness the birth of our child to be born into our beautiful world of ours. So after hearing those very kind words from Elite's mother Ms. Wonda Windgate as I thanked her ever so kindly as she taking me to right to her daughter. And when I finally arrived inside the deliver room to see just how Elite was doing as she was about to be giving birth to our baby I asked her was she about ready to bring our new born into the world that day? And Elite answered yes and that she was know ready to get our baby out of her stomach and bring it into the world that day.

And it turned out that even though Elite water broken indicating that she was now do to be giving birth to our baby as she been trying to push our baby out into the world but she could not do so as of yet. So her physician whose name was Dr. Cleo Morey told us both that Elite needed medicine to help her to induce her laboring of our baby and from there she given him the okay to do so. And the inducing of Elite and my baby taken twelve hours until she was finally ready to give birth and as she was giving birth to our child as Dr. Cleo Morey first had asked me to help my future baby momma Elite to help push to bring our baby into the world as I did just as he instructed me to do and from there he call me down to her birth canal area so that I may see the birth of our baby and when I finally did witness the birth of our baby boy I instantly felt like a band new man of honor. And from there after the nurse taken Elite and my baby from the mother womb area to go and get him all clean up as she placed our child in the doctor care and from there he given our little infant boy to his mother Elite as he place our little infant boy in the mother arms first as we both welcomed our baby boy in his mommy and daddy's life as we said our very first hello's to our new buddle of joy of our baby boy.

And it finally had been my time to first take hold of our baby boy and when I finally had did so I instantly had felt so very proud and honored to being a new baby dad as I began to shed a few tears of joy right along with our child mother Elite Windgate. So from there Elite told me that she would like for her mother to come and see our baby boy who is other wise known to be known as one of our baby boy grandmother. So from there I went to locate Elite's mother Ms. Wonda Windgate so that she may finally get the blessing of a chance to than visit her new infant baby grandson for the very first time as I said come on in the delivery room Ms. Windgate to see your handsome grandson and from there she said oh arighty than Romeo as I led her by her arms in as I helped her to get there as she be so very much exhorted from helping her oldest daughter Elite to prepare her to give birth to our son. And once we gotten to the delivery room doors Elite mother Ms. Wonda Windgate very softly said her hello's to her oldest daughter Elite and her brand-new infant baby boy of a grandson and once she laid her eyes on our bundle of joy of her grandson she shouted out thank you heavenly father for our family's gift from heaven.

So shortly after our family miracle birth of our little infant baby boy I started to remember that my mother told me to be sure give my own family a call at our house to let them know that the baby been born and from there do to they were already proud grandparents to my older brother Damian Jr. son whose name is Rashad Devine who is also my nephew they said that they wanted to come up to the hospital and see there new miracle of there baby grandson. And from there I told them yes and that I was hoping that they would say that and from there my mom and dad told me that they were going to to get my brother Damian Jr.

to baby sit our two sister Tameka and Fatima while they would be there at the hospital with Elite and her mom Ms. Windgate along with myself. And from there I said that sounded like great news for me to hear and that I would see them both here in the hospital when they were to soon arrived to see us all there. And once my mother Jahtayshia and father Damian Sr. arrived at the Long Island Island City Hospital in the Queens New York area as they gotten there by a taxi car service as they called me on my cellur phone for me to come downstairs to the lobby area to meet them both so that I may take them both to see our new edition to our family. And when I picked them both up to come and see my new born son my mother given me a big kiss on both sides of my facial cheeks and my dad given me a very firm handshake and a very manly hug as they I said congratulation to me son and that they also wanted on to than say that they were so very proud of me to becoming a very proud father.

So once we arrived to see my now mother of my child Elite Windgate my parents congratulated us both on our band new son as my parents also very warmly embraced us both as they congratulated us this time both together for the first time as one family. And as we said our thank you's to them both my parents said that they wanted to see there newest grandson and I said to my mom and dad sure it would be my honorable pleasure for me to take them both to see there grandson and from there we asked my fiance/mother of my child nurse to take my parents and myself to the infant nursery room where my son was being kept. And as we arrived there as we been looking through the hospital glass widow we saw my son as we waved and said our hello to my little youngster child as my parents who is also my son grandparents also had began to shed tears of joy just like I did a little early that very same day. shortly after that we came back into Elite's hospital room to see just how she and her mother were doing after all of the excitement of the baby finally being born as my mother also taking the sweet liberty of giving Elite's mother Ms Wonda Windgate yet another warm embrace of a hug as she went on to say that we are now officially family as we are all going to do right by the baby and we all agreed on that fact of that particular matter as we all said our Amens to that.

And shortly after that all three of our parents said there good byes for now back as they went to our two family homes and I spented a few nights in the hospital until it was time for Elite to go home to her own family. And as a few days pass as Elite been there in the hospital for about 4 days now when the nurse came to us both so that we may filled out the form for our infant child name selection and I told my son's mother that since we were both bless by the heavenly father the good God Almighty that I wanted for my son to be named after me, but she told me that she wanted our son to also have her own family name and I said okay that our child should in fact have both of our family last name even though we were not married to each other. So from there we called the lady that was assign to handle the hospital birth certificate records as we filled out the forms as when completed our child record of birth for his name to be as on record as Romeo Windgate-Devine and as everything been completed it been time for my new baby mother Elite Windgate to finally go to her family home from the hospital. So she told me to give her mother a call so that she may pick us both up from the hospital to take us all at our families homes and I said that I would do just want she be asking of me. And soon after Elite's mother came by to bring us both to our two homes.

And once my fiance Elite and her mother Ms. Wonda Windgate and our new family buddle of joy of a new born baby boy Romeo Windgate-Devine arrived back at there family townhouse home in the Long Island City New York area as I helped my new baby momma out of her family vehicle along with me holding our infant child of a son as we walked to her family door my son mother told me that she and her family was still not ready to let me in there family household as of yet because they were not yet comfortable to having any men in there home since her father Faarooq Cutler left them to go and live with his sister Victoria and her husband Uncle Tyson Fonzelrelly because he a hard time getting along with her mother Ms. Wonda Windgate. So from there Elite than asked her mother if she would bring baby Romeo Jr. inside there family home and my son new grandmother said yes and that she certainly would be very glad to take her baby grandson inside so that she may make him feel warm and comfortable as she said that she would feed him a bottle of milk because she said that he must be very hungry by now. And I told my fiance Elite Windgate that I totally understood before our new baby boy was born into the world that it been okay to not to let me inside their family home but as I explained to my baby momma that as we would all be in our little baby boy Romeo Jr. life as he will continue to grow up that we would always wonder why his mother side of the family would never want his father to come inside to be spending time with his mommy side our his family inside their own home. And Elite agreed that I been absolutely right in what I was telling her as she told me that she would discuss the matter over with her mother before they were all to let me in there family home and I said okay that would be just fine for now and that she should give me a call after she finish discussing the matter over with her mom and from there I given my baby mother Elite Windgate a big wet kiss on her lips and from there she said that she would called me much later on that very same night.

On February 17, 2000, I received a telephone call from my fiance/baby moma Elite Windgate as I asked her just how she and our little buddle of joy was doing? And she told me that she and our baby boy little Romeo Windgate-Devine was doing quite well but she felt so very exalted from just recently giving birth to our child. she went on to say that she talked things over with her mother Ms. Windgate and the rest of her immediate family members about know that we are official all family to each other that it's very important that they all start to open up there family town house home to me so that our little infant baby boy little Romeo would be able to enjoy his father company with the other side of his own family members. And once I was finally inside Elite family town house home I taking the liberty of embracing Elite's family members that consisted of her oldest brother Mason, youngest brother Epico and younger sister Epiphany Windgate with multiple hugs for her female family members and handshakes for the male family members as well.

So from there I began to take notice of Elite's family townhouse home as once I taken a good look around there place were there all live for over thirty-something years now I taken notice of just how all of their family clothes were just thrown all over the place such as there floor right along with a few pieces of garbage. And I begin to wonder just how people could live in such unclean condition such as that as I just been thinking to myself as I was holding Elite and my son little infant Romeo Windgate-Devine just how people could possible live in a dirty household such as that. I just put my fiance Elite Windgate family unclean family house home condition out of my mine at that particular time as I just focus on our new born son who I will always refer to him as Romeo Jr. even though our names were not the exact same. I told my son mother Elite that I to use her family bathroom facilities and the she taking me right upstairs for me to use it and from there she said that she would be waiting for me with our baby boy back downstairs with her family and I said okay.

And once I finish using the rest room as I been looking around Elite's and little baby Romeo Jr. upstairs family town house home I taken notice that there family only a one bedroom household and from there I really felt kind of bad for my baby boy little Romeo Jr. that he to live in a one bedroom townhouse with a family of five other family members along with it being rather unclean as well as I just kept that thought to myself. But Elite been helping her mother Ms. Wonda Windgate to prepare a good family meal for us all that consisted of a surf and turf meal of steak and seafood along with a bake potatoes. And the entire meal turn out one of the most delicious meals that I every had tasted just almost as good as my mother Jahtayshia Devine and my grandmother Alicia Gilbert tasty delicious cooking. And my fiance Elite asked me to spend a few nights with her and her family members to help her with our baby. And when I used to help take very good care of our baby boy I realized just how much it took to dealing with a new born baby of my very own as Elite me to be the one to get up with our child so I may start to giving our baby his early frequent bottle feedings. And it really made me feel very proud to do that for my little one to the point that I went out to purchase a swing set for the baby along with me to purchase a infant stroller for him.

On September 12, 2000, my youngest uncle whose name is Solomon Gilbert on my mother Jahtayshia's Devine side of the family came in our family home to informed me that there was a World Heavyweight Championship boxing match on cable television that same night between the champion Axel Mc Folly Vs Travis Ruckers and he asked me if I wanted to see the fight and I said to him hell ya I wanted to see that fight and from there we were both on our way to our Astoria New York Queens corner grocery store that is called Astoria Delicatestant. And as my uncle Solomon Gilbert and I said to the store owner whose name was Troy Munoz hey guy thanks a whole lot for letting us all watch the fight together and he replied back to me that I was quite welcome. So as the heavyweight boxing championship match was going on a middle aged lady walked into the grocery store as well as she sat right next to me as we both been sitting on a couple of milk cartoon crates and she said hello to me as she also went on to asked me if I work into the mid town building at Time Square Plaza and I responded back to her yes I did. And from there the middle aged afro American lady introduced herself as Theresa Lasey. And she told me that she worked for another company that was inside of the same building were I was employed at called Classey Fashionables Wares and she went on to say that she recognized me from the company office building.

And from there I began to get rather worrisome that even though that lady did not worked directly with my own employer at O'Conner, Sapp, Dash & Marshall LLP I suspected that she been informed by my coworkers at the corporate law firm was saying about me to be possibly apart of a New York City organized crime family. And once I saw that lady whose name she told me was Theresa Lasey introduced herself to me that evening I began to suspected that the corporate conspiracy was going to be possibly spreading the word in the streets of New York about me being possible a member of a New York organize crime mafia family member. from there my employer at the corporate law firm of O'Conner, Sapp, Dash & Marshall company building neighboring mate that was called Classey Fashionables whose name she was claiming to be as Theresa Lasey began to question my neighboring corner store owner whose name was Troy Munoz about just how well that he known me? And from there Troy told my building mate neighboring female coworker mate that I been his customer for a few years now as he also went on to say that some of my family members also shopped in his store and that he usually saw me walk from around the corner to make purchases at his store.

And from there my neighboring building mate whose name was Theresa Lasey told the corner grocery store owner Troy that my employers at a midtown Manhattan corporate law firm at O'Conner, Sapp, Dash & Marshall LLP reason to believe that I could possibly be connected to a New York organize crime mafia family but she also went on to tell the grocery store owner that no one in the company was for certain about me outside of my workplace. And from there the middle age lady whose name she claimed was Theresa Lasey asked the dedication store owner whose name is Troy Munoz if he along with him to spread the word to all of his neighborhood customers for them to all keep a close watchful eye of me to see if lam involved in any criminal unlawful activities of any kind? And to my very disappointing surprise Troy totally had betrayed me by agreeing with that crazy lady female neighboring building mate coworker of mine saying yes that he would spread the word about me to possible being a New York mafia gangster of some kind and from there the lady Theresa shook Troy Munoz hand and thanked him ever so kindly. And after the heavyweight boxing match ended that very same evening I the ran out of the store and my uncle Solomon chase right after me as he eventually caught up with me as he began to asked me what was wrong with me running out of the grocery store like that so dam fast? And I told him about my corporate conspiracy situation that originated at my employer corporate law of O'Conner, Sapp, Dash & Marshall about how a very false rumor started of me having ties to a New York mafia family. And when my uncle Solomon heard what I told him he been in totally disbelief as he said wow that sounded like a very crazy bad situation that I was in. And I asked him did in he hear the store owner Auturo tell that middle age lady that he was going to be telling his neighborhood customers that everyone in there area should keep a very closely watchful eye on me to see if I was actually participating in any illegal organize crime activities of any kind? And from there my uncle told me that no he did not overhear that lady conversation and that he just been enjoying the heavyweight boxing championship boxing match along with him drinking his alcoholic beer beverage. And from there I said okay their uncle Solomon since it been a very shocking night for me to find out that one of my neighboring building coworker mate wanted for my neighborhood corner delicatessen store owner to spread the very negative word of me possible being a New York organize crime family member and that they wanted me out of the employer corporate law firm of O'Conner, Sapp, Dash & Marshall LLP and place me into police custody just like any other New York mafia gangster of New York.

And from there after my uncle Solomon Gilbert and I came inside our family home in our home town of Astoria New York area I and I told my two parents Jahtayshia & Damian Sr. what just happen to me concerning my corporate conspiracy situation about how one of the company building neighbor mate whose name she informed me was Theresa Lasey that she recognized me mr from our office building in the Time Square Plaza area in the Manhattan New York area about the false rumors that was being spread around the entire office building in the Time Square Plaza area were a whole lot of the other employees worked right along with me to constantly hear them saying about me to possibly to be connected to a New York organize crime mafia family as one of the ladies from another neighboring offices that was also located in the same exacted building were I worked at come right in the corner delicatestant store and began to start questioning me about what actual company that I worked for and from there I told her the corporate law firm of O'Conner, Sapp, Dash & Marshall LLP. And all of the delicatestance customers of Troy Munoz really very much enjoyed the good entertaining heavyweight boxing fight that been going on as me and my uncle Solomon Gilbert been also enjoying ourselves quite a bit until a middle aged lady who came into our family neighborhood the corner that was called Astoria grocery and Delicatestan store and sat herself down right next to me as she was asking me hey there guy don't i know you from somewhere in the midtown Manhattan area in the Time Square Plaza area? And from there I informed both of my parents that the middle aged lady who said that she hand recognized me from the Time Square Plaza area told me that her name was Theresa Lasey. I went on to informed my mother Jahtayshia and my father Damian Sr. Devine that after the world heavyweight boxing match was over with that same lady began to questioning me about what was my name and where did I live at?

And I told my parent that I just thought that my neighboring building mate who been claiming that her real name was Theresa Lasey was just been trying to be very noisy as she was trying to all up in my very private and personal pleasant life style as I just informed her that I was one of the O'Conner, Sapp, Dash & MarshallLLP inter-office mailman. And I went on to tell my parents that the crazy lady from my employer of the corporate law firm job building neighboring mate whose name she told me was Theresa Lasey began to questioning the corner delicatestant corner grocery store owner who everyone in our neighborhood town of Astoria, Queens New York known Troy Munoz for over ten years now about how much could he tell her about me and if he known where I live at that particular time? And I went on to let my mother Jahtayshia and father Damian Sr. know that he was not for certain where I live at as he also had went on to betray me even though I been a long time customer just like everyone else in our Astoria neighborhood that whenever I would come to purchase some groceries from his store that the only information that he was a to give me female coworker was that I usually walked from around the corner. And my parents said that I better watched myself whenever I was at my place of business at that Law firm of O'Conner, Sapp, Dash & MarshallLLP because those guys are just trying to make your job a very uncomfortable workplace.

was Troy Munoz that he should never again work for that man and his other family member who also worked into the store right along with him. And from there my uncle Solomon Gilbert told me that as long as that corner Delicatestan grocery store man Troy Munoz the money to pay him to work for him that he would always continue to do work for him and his family and anybody else in the neighborhood because that was the only way that he told me was the fasted legally way to make his money. And when I heard my uncle Solomon Gilbert speak to me that way I began to get a little discussed with him quit a little bit.

from there my mother and father told me that I should try to get a tape recorder to try to record most of my employer harassment issues in multiple conversations that I was having with those troublesome coworkers of mines and I told her that were I been assign to work inside the Telecopy/Fax Department Center workstation be rather noisy with there office machines constantly running loudly to the point that I told her that by the telecopy machines would been running as I the explain that it might drown out the sounds of my harassment issues verbal face to face conversations to the point that I might really get caught with the company coworkers. So from there I thank my mother Jahtayshia Devine for at least trying to help me with my New York man mailman corporate conspiracy issues as I told her that I was going to find another way to legally prove a New York Corporate Conspiracy Situation that really did actually existed first at my place of my employment at the corporate law firm of O'Conner, Sapp, Dash & Marshall LLP some way and some how. The whole dam New York corporate conspiracy situation really to once again begin to bother me about how a false rumerous lies about the word in the law firm of me to belong to a New York crime family of some kind of gangster organization. I felt that now that my female neighboring company coworker whose name she said her name was Theresa Lasey totally went to far to start to find out about me out in the streets of New York instead of just keeping the whole non sense of my former employers at the corporate law firm of O'Conner, Sapp, Dash & Marshall LLP false silly rumors just inside there company walls.

So on September 15, 2000, when I returned back to my former employer corporate law firm of O'Conner, Sapp, Dash & Marshall LLP as I been still assign to be the mail clerk to make all of the hand deliveries for the company 4th floor copy center department as I entered the area where I saw the day time copy center supervisor Carlton Circuit and he asked me was the baby born as of yet? And I told him yes and that I was the proud father of a healthy baby boy who I said I name my child first name after myself as his father. And from there Thomas congratulated me with him also to shake my hand as he also insisted that I broke the good news to the rest of the 4th floor copy center department guys and when I did they all seemed very happy for me as they also informed me that it always been a traditions for a brand-new father to bring into work a box of cigars for his fellow coworkers. And even though I did not like a few of the support staff members that I to work with I put on a fony smile and said that I no ideal of tradition but I told the 4th floor copy center guys that I would bring in some cigars by the very next day and they said okay that great news for them to hear that the whole department would get a free smoke of cigars.

So when I went back into my employers corporate law firm of O'Conner, Sapp, Dash & Marshall LLP as I brought in the cigars to properly celebrate the very birth of my young infant son Romeo Windgate-Devine with my coworkers guys of the 4th floor copy center department and I began to started to passing the cigars all out to to all of there staff members as they all had said there thank you's and with them all giving me there congratulations of me to being a brand-new parent to my son. And from there I giggle and laugh with them to as they asked me just how my little boy was doing right along with his mother? And I told the 4th copy center staff members that my son mother and child were just doing quit well as I thank them all for asking of my new family. And for a couple of weeks things seemed to be quit calmed down with the guys as there department day time supervisor whose name is Carlton Circuit been sitting at the copy center front desk as the company telephone rang as I been working at my workstation as he told me that it was my sweet heart of a fiance Elite that was calling for me as he began to laugh out loud as he told me to come get the telephone call that was for me as I told him that I was on my way over to the desk.

And from there I said my hello to my fiance/baby momma Elite Windgate and as we began to talked to each other the day time copy center supervisor Carlton Circuit once again began to laugh as he was also asking me just when I and my fiance Elite was going to be bringing up our little buddle of joy of a baby boy to pay him a visit? And he insisted for me to give him the telephone so he could asked my fiance Elite himself. So from there he said his hello to Elite as he introduced himself to her as a close coworker friend of mines as he also went on to say to her that he considered me to be like a son to him. And from there he asked us both while she was on the speaker telephone if she could bring our baby boy by so that he may shower him with many gifts as he asked if he could become apart of our family as our infant baby boy Romeo Jr. God Father?

And we both tried to humor him that we were not for certain when it would be the very best time to bring our infant baby boy Romeo Jr. by the corporate law firm but we also told him that we would have to get back to him on that matter because she was mostly busy a hole lot. And the day time supervisor Carlton Circuit told us both to please keep him posted of the matter and my fiance Elite Windgate and I just told him that we would have to let him know when she could make it up to the my job.

And even though Elite and I told the day time copy center day time supervisor Carlton Circuit that we would have to get back to him on when his mother would be able to bring up our baby boy little Romeo Jr. into pay him and the staff a visit. But I already knew that with all of my harassment/sexual harassment issues that I was having with some of my former coworkers that there was no way in hell that I was going to ever expose my child to those crazy foolish people that I worked with as I informed my son mother Elite Windgate. And as the copy center staff members kept on asking me just when they would get a chance to someday see my son pay them all a visit with his mother to bring him into the office I kept telling them that she just did not have the time to come to our office because she was always to busy with our baby boy. So about two weeks of September 30, 2000, I was later reassign out of the copy center department as I been placed back into the company telecopy department by my mailroom manager Henry Hernandez. And as I been on my way to the forty-second telecopy/fax department as I been on my way walking into my workstation area I saw the originator of all of my employees corporate conspiracy problems whose name was Stone Casey as he said to me that even though I been trying to escape the mailroom talks of me to be possibly to have some sort of a New York mafia family gangster crime connection trying to ruin the law firm of O'Conner, Sapp, Dash & Marshall LLP that as long as I continued to work inside the company that all of the employees would always think of me as a criminal master mine of sorts just trying embesell money from the rest of the company.

And my former coworker whose name is Stone Casey went on to say that he heard about that middle age lady whose name was Thereasa Lasey who worked for the corporation of a company called Classey Fashion that I saw her in my neighborhood of the Astoria Queens New York area in my local town corner grocery store as he told me that he and the law firm of O'Conner, Sapp, Dash & Marshall LIP was told all New Yorkers watching me and even my family members just to see if anyone of us are participating in any kind of criminal activities of any kind and he walked off away from me as I been so very much relieve that the crazy former coworker did so as I just went all to making my mail deliveries of the company telecopy/fax documents along with some mail deliveries as well. And from there I was just trying to figure out why my crazy former employers at the midtown Manhattan law firm of O'Conner, Sapp, Dash & Marshall LLP was still trying so hard to prove me to be such a guilty criminal mined type of a man when in fact I would always be a very law biding citizen who would never want to see the inside of a prison cell. So soon after my work week ended I was so exhorted from all of my very stressful work week conspiracy situation once again that I just wanted to go to my family home where I lived and just lay around and relax myself. And once I arrived back at my parents Jahtayshia and Damian

Sr. Devine family home that asked me just how my work week gone that time around?

And I told my folks about how when my mail clerk coworker whose name was Stone Casey approached me to say that he heard about the middle lady who also worked inside the same exact building that we did as the rumor of me to be possibly to be connected to a New York criminal mafia family of some kind started to spread around our very own family neighborhood of the Astoria, Queens New York area straight to our town corner Delicatestan store with the owner whose name was Troy Munoz with the company New York corporate law firm of O'Conner, Sapp, Dash & Marshall LLP in the midtown Manhattan area at the Four time Square Plaza area conspiracy story slanderous lies of me to being a Mafia gangster of New York. And after confiding all of my problems once again that I than had at my employers midtown corporate law of O'Conner, Sapp, Dash & Marshall LLP my parents once again begin to doubt me to the point that they become once again paranoid of them once again believing that there could be some actually truth to the story as I would overhear my very own mother and father whispering to each other as they step back away from me with me as I would also would overhear them say that our own family better beware of me because of me as they said that I could maybe be possibly actually connected to a New York mafia criminal family of some kind and that our very own family not been yet aware of as of yet as they would once again to have themselves to bow there heads toward me as they would also turned themselves away from me as they decided to face the wall leaving themselves to becoming so very much so once again paranoid to still believe that it could be some actually truth to the slanderous rumerous lies and deceit of my former employer law firm of O'Conner, Sapp, Dash & Marshall LLP.

And shortly after I discovered that my employer building upstairs neighboring building mate whose name she claimed was Theresa Lasey who come into my home town of Astoria, Queens New York and started investigating me with my neighborhood corner grocery store owner whose name was Troy Munoz and I than began to take notice that many different people around the area began to than bow there heads toward me just like my two parents Damian Sr. and Jahtayshia Devine did as a way to acknowledge me to the point that many people began to fear me like some kind of New York mafia gangster member of some kind. And as my two parents continued to still than treat me so very badly just like some kind of a criminal suspect as they still believed in the very slanderous lies of a rumor of my former coworkers of the corporate law firm that is called O'Conner, Sapp, Dash & Marshall LLP with them spreading the word in the New York City streets that I could actually be a New York mafia gangster family member that I even told my mom's younger brother my uncle Ronald Gilbert as he also had come over to pay our family a visit for a short while that I suspected that my mother was calling my former employer behind my back as she also had asked me for my job telephone # just in case my family was to have some kind of emergency of some sort. And shortly after I did that I would overhear that my mother Jahtayshia Devine would sometimes would go behind my back to try to find out what my former coworkers at the corporate law firm of O'Conner, Sapp, Dash & Marshall LLP still been saying about me with everyone on my job stilled had there reasons to believed that I was a New York City mafia gangster of some kind just trying to help a New York mafia family steel from the my job. But on October 8, 2000, I could not understand just why when my former mailroom coworker whose name was Craige Stoneson told me that my mother Mrs. Devine called for me on the company telephone line as she left a message with him for me to give her a called back at my home as he went on to tell yet another coworker who was also the ring leader of a II of my former employers at the corporate law firm of O'Conner, Sapp, Dash & Marshall LLP whose name was Stone Casey that the company now even my very own mother trying to find out what was the proof that my employer come up with?

And my former mailroom coworker Craige Stoneson went on to say that my mother Mrs. Devine also went on to say that even though my employer at the Corporate law firm of O'Conner, Sapp, Dash & Marshall LLP there own personal suspicions that her son could have some sort of a criminal connection of a New York mafia crime family that the company no actual real proof of the matter and that she also added that the midtown corporate law firm better stop harassing her son because as I heard that she said that I medical condition of some kind that was very visible but also very private for only his family concern of the matter. And my mother Jahtayshia totally denied my accusation of her to never called my employer job unless it been an actually family emergency of some kind. And my parents Damian Sr. and Jahtayshia Devine and I gotten into a slight argument about me accusing my mom of doubting me to the point that I overheard from my former coworkers whose name was Craige Stoneson that my very own mother was calling into her son's workplace trying to spy on me behind my back to try to figure out just what still been going on with me at my employers corporate law firm of O'Conner, Sapp, Dash & Marshall LLP by her also began to start to questioning my former coworkers to see what they found find out about me and if there was any new criminal true information about me. And my former mailroom coworker whose name was Craige Stoneson also went on to say that my mother Mrs. Devine also find out that there was no new news about me to be in any criminal activity to report to her. And than as I also heard Craig O'Brien say that my mother also gave a verbal warning to my employers at the corporate law firm of O'Conner, Sapp, Dash & MarshallLLP to back up off of me because as I overheard some of the guys in the mailroom saying that my mom warned them all that they better beware and back off of me simply because I a very serious noticeable medical condition that was a very private family matter that was none of the employers concern. So after accusing my mother Jahtayshia about what I heard about what she possibly had done my father Damian Devine Sr. hand stepped into between my mother Jahtayshia and my argument as he told me now wait a got dam F*ckin minute there son and that I better started to back the hell up out of my mother face as he insisted that I was falsely accusing my mother for know good reason at all. And my dad went on to started to questing me just why I was accusing my mother/his wife of calling that crazy problematic job of mines?

And I just told my parents that what my former coworker guy whose name was Craige Stoneson been telling the rest of the guys in the company 4th floor mailroom center. But my mother Jahtayshia and Damian Sr. insisted that wasn't actually true as they claimed that my former employer at the corporate law firm of O'Conner, Sapp, Dash & MarshallLLP been totally lying to me to just trying to drive your whole family apart from each other as my father Damian Sr. said that I should not believe my former coworkers lies and deceit. And I began to question if what my parents were telling me was the actual truth than why on some very strange occasions that my very own two parents would seem to become very paranoid to the point that they would both bow there heads and turn there faces toward the wall? And after hearing that my mother and father asked me just how I could believe in those insane things that my coworkers were saying about your very own parents as they been in totally actual denial of what I accused my mother of doing? And I just told my parents that I don't know why my coworkers at the corporate law firm would say those bad things about my very own parents and that was just what I heard from the mailroom guys talking about our own very family.

And my mother Jahtayshia and Damian Sr. hand said that after all of that craziness that was going on with my very disturbed minded corporate law firm employer at O'Conner, Sapp, Dash & MarshallLLP that they as my parents stared to realized that my former employer were trying to turn me against my very own family members by telling me all those lies that my mother was trying to spying on me by calling to speak to my coworker while just trying to find out any information that they were not yet aware of as they also had stilled claimed was true. And from there I asked them both how come sometimes when I been in there very present they all of the sudden become very paranoid toward me by me to see them both bow there heads to me as they would also would be standing around our family home as they would began to turn themselves toward the wall? And after hearing me saying all of that they totally had denied what I be telling them as they said they never reacted in no such of a way at any time. And from there they stood by what they told me as they told me that I better started to get a good night rest and began to start to enjoy my long three day weekend of the Labor Day and from there I said good night to my parents as I just went on downstairs to our family basement home to call my fiance Elite Windgate and our young son Romeo Windgate-Devine. And once I gotten myself very much so very comfortable as I gotten myself undress from my mailroom clerk uniform and into my night time pajamas I decided to fix myself something to drink and eat and afterwards I called my baby momma Elite Windgate and our little son Romeo Jr. And when I finally had gotten around to doing so I confided with my fiance about how I was so very stress out from all of my harassment issues that I was having with my former coworkers at the corporate law firm of O'Conner, Sapp, Dash & Marshall and that was really stressing the hell out of me. And from there Elite said ahhh and that she felt so very said and sorry for me and my troubles that I at that time as she also suggested that I should come over to pay her and our baby little Romeo Jr. and family visit and I told her that sounded like a very wonderful Ideal and that I would be right over to her family town house in the long Island City New York area and from there she said that sounded like a very good ideal to come and see her whole family as well and I said that I would arrive the following day just as soon as I could do so.

on October 29, 2000, while I was on my way to visit my son's mother/fiance Elite Windgate and our toddler son Romeo Windgate-Devine in there home town of the Long Island City New York area and as I was getting off of a New York City Transit Authority Queens New York bus as I saw a Spanish lady who I recognized from my employer at the corporate law firm of O'Conner, Sapp, Dash & Marshall LLP in the midtown section of the Time Square Plaza area and from there with all of the false rumors of a very slanderous lies that was still going on at that time saying that my employer coworkers wanted to know whatever I was doing in the New York City area and even whenever I was in the streets so that someone could possibly catch me doing some sought of a illegal criminal activities of any kind so that I would be tried and convicted of some unlawful crime of soughts. So on October 30, 2000, even though I became quite worrisome of me to possibly to be starting to be spy on in my extended family in my son family neighborhood of the Long Island City New York as I just went on with my very own personal and private life as I called for my son's Romeo Jr. and his mother Elite Windgate to come and open there door to please let me in so that I may pay them a visit for the weekend. And once I arrived inside of my son's Romeo Jr. and his family townhouse home I said my hello's to my new family of the Windgate family as they did the very same as they all welcomed me inside with a very warm embrace. And from there after I received such a warm hospitality from them back my fiance Elite Windgate came up with a very good ideal of how she thought that it would be such a wonderful idea for she along with our son Romeo Windgate-Windgate alone with his grandmother Ms. Wonda Windgate as-well as myself was to go outdoors and to have a nice family picnic in there neighborhood park called Mc Kinely Park and I said that sounded like a great ideal for the family as I also said that I was ready whenever ever they were. And once we arrived at the park Elite and I rolled out two blankets for the four of us to set and eat on as Elite previously pack up a picnic basket that was full of sandwiches, salads, fried chicken and some sodas for some refreshments.

after my new family and I enjoyed such a wonderful and delicious meal my son's Romeo Jr. mother Elite and brought out of her digital camera so that our family would always remember this good family day that we shared together. So my fiance/mother of my child Elite Windgate and I asked her mother Ms. Wonda Windgate if she would be so very sweet and kind to do us the honor of taking some photographs and videos of our little family and my common law mother in-law said why ocource and that she would love to as she also went on to say that this should be a whole lot of good fun for you two new parents and our baby who she given our son the nickname of cuddles. And after we all went to the Mckinley Park area where my baby momma Elite took myself and our family to the baby swing set section were she and I began to placed our son little Romeo Jr. inside as she and I began to very gently swing him back and worth just until our little baby boy was to fall him sleep and it actually worked. And shortly after that little baby Romeo Jr. grandmother Ms. Wonda Windgate took her baby grandson out of the public park swing set as she whispered to him saying that it was time for him and our family to finally go home as she also went on to say that she love him so very much so has she called him cuddles once again and from there my son's mother/Elite and I began to smile at her mother as we both said that was a very sweet and loving nickname that was giving to him by his grandmother.

So after that day finally ended I received a called from my very own mother Mrs. Jahtayshia Devine on my mobile phone saying that she just been wondering how Elite, little baby Romeo Jr. and I enjoyed our day together as a family? And I told my mom that everybody was doing just fine as we all a good day in Elite's neighborhood family park. So from there my mother informed me that she and the family really started to miss little baby Romeo Jr. as she also went on to asked me to asked my son's mother Elite if she would be so very sweet and kind to bring her grand son by my family home in the Astoria section in the Queens New

York area so that our kids could enjoyed the October 31, 2000, hallowed day together? And I told my mom that I wasn't yet sure and that I to asked my son's mother Elite if she felt like bringing our baby little Romeo Jr. by my family home in the Astoria Queens section? And from there my mother told me to just shut my mouth Romeo Sr. and for me to pass the telephone to Elite because she very quickly decided that she was going to do the grandmotherly thing and asked my son mother Elite her own self as she began to laugh at her very own self. And from there I given my fiance/baby mother Elite the telephone as she said her hellos to my mother as she herself began to laugh at what my mother been saying to me as she told my mom that she herself hand overheard her my mom's conversation as she told my mother that wright Mrs. Devine and that she also told her that she totally had understood where she was coming from as Elite went on to laugh out loud to say to my mother that sometimes we as women have to tell our men to just shut there mouths up from time to time and for them to leave certain things to be discussed between the ladies of the family.

And from there I said well occurse their ladies and that I did not mean to get in between you ladies momma's conversations. And after all of that joking around of a very hilarious conversation my mother Jahtayshia Devine asked her about her youngest grandson little baby Romeo Jr. could come over to pay our family a visit and Elite said yes and that we would all be there the following day and than my mother said that was great news for her to hear because of my to younger two stepsister Tameka and Fatima Devine began asking for there baby nephew Romeo Jr. So from there after I spented the night with Elite and little baby Romeo Jr. the next afternoon day of October 31, 2000, of Halloween that little baby Romeo Jr., Elite and I had said our good byes for now to her side of the family we also told her people that we were on our way to visit my family home in the Astoria, Queens New York area and from there my child mother asked if she could borrow her mother car and after she said yes and that it would be fine for us to do so and from there the three of us where on our way to my family home but before we were to leave out my son's mother pulled out a very cute looking Halloween outfit for our baby so that he may be dress up as a amazing super hero of the Batman and from there we were on our way to see my side of the family. And from there after the three of us finally arrived very safely to my own family home my two little stepsister Tameka and Fatima been all stress up just jumping up and down as they said there hellos to Elite little baby Romeo Jr. and I as we gotten inside the house and the girls asked Elite to please take a set so that they may play with there little nephew Romeo Jr. as my son's aunty's said there hello's to little Romeo Jr. how's it going with you But he was to young to talk as of yet. So from there my two little stepsister Tameka and Fatima asked our mother Jahtayshia Devine if they could get themselves dress up so they may all go out with Elite and I for trick or treating?

And our mother Jahtayshia said that it was okay with her if your big brother Romeo Sr. and his fiance would agree to take them both out just as long as we were to all to stay on the our family block. And Elite and I agreed with my mom as we began to start to dress up our little baby Romeo Jr. and my girls went upstairs to dress themselves up so that they may join in on there Halloween hunt for there best cadies that they could possible get there little grubby little hands on. So once we all been ready to go my two little stepsister Tameka and Fatima asked Elite and I if we were going outside for trick or treating with them all while wearing a costume of our very own? And from there we told the girls no but that it really will bring joy to our hearts for us to see all three of you kids to get as much of candies as they can possibly get there grubby little hands on and about thirty seconds later as there girls been dress up as Cinderella with there magical wands as they rang as many door bells as they possible could as they shouted out trick or trick as they asked the neighbors can we please have some candies?

And Elite and little baby Romeo Jr. and I also gotten into the action of getting a few pieces of soft candies for the two of us and a little for our baby little Romeo Jr. And afterward my mother shouted outside that it was time for all of us to come inside because she said that it was starting to get very late. So once we arrived back inside my family home my to stepsisters Tameka and Fatima started to open up a few pieces of the cadies as Elite and I also did the very same thing for ourselves as well as for our son Romeo's Jr. while he nippled on little pieces of cotton candy and marsh mellows. And after all of that excitement for the children in our family finally had ended we all said our good nights to each other as Tameka and Fatima and both said there thank you's as they both gave

133

us a kiss on our cheek bones as we were all wishing each other to have a good night rest and relation for the night as we said that we would see each other all in the morning time.

So when my family and I awaken up the very next morning of November 1, 2000, my mother and father Jahtayshia and Damian Devine Sr. made us all a nice family delicious breakfast that we all enjoyed very much so. afterwards my two little stepsisters Tameka who was the age of 8 years old at the time as Fatima was only 6 years old at that particular time began to play with my son/there nephew little Romeo Jr. with some of there toys that the family for the kids to play with. So a few hours later my two stepsisters Tameka, Fatima, little baby Romeo Jr. along with his mother and I all sat around my family living room area as we started to take multiple family photographs of one another with us all to have very bright and beautiful smiles in each and everyone of them. So later in the afternoon my son's mother Elite told me that she was getting to be rather sleepy and that she wanted to go downstairs to our family basement to lay herself down for a little while as she told me to make sure that I would take good care of our little son Romeo Jr. and make sure my stepsisters don't play to rough with him.

And shortly after my son's mother awaken up from her short nap time my two little younger little stepsisters Fatima and Tameka rushed in to our family basement bedroom were I lived for many years back in the day as they were all so very cute and little as they said there hello's to her as they also went on to asked her if she would get herself up out of the bed to come and play pin the tail on the donkey with them and our son little baby Romeo Jr? And so we did in fact play plenty of other games as-well such as peek aboo with little baby Romeo Jr. as we covered and uncovered our eyes with our two hands as we all also made plenty of funny faces. shortly after that my fiance Elite Windgate told me that she really enjoyed my family so very so but as she also went on to tell me that her very own family called for her to come back to there own family townhouse home in the Long Island City New York section of the Queens New York. And I said okay baby momma Elite and that I totally had understood that she to get back to her very own people. But shortly after that Elite told me that she wasn't feeling very well at that particular time and she told me that she wanted me to call a taxi cab car service for her and our little young son Romeo Jr. and she also said that she also wanted me to come along with her and our child a spend a few days with her family to help her to take care of our baby.

So about thirty minutes later after that Elite gotten herself dress up ready to go back to her mother family town house home we all went back upstairs from the basement to sit with my family for a very short while to say our good afternoon to my immediate family members that consist of my mother Jahtayshia. my father Damian Sr. my older brother Damian Jr. and my two little stepsisters Tameka and Fatima. And my big brother Damian Jr. asked his common law sister in-law my fianance/baby momma Elite Windgate if it would be alright for him to hold his little nephew little Romeo Windgate-Devine ? And she said sure as she given our baby to him as he began to say hey there little baby Romeo Jr. and he introduced himself as his uncle Damian Jr. as he given him a very warm kiss on both of his cheek bones. And as my parents said that it was actually there turn to hold there baby boy of there grandson Romeo Jr. And when they finally did little Romeo Jr. began become so very happy just smiling at everyone of us. And shortly after that it was time for us to call a taxi cab service to take my my son mother Elite Windgate, Romeo Jr. along with myself to come take us back to her family home and when it arrived we given everyone in my family quick hugs goodbyes and than we were on our way to Elite and little Romeo Jr. townhouse home in the Long Island City New York section of the Queens New York area.

So once my son Romeo Windgate-Devine, his mother Elite Windgate along with myself all arrived back in the Long Island City New York section of Queens after we all gotten ourselves settled back in my common law in-laws town house home we just sat around to relax ourselves from all the fun we with my side of the family. my common law mother in-law Ms. Wonda Windgate asked her oldest daughter Elite and I the question of just how did we and our little buddle of joy of our baby boy little Romeo Jr. enjoyed our Halloween treats that year? And we just said that we all a great time with us to taking all three of thee kids which also included my two stepsisters Tameka and Fatima for there trick or treating were we told her mom that all three of the kids in our family received plenty of candy treats to last them for quite some time. Elite's younger sister Epiphany Windgate come inside her own family living room to set with her older sister Elite and her nephew Romeo Jr. and myself as she said that she miss all three of us a whole lot. on November 8, 2000, Elite's two brothers whose name are Mason, Epico Windgate and I decided to go to there family neighborhood grocery store that was called Long Island City grocery and delicatestant store.

So once my two common law brother in-laws Mason, Epico and myself arrived at the store I recognized a middle aged Spanish lady from my former employer at the corporate law firm of O'Conner, Sapp, Dash & Marshall LLP as she was just crossing the street as she walked herself up to me as I tried to hide myself away from her while ducking my head in a downward position in a nearby neighborhood telephone booth as I told my two common law brother in-laws Mason and Epico Windgate while I was trying to use them both as a blocking shield just hoping that my corporate neighboring mate of a female would not see me hanging out with my common in-law male family members. But I was unsuccessful in doing so as that Spanish lady from my former place of my employment at the corporate law firm of O'Conner, Sapp, Dash & Marshall LLP walked right up to me as she said ahhh haaa there you are you New York mafia gangster man as she said that she finally caught up with me and your New York mafia organize gangster crime family members. And I told her that she should mine her own got dam f**king business and go the hell away from me. my two common law brother in-laws whose name was Mason and Epico stepped into enter vein and as they both asked that lady just what are you accusing Romeo of? So from there the Spanish lady told my common law brother in-laws that the corporate law firm of the midtown Manhattan law firm that is called the O'Conner, Sapp, Dash & Marshall LLP has reasons to believe that Mr. Romeo Devine could be apart of a New York City organized crime mafia family. And at the same dam time my common male in-laws asked the question of what in the hell are you talking about there lady?

This man Romeo Devine that you see standing her before you is a very honest and very hard working man who is taking very good care of his own family which happens to be there own sister and there baby which is also nobody's business at all that works in your corporate law firms. And from there I myself shouted out at my corporate office building neighboring female mate to say that's right you noisy behind middle aged

Spanish lady. the middle aged Spanish lady shouted at me to tell me to shut the hell up before she was going to be calling the cops on all three of us for a public disturbest charge of us speaking to loud as my son's family lived just right across the street from there neighborhood police station. And me and my two common law brother in-law Mason, Epico and I just back ourselves away from that crazy Spanish lady that worked inside my employers midtown Manhattan building as all three of us back the hell away from her as we said repeatedly at the very same time please lady don't call the cop, please don't call the cops,. don't called the cops and we wented back inside there family town house home. And once we gotten back inside I to explain my entire corporate conspiracy situation to Elite's family members of how a false rumor started on my place of employment about how when I taken out a female coworker mailroom head manager secretary whose name was Gloria Knight out on a lunch date as I also taken the liberty to purchase for her some long steam dozen of roses and how there was my mail clerk coworker whose name was Stone Casey who started to make funny jokes of how I become so very sweetly fond of our mailroom bosses secretary that he said that I really must of thought that I was going to be starting a brand-new office romance with the woman. And as I gotten myself rather upset I given my male coworker Stone Casey a very cold hearted stare of my eyes and from there he told another male coworker of ours whose name was Craige Stoneson that I look so very mad at him that he made a 2nd floor mailroom announcement how everybody better keep a very close and watchful eye on me because I look like I could be a New York City organize mafia crime family member of some kind. And when they all heard that Elite's family was in totally shock but I I just told them all that it was just a very silly office rumor and that there was one of my office mate that approached me at there own neighborhood store. And my common law in-law family member told me that I better be very careful on that very crazy jobs on mines as I said I will do my best to do so.

On November 12, 2000, while I overheard a conversation being decused by my coworker who worked in the midtown Manhattan corporate employer that is called The O'Conner, Sapp, Dash & Marshall LLP law firm whose name is Leon Abrames about how he said that he heard that the job finally discovered exactly just what home town that I a secondary family in with a mystery lady that I been involved with in The Long

Island City Queens New York area as it was also said by that very same guy that the company had there corporate spyes as of such as one Spanish lady that also live inside one of his other family neighborhood as it was even said that very same exactly Hispanic woman usually saw me go to that very same town sometimes after my Friday work day hand end as she been instructed to keep on watching me just whenever she could possible do so just like everyone else in the company building that was located in The Time Square Plaza section is in the Manhattan section area just in case something was to happen to them all such as a get away high way robbery to have me according to my former coworker of the company that is called The O'Conner, Sapp, Dash & Marshall LLP have as they said it as they should have all New York City people put on very high alert to help the Time Square Plaza corporate law firm to very closely monitor me to see if anyone could catch me just being apart of a New York City organize crime family who might been sent in there employer office to come and tear and shake down there place of corporate employment. And came the Telecopy/Fax Center operator whose name was Leon Abrames as he came out of his forty-second floor departmental office area to went onto to say even though he heard about how one of that guy Romeo Devine own immediate family members been very secretary went behind his back to warned the corporate law firm of my employer that was called The O'Conner, Sapp, Dash & Marshall LLLP to back the hell up off of me, as it was also said to my very own immediate family member that it was too little to late simply because I already been made to be a New York City public allege organize crime figure just to let the public know if they were to ever see me to be associated to be apart of in unlawful crime family as they said as I overheard it that all criminal action should always should be reported to any part of law enforcement that any one was to see fit. very soon after the day time 4th floor Supervisor whose name is Carlton Circuit came up to the forty-second floor Telecopy/Fax Center front desk area as he began to asked me well there Romeo just how it was going with me and my fiance Elite Windgate and our little baby boy? And I felt so very bad for myself because even though of the corporate law firm of my employer that was called The O'Conner, Sapp, Dash & Marshall LLP day time Copy Center supervisor whose name was Carlton Circuit never physical harassment me or ever even sexual harass me just like the other two male coworkers of Neil Harry and Exodus Franklyn once did but I thought that at that particular time that he had very real bad timing to start back to questioning me about my very personal and private life because of the just recent talks that I just heard about what other New York City neighborhoods that one of the office building neighboring female mate very much so recently saw me with my son Romeo Windgate-Devine two family male members as I just been thinking that very same thought in my own state of mine at that time in my very own private thoughts.

And from there I told my them employer company daytime supervisor who was Carlton Circuit that my baby momma and our young son were doing just find as I said to him thank you for asking me. on November 21 of the year of 2000 as I received a telephone call from my son Romeo Windgate-Devine mother Elite Windgate with her to to asking of me to come by her family townhouse home in the Long Island City Queens New York area so that she and our baby boy and I may than spend some family quality time together and I felt so very glad to received her verbal invitation to having the very good chance to see my son little Romeo Jr. and his mother Elite Windgate as I told her that I would be right over to see them both just as soon as I could possibly could do so. And from there my child mother Elite Windgate told me that sounded like great news for my little family to her as she also put our son on the telephone so that I could tell him myself that his Daddy is on his way over to see him and his mommy as I just heard our child laugh and giggle through the telephone as I just figured out that he was just so very much happy to know that his father was on his way over to see him and his immediate family members. And once I arrived at my fiance/baby momma Elite Windgate family townhouse home as I rang her family door bell and when she and our son answered the door as I said my hellos to them both as I was at there door way as I was so very surprise to see our son Romeo Jr. start to learn how to walk while he was in his baby walker that I recently brought for him at a baby store that was called Baby 'R' US as I thought back about how cute and cuddly our son was as I just the father urged to pick him up and huge and kiss my son as I have also given him a high five hand slap as I said to him well alright there Junior that a good little man that your very proud Daddy has there. little Romeo Jr. mother Elite called me into her family kitchen area where her mother Ms. Wonda Windgate was helping her eldest daughter prepare a very tasty looking surf and turf meals that consisted of steak, Lobster and potatoes dinners for all of us to feast on. And once we began enjoying our very delicious meals my fiance/baby momma Elite Windgate oldest brother who was Mason Windgate come by his family townhouse home as he started to demand money from his mother Ms. Wonda Windgate because of his drug dependency problem that he for many years as he no source of income to support his substance abuse problem.

And from there my oldest common law brother in-law whose name is a Mason Windgate would began to start to verbal and physically harass his very own mother to the point that he would begin to push and shove at his very own mother in order to try and scare her enough to try to intimate her to give him some money for his very terrible drug habit as he also wanted even more money from her to give to him for some food and some alcoholic beverages do to he was no longer legally allowed to live in his very own family town house home where he once grown up as a kid as he had lived with his mother sister which is also his aunt Ivory Fox and his uncle by marriage Terry Fox. And whenever my fiance/baby momma Elite own mother Ms. Wonda Windgate would have no more money for her oldest son Mason Windgate he would began to push and shove around his very own mother to the point to where she would began to scream at him to back always from her. And from there my fiance/baby mother Elite Windgate to constantly step in between her older brother Mason Windgate and there mother to tell him that he better start to head out there door way before Elite was going to have to call in the police on him for treating there mother so very badly and from there he was push out of his family home by brunt force of his oldest younger sister and there mother. And from there I could not believed what was going on with my son Romeo Jr. and his mother Elite Windgate family members and her oldest brother Mason Windgate as I really had felt so very bad for my son to having to have a drug addict dependent uncle that he to witness him to have several violet outburst of anger as he constantly man handled his very own mother by grabbing her by the arm at least once ever 4 hours on a daily bases. So after witnessing the very constant outburst from my fiance/baby mother Elite Windgate older brother Mason Windgate older brother I made a very concern fatherly suggestion of that since her big brother seemed to be so very much aggressive toward his very own mother because of him trying to repeatedly strong armed her in order to try to come inside there very own family town house home to steel her money I made the suggestion of that I thought that it would be in the very best interested of our child to have him to start to come and lived with my sided of the family as I went on to say to her that It would be the very best thing for our son Romeo Jr. to grow up in a daily non hostile environment household rather than a very frighten one that was going on at her family household. And when my fiance/baby momma Elite heard what I suggested to her, she said no thank you and that she went on to say to me that she and our son would be just find with him to always to lived with his mother side of the family as she informed me that whenever her big brother would start his physical and aggressive grabbing on there mother that she would have him very firmly man handled by the New York City police department. So from there I went on to say to her that sounded like a good solution to than have her brother physically handled by her neighborhood of the long Island City of law enforcement to properly man handle him. And she went on to say to me about all of the stress that I been going on in my life with my coworkers at the mid town Manhattan corporate law firm that I confided in her that how that I a very emotional stressful job life style in constantly having to deal with those very crazy coworkers of than harassing me about how my employer believed that I could actually have a criminal connection of some kind to a New York City organize crime family even though that was not actually my real truth as it was just a very disturbing rumor.

And from there she went on to asked me just how I than planned to raise our child of all of the stress that I was than going through with my very stressful job harassment situation? And I just told Elite that she shouldn't worry herself of that matter because I told her that Iam a very strong mined typed person who could indeed handle both my very stressful place of employment at that O'Conner, Sapp, Dash & Marshall LLP corporate law firm as-well as the raising of our son as I also went on to say that at least that I would know that no physically and emotional harm or stress would come to our son just as long as he was away from her drug addict uncle Mason. And after hearing all of what I to say of that matter she still refused me to have my son Romeo Jr. come and live with me and my side of the family. So from there I became so very frosted of her not wanting me to keep our baby little Romeo Jr. safely out of harms way of her drug addicted brother Mason Windgate I immediate became so very much upset with my child mother Elite I just felt like just walking right out of her family town house home and began to go to my very own home family house in the Astoria New York.

But Elite said to me that I couldn't leave her and our baby just yet because her big brother Mason just might come back to get them all. So again I said to her that is why it would be in our son very best interest if he would come and stay with me and my family were he could also grow up with my two stepsisters Tameka and Fatima but she once again denied my request as I argued with her that I felt that she wasn't being fair to our child, but she just sat there as she ignored me in what I been saying to her.

On November 23, 2000, as my fiance/baby mother Elite Windgate told me that she wanted to get a breath of fresh air as she informed me that she and our son Romeo Windgate-Devine were going to be on there very way to their neighborhood corner store to make some purchases of a few grocery items for our family, and from there she was on her way out of her family door way. And shortly after she arrived at the corner store Elite called me from her mobile cellur phone to tell me to come meet her and our child at the store so that I may help them both with carrying most of the grocery's back to there family town house home and from there I said that I was on my way to pick them both up to bring them back to there home. And when I finally did arrived at my fiance/baby mother Elite Windgate neighborhood grocery store that was called the Long Island City grocery and delicatestant as I saw my little family as she been signing a neighborhood partisan to help them keep there town safe from criminals as I approached her I saw that the lady that was gathering up as many signatures as she possibly could and to my very own surprise it was that very same Spanish lady who was also my former employer at the corporate law firm that is called the O'Conner, Sapp, Dash & Marshall LLP in the mid Manhattan area in the Time Square Plaza section. And from there after Elite already sign her name and address to the neighborhood partisan coming from my female neighboring office building mate she began to asked my fiance/mother of my child if she known of this guy Romeo Devine ? And from there she very quickly answered yes this is my son father who is also my fiance.

And my son mother Elite asked that Spanish lady that was collecting the signatures well just how did she know of her fiance Romeo? And my former office female neighboring building mate told my son mother about how there was a rumor that was going on at my employer corporate law firm of a midtown that was called The O'Conner, Sapp, Dash & Marshall LLP with many of his other coworkers saying that I was a New York mafia criminal gangster family member that was sent into there company to try to extort money from the company. And from there I step in between my son mother Elite Windgate and that Spanish lady to tell my former neighboring building female mate that she better back up off of me and my family while I informed her that I was getting very tiresome of most of our office coworkers first bothering at work while I was doing my 5 day of the week job as of one of the company mailmen and I also went on to say and future more as far as my very personal life is concern it is none of her or anyone on that job got dam f**ckin business. And did I asked her did ya heard me?

And I taking the liberty to snatched my female office mate former coworker little neighborhood partisan right out of her hands as I told my fiance/baby mother Elite Windgate to stuff that neighborhood partisan right into her pocket book bag as she already paid for our family groceries. And from there my son Romeo Jr. mother Elite told my employer office neighboring female mate that she really a whole lot on crazy nerve to bother her fiance Romeo while he was there company mailman while I was just trying to do a very good job in order to service the people and my child mother continued to say that she and that company of hers better stay the hell away from our family if they all did not want to face any criminal charges of there very own and from there we left out of the Long Island City corner grocery and deli store and went back to Elite's family townhouse home. And once we gotten back inside after being totally stress out from my female building office mate Elite and I went on to tell just what happen with us both while we were just at the neighborhood grocery store and Elite's mother Ms. Wonda Windgate could not believe what we been telling her what just happen with us and my former female office building neighboring mate of that Spanish lady that worked on my former job as Elite and I told her mom that we curse the crazy Spanish lady out and as we been laughing at what just happen as we told her mom that we told that Spanish lady off as I rip a neighborhood partisan right out of her hands. And from there my fiance/baby mother Elite Windgate's very own mother Wonda Windgate began to laugh at what we both been telling her.

So after all of that incident of the invasion of my privacy happen in my son Romeo Jr. and his mother Elite Windgate neighborhood as I did not want to over stay my welcome at my fiance family town house home I told my common law family members along with my son that I was going to started to head back home to my mother and father house in the Astoria, Queens New York area as I given my son, his mother and his grandmother Ms. Wonda Windgate a big hug and a kiss good bye for now and from there I called my own parents to tell them that I was on my way back home to see them all. And once I arrived back on my family street of 212th Place in the Astoria, New York area where we than live at I ran into two of my childhood female friends whose name were Layla Gracey and Nichole Berman as we greeted each other with a big hug and a kiss on the facial cheeks. And as we all started to converse with each other just about we all been living on the same block of 212th Place as we learn about each other of how all three of us worked in the midtown Manhattan area all that time as were not even aware that fact as we caught up with each other. So from there my two lady friends Nichole Berman, Layla Gracey and I made plans for us all to go out for a friendly luncheon the following day. And shortly after that we wish each other to have a good night rest as we said that we would see each other in the noonday as we went our own separate homes.

And once I gotten inside my mother and father home as I said my hello's to every one of my immediate family members said there hello's and that they were so glad to see that I made it home from my fiance Elite and little baby Romeo Jr. town house home in the Long Island City New York area to spend some good quality time with my very own family instead of me to mostly wanting to be over there with my new common law family. And from there I asked my mother Jahtayshia if she was a little upset with me spending too much time with my fiance Elite's family members? And my mother claimed that she was not mad with me and that she and my father Damian Sr. thought that I should also spent some good quality family time with my two parents and my two little sisters Tameka and Fatima Devine. So after I heard my mother say that I since that she became rather a little jealous of me to finally to have a brand-new family of my very own but I totally understood just how they must felt as they must miss seeing me around our family home. So I said that I was going to slow it down a bit and spend some good times with immediate family members as I sat down with my two stepsisters Tameka and Fatima Devine as they given me a big fat juicy kiss on both sides of my cheek bones as I began to cry just a little bit of tears of sadness and joy with me not realizing that I was neglecting my very own family where I live with.

on November 24, 2000, as I been making multiple hand deliveries of the company incoming mails and telecopy faxes documents as I been assign to work inside the company forty-second-floor conveyor station I would overheard one of the telecopy/fax operator whose name was Denise Hailey say while I was sitting in department back room how I been once again tracked down by one of the company neighboring female mate as they reported back to the corporate law firm of the O'Conner, Sapp, Dash & Marshall LLP as the Spanish lady told the company that she gotten herself into a one sided argument with me and my son's mother right in front of his child and that he also went on to say that he heard that my very own fiance and Romeo as well told that Spanish lady to back the hell up off of her and her man Romeo. And shortly after hearing that I shouted out you dame right as I grab a bunch of the company mail and fax deliveries as I went out to do a distribution mail runs. afterwards I finished my hand deliveries I was on my way to my luncheon with my two lady friends Layla Gracey and Nichole Bermen. So once my two neighborhood lady friends Layla Gracey, Nichole Berman and I all called each other for a friendly lunch get together I known of a good restaurant that was called cold water seafood bar and grill and as the three of us decided that was a good enough place for us to dine out at we been on our way there. So as Layla, Nichole and I been enjoying our very delicious seafood meals that consisted of lobster tails, salads, baked potatoes and softdrink as we have been very much so also having good talks about the good old days to my very surprise in comes into the restaurant a small camera crew with the lights shining directly in our faces as the three of us been slightly blinded for a few seconds as it been pointed directly in our faces with the man who was holding it asked me and my two lady friends Layla, Nichole along with myself if we all were camera shy because we were about to become public figures? And from there I very quickly figured out what was going with that camera being pointed directly at me and my friends as I has strongly suspected that it was my very disturbing employer at the corporate law firm of O'Conner, Sapp, Dash & Marshall LLP trying to now catch me on video tape so that the entire New York City public would know exactly who I am and whoever I could be associated with and from there as my two friends and I just finished our good meals I told Layla and Nichole that I was in a very crazy corporate conspiracy situation that to do with my employers at a corporate law firm that is called O'Conner, Sapp, Dash & Marshall LLP and from there I said to them both let get up out of her and run off away from those video camera men that were than in our faces and we than ran our way out of the restaurant doors. And from there after all three of us ran away from that crazy camera crew I felt so very bad and embarrassed that I to apologize to my childhood friends for that very bad inconvenience as I to explained that how my employer started a very disturbing office rumor with them all saying that I could be a part of a New York City Mafia crime family as I also told my dear sweet lady friends that my job even tracked me down to our family neighborhood in the Astoria, Queens New York area as well as my son Romeo Jr. and his own mother neighborhood in the Long Island City area in order to try to have me convicted of me possibly wanting to steal my corporate employer law firm money. And when my two long time neighborhood friend Layla Gracey and Nichole Bermen heard about my crazy situation they said that I should try to leave that job and find a much more better one because they know that lam a very good kind hearted type of a man and that the people who then started all of my problems that I was having on the job should have not ever happen in the first place and I told my two lady friend that I totally agreed with them both but I also went on to say that I had to get myself back to my workplace before the job tries to fire me. And from there my two lady friend Layla and Nichole given me a quick kiss on the cheeks as I did the very same thing and from there we said that we would see each other back on our block on 212th place.

On the very next day of November 25, 2000, it been time for our two families to have a Thanks Giving day family feast with a big fat juicy 20 lbs. turkey to eat off of along with all of the delicious trimmings to go right along with our family meals. So I decided that I was going to invite my son Romeo Windgate-Devine along with his mother Elite Windgate to enjoy our family traditional holiday with my side of the family. And once I giving them the call my son mother told me that yes she would be very much delighted to joined me and my family members. So from there I told my new now common law wife Elite Windgate that I would be so very happy to see her and our baby boy Romeo Jr. once they both arrived at my family home in the Queens New York area, as she also said that she and our child would be there just as soon as she packed the clothes up and put them in a suit case because she also added that she was getting rather stressed out from her drug addicted oldest brother Mason Windgate with him always bother her to try to demand money from her as she also added that she gotten so very tire of her mother letting him into their own family town house home in the Long Island City Queens New York area. So from there I said that I would be very glad to see her and our baby boy when they get at my very own family home where I said it was at least very peaceful and pleasant around the holiday seasons.

And once my son Romeo Jr. and his mother Elite finally arrived as they both entire my family home I showered them both with multiple hugs and kisses as my mother Jahtayshia, two stepsister Tameka and Fatima did the very same exact thing as I did as my dad Damian Sr. just said his hellos as he waved his hand to the mother of his second grandson. And soon afterwards my common law wife Elite offered to help my mom with them preparing the food for that evening, as the extra help was gladly accepted as I said that I felt so very special to see my favorite two ladies working so well and hard together in order to give our family such a terrific dinner, so from there they laugh at what I just said as they also went on to say that sounded like some great appreciation for me to give them both as said that was a very kind complement as they made the serious joke of that sounded all good because I was going to be the one held responsible for washing all of our family dishes and cleaning up our family household entire kitchen area, and from there I said that I didn't mind at all not even a little bit. So my big brother Damian Jr. and his fiance whose name is Tara Dunkins also had arrived at our family home as they decided to join all of our family festivities. And my big brother and his fiance Tara made a big announcement that they wanted to get married by December 25, 2000, Christmas Day which was the birth of Jesus Christ our Lord and savior and our family said that was such wonderful news of joy for us all to hear.

So after our family thanks giving dinner been over Tameka and Fatima jumped right into our big brother Damian Jr. lap as they asked him if they could be Damian Jr. and his fiance Tara Dunkins flower girls for their wedding? And our big brother Damian Jr. and his soon to be wife Tara Dunkins said yes that they would love to have them both in the family wedding and the girls said that was great for them both to say that as our two stepsisters Tameka and Fatima had asked our mother Jahtayshia if she could buy them both the prettiest dresses for them both to attend our brother wedding? And both of our mother and father told them both yes and that they defiantly will do so. And shortly after that my big Damian Jr. his fiance Tara Dunkins, my common law wife Elite Windgate along with myself, my son Romeo Jr. and his two aunts Tameka and Fatima decided to take some photographs of each other as we struck many different picture possess as we all many good laughs on that very special holiday season as we were all also began thinking about how we were going to prepare for the wedding day as my big brother Damian Jr. and I hand also decided to do a little bumping and grinding dancing the night away with our two very special ladies Elite and Tara.

So the very next day on November 26, 2000, our grandmother Mrs. Alicia Gilbert called our family home in the Astoria, Queens New York area just to her about how we were all doing as the call been placed on speaker phone. And from there our oldest brother Damian Devine Jr. hand informed our grandmother whose name is Alicia Gilbert that he and his fiance were going to be soon getting married to each other on Christmas day the year of 2000. And from there our grandmother congratulated him and his soon to be wife Tara Dunkins on there soon to be wedding. shortly after that our grandmother Alicia said that she miss our family all so very much and that she wanted for us to stop by and pay her and our two uncles Solomon and Ronald Gilbert a long overdue family visit. So from there we agreed to do so as we told her that we would be right over very shortly after we were to get my son little Romeo Jr. ready for a nice little drive to the Propect Park Brooklyn area to come see my mother Jahtayshia side of our family.

So from there my brother Damian Jr., his fiance Tara Dunkin, my common law wife Elite Windgate, little baby Romeo Jr. and I gotten into a taxi cab car service and began to be on our way to visit my grandma Alicia Gilbert apartment. And once we arrived there safely as we gotten ourselves out of the car service vehicle we all heard people cheering, whistling and clapping of the hands and at that time we could not figure out why as we were all just headed inside to visit our other family members. And once we all gotten inside my grand ma Alicia apartment she immediately extended her arms out to reach for her second great-grand-son from her oldest daughter Jahtayshia little baby Romeo Jr. as he received plenty of sweet and wet kisses from her. And from there the new ladies that were just a part of my big brother Damian Jr. and my life sat down to get to know my grandma Alicia a whole lot better as they just their girl talk of soughts.

And shortly after we all enjoyed a very wonderful family dinner together my two uncle Ronald, Solomon, Damian Jr. along with myself decided to take a walk to the neighborhood store that was called Mandy's groceries. And I began to think back at my employer corporate conspiracy situation that was going on from the Queens and Manhattan area about how my employer vow to make me a allege public New York mafia criminal figure by according to what I heard as I was still employed at the midtown corporate law firm of O'Conner, Sapp, Dash & Marshall LLP that they wanted all New Yorkers to know just who I was just in case I was to try some criminal act of some kind so that would be reported to the police by a honest citizen. So as I explained my entire former employer situation to my older brother Damian Jr. and our two uncle two Ronald and his younger brother Solomon once again of one day when I been enjoying some lunch with our good friend Tyrone Gracey younger sister Layla Gracey and our friend Nichole Bermen a some camera crew came into the seafood restaurant were all three of us dine at as those men put me and my lady friends on a Television camera set as they said directly to me that I should smile for them all as the also referred to me as a allege New York mafia mailman of some kind and I also have told my grandma and her two sons Ronald and Solomon that me and my lady friends to run the hell up out of there in a very quick and fast hurray in order to try to avoid me to be seen and placed on the local T. V. news. And from there I told my two uncle and big brother that I thought that I was being acknowledge now by the Brooklyn New York people because all of that sudden noise that I took notice of just before we than entire my grand ma Alicia apartment building as I said that I was getting very worrisome because of the prospect park Brooklyn New York area was a high crime neighborhood.

So from there my male family members said to me not to worry so much about all of my jobs problems while I was with my very own family because they said as we were to go out the door that they were all going to be caring there license firearms to protect us all so that we would make it back home to our family safe and sound but they only offered me a stun gun for some added protection because I was not legally register to carry a hand gun. So once we gotten outside I heard people shouting out with me to hear them say hey there goes that guy Romeo Devine from the news that was broadcasted on the television. And from there I was in totally shock that I made it on the news all because of that slanderous former employer at the midtown Manhattan law firm of O'Conner, Sapp, Dash & Marshall LLP spreading lies about me to possible to have some kind of a criminal New York mafia connection but after that we just kept ourselves moving right along to the corner store and back to our family home as the people just kept on cheering and whistling with them saying as they were joking around with them laughing and saying that they wanted the mail right on time as I just gave the small Brooklyn crowd a quick and friendly wave and a friendly two figure peace hand sign. And Once my male family members and I arrived back inside my grand ma Alicia apartment I to explained what just happen and from there my common law wife Elite Windgate said that was a very similar situation that happen in her neighborhood in the Long Island City section of the Queens, New York area with Romeo Sr. office female coworker who was a middle aged Spanish lady hand recognized her son father with her saying that his employer was having him watched very closely as a allege criminal.

And from there my Common law wife Elite told my Prospect Park Brooklyn New York family that she curse that dam crazy b**tch a**s Spanish lady out and told her to stay away from our family and after all of that was explained to my people we all just sat around just having ourselves a big bunch of laughs and my grand ma said to Elite you go girl and that was good looking out for her and her baby grandson and her baby daddy Romeo Sr. And so a few hour later it was tine to head back home to my mother Jahtayshia and father Damian Sr. home so we kiss my grand ma Alicia Gilbert good bye for now as she thank us all for coming by to his her and from there my brother and his fiance along with my very own little family call a taxi cab to bring us back to the Astoria, Queens New York Area.

And so while my brother older Damian Devine Jr. and his soon to be wife whose name was Tara Dunkins began to start to make their preparations for their very first wedding right along with our mother Jahtayshia Devine it was time for me to take myself back to my place of employment at the midtown Manhattan corporate law firm of O'Conner, Sapp, Dash & Marshall LLP in the midtown Manhattan Time Square section area. And when I arrived back at the corporate law firm of making multiple hand deliveries of bulks of telecopy/fax documents and incoming and outgoing letters and packages of mail as I had been also assign to partly also work into the company forty-second-floor conveyor station area. And on December 1, 2000, as I been rather tired and sweaty from working so very hard came into the conveyor station a woman whose name was Connie Conner and when she saw me working so very hard she began to also flirt with me to the point that she would take a clean tissue right out of her very own bra bosoms and would began to hand pat and wipe down my forehead that was full of perspiration until I was dried up. And she would go on to say to me how I really did look so much more better to her as she would also proceed to massage my neck and back as she told me to just try to relax myself some.

And because of that woman Connie Conner who was one of the company associate secretary appeared to look always so very beautiful looking to me I once again found myself to becoming so very much more attracted to yet another company coworker associate secretary. So after a few days pass even though on December 7, 2000, I was already still in a very serious intimate committed relationship with my fiance Elite Windgate who is also my son Romeo Jr. mother as I could not stop thinking about how very fine looking that I thought that my employer associate secretary was. So when I went home for that very same evening I called my common law wife Elite Windgate and our son Romeo Jr. to hear about how they were doing as my son mom said to me that she a very stressful day with our son Romeo Jr. because he was in a very playful and loud mood and as she continued to tell me that he did not even take his usual daily midday rest for that day. And Elite asked me well just how my very own day went F?. As I just told her that it was slightly a little bit better that day and she said that she was glad that I was not as stress out as she was. But I of course refrained from telling her my real truth for that day and what actually did happen because I did not want her to become very jealous of another woman giving me a back and neck rub down massage.

So after a few days passed on December 14, 2000, as I been still making multiple hand deliveries of the midtown company of the O'Conner, Sapp, Dash & Marshall LLP corporate law firm as I to make a mail run stop at that very same company coworker secretary Connie Corner desk as she asked me well there handsome just how is my very favorite New York mailman doing with his self today? As she taking the liberty to grabbed a hold of my two hands as she also stood up to pinch me on my right buttock cheek area. And I said to her that I was doing quite fine with myself and from there I asked her if she would want to go out with me sometime in the very near future? And from there the company associate secretary said that she did not know if that was a very good ideal for us to become that personal with each other because she was already in a very serious and committed relationship with another handsome man just like myself as she just told me that she just been flirting with me simply because that is what she loves to do to most men to tease them as she just blew me a kiss and a very light slap on both sides of my facial cheeks bones structures.

So from there I found myself to once again to be very foolishly infatuated with yet another former female coworker. But when I arrived back at my family basement home I had find myself to still be very much smitten with the company of the O'Conner, Sapp, Dash & Marshall LLP associate secretary Connie Conner as I began to listen to her out going voice mail messages from our employer company telephone at night time after I gotten myself home as I also left her some voice mail messages for her to please reconsider and go out with me. So on December 15, 2000, the company associate company Connie Corner waved her hands to me to asked me to come right over to see her for a minute to tell me that she was so very sorry but that she could never have nothing but a very professional relationship with me because again as she told me once again that she was still very much so involved with a good man as she told me that I better stop leaving her any more voice mail messages in order to avoid any conflict that might become between she and I and after that she demanded me to go away from her and that I should start back to focusing on doing the best mail man clerk job that I could possibly do and from there I walked off always from her feeling very much broken hearted by yet another former female coworker that once again turn out to be yet another female coworker in fact that was also trying to emotionally hurt my feelings because of the ridiculous rumor that began with the midtown Time Square Plaza law firm telling many New Yorkers that I could very well much be a New York mafia gangster of some kind and so after all of that I realized that it would always be in my very best interest that I never should think about having a romantic and intimate office romance with any of my female coworkers.

on December 24, 2000, on Christmas Eve that year my older brother Damian Devine Jr. and his thin fiance whose name is Tara Dunkin right along with our mother Jahtayshia Devine were still very much so preparing for the big family wedding day as I expected for my big brother to asked me if I would do him the good family honor to be his best man at his and his wife Tara Dunkin wedding but he never taken the liberty to do so. So instead of him asking me to stand by his side to watched him wed his soon to be wife to be his best man he made the decision to asked his best friend whose name is Tyrone Gracey who was a good old neighborhood friend to my family. So my soon to be sister in-law Tara Dunkin very own family members of her mother whose name is Felicia and her younger sister whose name is Maxie Dunkin came over to also join in the family wedding celebration. And my soon to be sister in-law ladies in her family pitched in to help with all of the cooking and cleaning of my family household as the extra help was greatly appreciated.

So from there my big brother Damian Devine Jr. best friend Tyrone Gracey also planned a big bachelor party for the groom to be as I along with my oldest sibling son whose name is Rashad Devine gotten rather excited of what was about to soon go down. And from there our neighborhood friend Tyrone Gracey pulled me to the side as he told me that we to think about getting my big brother Damian Jr. some dancing ladies strippers for his very last big night of him to still to be a single man. And our friend Tyrone Gracey along with myself decided to get some of our neighborhood sexiest ladies that we know right up the street from our neighborhood of the Astoria, Queens New York 212th Place area that lived right up the street from us. And so once Tyrone and I gotten in contact with all three of our ladies friends whose names was Vivian Green, Delotta Blackwell and Lowla Spears they very happy agreed to do a strip tease show for my big brother Damian Devine Jr.

So from there all three of our neighborhood lady's friend of Vivian, Delotta and Lowla sat my older brother Damian Jr. down in a armless chair that was in our friend Tyrone Gracey family basement apartment as our very womanly friends began to put on a very sexy show by beginning to striptease down to their birthday suits as they also gave him a very sexy and exciting lap dance along with them to also spray whip cream all over him and some of us guys as well. But came a very hard knock at our friend Tyrone family sidedoor entrance as it been his very own soon-to-be wife Tara Dunkin and her younger sister Maxie Dunkin showed up, also been single and much ready to mingle in with my big brother Damian Jr. fun parting time moment. And from there my soon to be sister in-law Tara and her younger adult sister Maxie pushed away our ladies friends that we all had arranged to enter name as my big brother future wife sat into his lap as she also brought out a can of whip cream and a bottle of Romeo champagne to begin to shower us all with it as we all cheered them both on as we given them both our sincere congratulations as I myself giving them a big shout out as it was the sound of me to say "Wooooooo! I here present a toast to you my big brother Davin Jr. and your soon to be wifey Tara!" and shortly after that the bachelor party ended and we all went back to our own family homes.

The on December 25, 2000, which was Christmas Day as it been my older brother Damian Devine Jr. wedding day for him and his soon to be wife whose name is Tara Dunkin as our whole immediate family members been so very much so very happy for them both as we along with my son mother/common law wife whose name is Elite Windgate taking the very sweet and thoughtful liberty to helped us all prepare the soon to be married couple to join together as husband and wife as they read several Holy Scriptures just before the actual wedding was to be taking place as my young son whose name is Romeo Windgate-Devine also came right along with his mother to witness his oldest uncle Damian Jr. and his very soon to be aunt Tara Dunkin blesset event of them both to be getting married to one another. And it been time for the actually wedding to be taking place inside our family home in the Astoria, Queens New York area. And as my big brother Damian Jr. and his soon to be wife Tara Dunkin gotten themselves all dress up with the groom wore himself a very handsome black tuxedo suit as his fiance wore a very fabulous pinkgust wedding gown of her very own as they looked so very fine together as it been time for them both to say there wedding vows to one another. And shortly after that there Holy minister than arrived at our family home as he announced himself as The Reveren Raymond Dougley as he gotten them both together to resight there wedding vows to one another as he asked just who was standing in as there best man for the wedding ceremony?

And from there our good neighborhood friend whose name is Tyrone Gracey said that it was him standing in as the grooms best man and very shortly after that the entire wedding ceremony taken placed. And as my big brother Damian Jr. Devine Jr. and his lovely soon to be his wife Tara Dunkin were than asked by the Reverend Raymond Dougley to began to start to say there Holy wedding vows to one another as they did just that and from there my older brother young son whose name is Rashad Devine been his Daddy's ring bearer while standing right along beside his him as the Holy minster asked for the two wedding rings to be be present before him as the best man Tyrone Gracey taken the two wedding bands from his best friend son little Rashad Devine right off of a red velvet soft pillow as he given them both to my brother and his soon to be wife as her very own mother whose name is Felicia Dunkin who also been her oldest daughter Maid Of Honor and her younger adult sister whose name is Maxcine Dunkin also been made her big sister Bride Maide as she also been there at the wedding ceremony as well. from there as the lovely bride and groom been resighting there very holy spiritual wedding vows to each other as they both been instructed to do so as the marriable question been asked from the Reverend Raymond Dougley do they both take each other as lawful husband and wife and from there my older brother Damian Devine Jr. and his very soon to be wife answered yes and that they most certainly do, than from there they both been announced to us all as husband and wife as the groom been instructed by the Holy Reverend that the groom may kiss his very fabulous looking bride as he announced them both as husband and wife the now Mr. and Mrs. Damian Jr. and Tara Devine. So shortly after that it was time for the two cute little flower girls who of course happen to be our two little stepsisters Tameka and Fatima Devine hand laced the floor with pink and white flowers as my family cheer them both on.

my family and I t began to start our family wedding celebration time by first feasting off of another delicious family dinner of a hot and spicy chicken and boneless spare ribs meal along with us all to have some wild rice and some sweet potatoes yams as we all agreed that all of the soul food tasted all so very delicious that we all asked for a second helping as my mother Jahtayshia and father Damian Devine Sr. said yes to our family request. shortly after that my big brother Damian Jr. and brand-new wife Mrs. Tara Devine began to cut multiple slices of there cherry vanilla wedding cake and ice cream as they both kissed each other as they did the very family wedding traditional thing of mashing each other in the face with two peaces of there very own slices of wedding cake from there my big brother went into our parents refrigerator to go and bring out the chilled bottle of Marlow champain and some wine glass as he popped the bottle cork as I myself giving the shout out of the verbal sound to say woooo and that it was all going to be such a good night tonight, as we began to make multiple toasts to the new bride and groom as we began to laughed and cheer for the both of them just as well as ourselves as we also began to turn up our music as we dance the night away as my family all joined in to gather ourselves into a family traditional line up of a Soul Train line up dance. after a few hours past by as it gotten rather late that same wonderful Christmas evening my big brother and his newlywed lovely wife who new marriage name is now Mrs. Tara Devine thanked there minister Reverend Raymond Dougley for performing such a wonderful and holy wedding service as he blessed them both with some spiritual holy oil as he place some on there foreheads as he wished them both nothing but the absolute best intentions that our heavenly father would have for them both. And from there he given them both multiple huge hugs as he shaken my big brother Damian Jr. two hands as he also given the bride and groom the new Mr. and Mrs. Damian Jr. and Tara Devine a good short spiritual marriage counseling of just how a good spiritual marriage should be between the two of them both according to the biblical words of the bible and soon after that the minister left our family home so that we may all continued our family after wedding celebration. shortly after that as it was beginning to get rather late as my older brother Damian Devine Jr. and his brand-new wife made the announcement that they were on there way out to start on there Honeymoon weekend and from there as they both were leaving out of our family home we all line up to throw the wedding traditional white rice directly at them both as we cheered them both on as they driven themselves away in a car rental.

shortly afterwards my son mother/common law wife Elite Windgate asked me the question of well now that my brother Damian Jr. and his brand-new wife the new Tara Devine wedding gone so very smoothly as she went on to asked me well how's about she and I to to start to make our very own planes for our very own family wedding as-well so that we may finally become husband and wife together for the goodness sake of our little baby boy Romeo Windgate-Devine ? And from there I told my common law wife Elite Windgate that I felt that it was way to soon for us to be thinking about for the two of us to be thinking about us to be getting married to each other as I explained that we should start off by us as a family to live together at first before we were to finally think about becoming husband and wife to each other. And from there she said that it would be so very fine for us to start looking for our very own apartment place for she and I along with our little baby boy Romeo Windgate-Devine to finally start to live together as she also went on to say that she wanted for us to have a three bedroom apartment rental because she explained that she also wanted us all to have our very own separate rooms. And so from there I asked her just why should we start off living that way in separate bedrooms instead of us to sleep together in the very same bed just like any other engaged to be married couple?

And from there my common law wife Elite Windgate explained that was the only way possible that she would accept our family to all lived together while we all were to be underneath one roof. And from there she went on to also explained that that she a good lady friend whose name was Bobbi Booney and that she herself been looking for a apartment as Elite went on to say that she also had wanted her womanly bi sexual friend to move in with us all. And after hearing that I asked my common law wife Elite Windgate if I was to agree with her lady bi-sexual friend to come in and lived with us all to help us to share all of our three bedroom apartment living expensive as I asked her the question of could the three of us sleep in the same bedroom so that we may also have a passionate sexual threesome relationship on a every nightly bases? And from there my common law wife Elite denied me of my request as she went on to say that she only wanted herself to have a intimate relationship with here woman friend alone as she told me that when it was our time to be intimate with one another that it would be just between the two of us and not her lady friend Bobbie Booney.

As she also went on to say that she really wanted to move out of her mother's Long Island City town house home so that she may also get away from her very violet drug addicted older brother Mason Windgate always having come by her family home were they all grew up at as he always demanded mother from them all until they were to give it to him. And she told me that she did not really trust to many men at all because she always feared that they might become very violet toward her and even our child as she even went on to say that she did not even really trust in me all that very well just because I was a man. And from there I tried my very best effort to try to convince her that she could trust in me but she said hmmmm and that she just wasn't yet to sure about me back and from there I realized that her emotional problems that she gotten from growing up into a violet household might be to much for me to try to deal with as I mad the decision as I told her that I reconsidered us to move in together as a family as I told her that I really did strongly think that she should really seek some therapy for her all of her emotional issues that she.

when the New Years Eve of December 31, 2000, finally arrived that year as my immediately and new family of both of my mother Jahtayshia and my father Damian Devine Sr., along with my two younger stepsisters Tameka and Fatima, and my brother Damian Devine Jr. and his wife Tara Devine and even my very own new family of my son Romeo Windgate-Devine and his mother/my common law wife Elite Windgate all brought in the New Years together as just as good as one's family possibly could. So from there when the clock trucked 12:00 AM we all celebrated by bringing in the New Years of 2001 by just setting together as we all said a very spiritual prayer that is in the Holy Bible of Mathew 6:9-12 the the Our Father Prayer. And as I remembered that was the very first New Years with my common law wife Elite Windgate and my son Romeo Windgate Devine as I remembered that we were so very much happy that we all taken a big family portrait together by a digital camera that and thirty-second timer on it. And from there we decided to video tape all of the kids as well as the adults just sat around laughing and giggling as the grown ups been just sitting around one another while we were all just sipping on some 12 oz. alcoholic beverage wines coolers as we all been making funny jokes of each other as we also laugh the night away.

And my son little baby Romeo Windgate-Devine came around on February 14, 2001, with his mother Elite Windgate as we thrown our child his very first birthday party at my family Astoria New York house as we also invited a few friends that consisted of our neighbors whose names were Willimeana and Alfonso Ramous and there 3 year old son Jerry Ramous right along with our other very friendly neighborhood family friends whose name were Louie Nicholes and his wife Aretha Nicholes and their daughter Marcia Duran who birthday also been on that very same day. And from there came the kids very big surprise of a knock that came to our door as all of the adults asked the question to our kids that we wonder just who could that be at the door way? So from there everyone told me that I should be the very one who should answered the door and when I finally did it been a totally surprise to all of our kids to see me to open up the door as I said to every wait just a minute as it been a made of custom character of Sponge Bob The Square in his full uniform suit. And once the kids saw him they all began to become so very happy to see him in person as he talked with the children that was at children birthday party as he entertain them all by making many jokes and hand tricks as we all cheered Sponge Bob Square paint on. And shortly after that the kids received some birthday cake and 3 flavored ice cream of Chocolate, Strawberry and Vanilla as all of our little kids enjoyed their birthday cake and ice cream so very much that there barely left any for the adult but we parents just humorously laugh it off.

And from there the rented character of The Sponge Bob Square Pants wished all of the kids to have a very happy birthday as they very cutely shouted out to him thank you Sponge Bob the Square Pants as it was time for him to leave the party as he made his exit out of the door. And from there our kids just played games of some of my son new toys presents that he received at the time of the party from his guest and shortly that our kids been so very worn out from being so very happy from there big exciting birthday party time that they all fell themselves right to sleep. And from there all of our guest decided that it was as good as any time for them all to take their kids home to lay them all down for some good sleep time and my family said our goodbyes for now to our neighboring friends as they all made there exits to their very own home.

On March 8, 2001, as I been on my very own way to see my son Romeo Jr. and his mother Elite Windgate in the Long Island City section area of the Queens New York as I bumped into one of my former coworker whose name was Denise Hailey who worked inside the company of my former employer at the corporate law firm of The O'Conner, Sapp, Dash & Marshall LLP as he been with his young son who he told me that his little boy name was Maleak Hailey as he explained that they were on their way home from them doing some shopping for his young child. And from there my former coworker Denise Hailey asked me just were I was on my way to? And from there I very quickly thought to myself that I better keep this very noisy coworker of mine out of my personal life as I lied to him as I told him that I was on my very own way to see a good friend of mine. And from there Denise laughed as he said to me that he thought that I was on my way to see my lady friend as in my son mother as I said no I was not headed there.

And from there even though he guest my truth were I was really headed to with all of the company corporate conspiracy situation at the former corporate law firm of the O'Conner, Sapp, Dash & Marshall LLP I thought that it would be in my and even my son Romeo Jr. along with his mother Elite best interest to try to keep any and all my employer coworkers strictly out of my very private and personal life as much as I possibly could as I constantly felt like I always been spied on quit to often from my former employer as I felt that it was an invasion of my very own privacy like some kind of actual criminal. So I told my coworker Denise Hailey that I to go and be on my very way over to see about my very good friend and that I would see him inside the corporate law of the O'Conner, Sapp, Dash & Marshall LLP law firm as soon as the next Monday morning arrived and from there he himself told to me okay Romeo and that he would see me. And once I saw my former coworker Denise Hailey as he told the company Telecopy/Fax operator Departmental coworkers that hey he saw this guy Romeo in the Kew Garden section in the Queens New York area. As he asked me right Romeo and from there I only been joking around with the company Telecopy/Fax operator guys as I said oh no that wasn't truth and that Denise really didn't see me at all as I went on to future joke with guys as I also said that maybe he just thought that he saw see me.

And from there as I just been only joking around with him and the other departmental Telecopy/Fax operator guys, Denise Hailey really taking my joke way to much seriously as he asked me if I was calling him a liar and once I saw that he develop a very serious attitude about the whole thing as I became rather serious with the other guys as I admitted to them all that yes he did so in fact see me in the Kew Garden Queens New York area. And from there he told me if I was to ever to ever try to make him seem like a very foolish liar ever again that he said that he would start to put a very serious and painful hurting on my a**s. And from there another of the employer company of the Telecopy/Fax operator guy whose name was Peter Wilkerson told his good friend Denise Hailey to back up off of that man Romeo Devine got dam it before things between the very two of us would really start to get out of hand to the point that the Time Square Plaza New York City police department to be called into our employer office of The O'Conner, Sapp, Dash & Marshall LLP to make an arrest of only him to be the aggressive one. And from there Denise Hailey been remind that what happen right between myself and that other departmental coworker of his who was Leon Abrames as he said that he almost to learn the hard way himself not to have too much conflict in the company office as he previously had his very own issues with me.

And from there my telecopy/fax operator coworker Denise Hailey agreed with what was being said to him to calm himself down as he told the fellows that he was going to take a quick cigarette break to try to calm down his nerves. And from there he left out of the forty-second floor for a little quick personal break time. And from there the company of my employer of The O'Conner, Sapp, Dash & Marshall LLP corporate law firm telecopy/fax whose name was Peter Wilkerson told me to stare clear of that guy Denise Hailey before some drama was to be happen on our place of employment as I said okay as I also went on to say that the department has my very own word of honor that I would keep my very own attitude right on strictly professional level bases without me to have any type of a bad attitude between us all and that is the way that I said that I would always prefer it to be for us all. And very soon after the day been over with I left the office for the day as I went right back to my family home in the Astoria, Queens New York area. And once I arrived back there as my mother and father Jahtayshia and Damian Devine Sr. asked me just how my day went at the office? And I just told the both of them that things were still very much stressful at my workplace of the Time Square Plaza corporate law firm of the company that is called the O'Conner, Sapp, Dash & Marshall LLP and very soon after that I just said that I was so much very exhausted as I said that I was just going to my family household basement apartment to get myself so that I may rest myself as I told my parents that I would see them both in the morning time. And once I gotten some alone time with myself I thought about just how things were getting to be a little too much rough around my place of my employment of the corporate law firm of The O'Conner, Sapp, Dash & Marshall LLP as I decide to make a purchase of an electric Taser stun gun that I saw online as I decide that I better start to protect myself for those male coworkers of mines as I had it shipped to me in an overnight United States Post Office delivery. On March 10, 2001, as I felt a little more secure about my very own self as I went right straight on into my employer place of business right along with my brand new Taser stun gun. And when I arrived back at my place of my employment at the corporate law firm that was called The O'Conner, Sapp, Dash & Marshall LLP as I once again saw that very same coworker man whose name is Denise Hailey who been one of the company Telecopy/Fax Department day time operators as he still himself a very bad attitude with me as he proceed to approached me one again as he very firmly bumped his right shoulder right into mine as he said to me that I better watch myself whenever I was to walk myself near him.

And from there I told the Telecopy/fax Denise Hailey that I wasn't going to be putting up with his bullying attitude any f**ckin longer. And from there Denise pulled out his sharp razor blade out on me as he grabbed me by my shirt collar as he put his blade right up to my face as he told me that he was going to cut and slice me up something bad. And little did he did not know I brought in my electric Taser gun as I reached in my paint pocket to define myself as I stun him twice on his very same hand that he his razor blade in as he dropped his weapon of choice. And from that it been a whole lot of other employees who eye witness the whole dam thing as the company security team once again to be called in for my second very physical altercation that I had with another employee as they no other choice but to call in the NYC police department to finally take the know former Telecopy/Fax operator away to the downtown jail house. And from there I been sent to my mailroom manager whose name was Henry Hernandez on 2nd floor mail room office to once again asked him to please resign me to another mail clerk workstation?

And from he told me that he thought that it would best for the mailroom management best interest to start to keep a very close and watchful eye on me to keep me out of trouble. from there the police department arrived back to my workplace to take me downtown to find out if in fact that I wanted to filed official menacing charges against the former coworker Denise Hailey and I told them yes and indeed as I told the police officer that I than gotten rather tire of that man trying to bully me while I was just trying to do my actual job as one of the corporate law of The O'Conner, Sapp, Dash & Marshall LLP as one of the mail men. And soon after I filed an official complaint charges against my coworker Denise Haily as the police department giving me a written order of protection that was against him to official have legal documentation for Denise Hailey to stay a good distance away from me as I went back to my place of my employment as I went right back to work just trying to make my hand deliveries of the company mail.

So after yet another very physical altercation with yet another coworker whose name was Denise Hailey who back used to work at the O'Conner, Sapp, Dash & Marshall LLP corporate law firm in the midtown Manhattan Time Square Plaza section area as I once again gotten rather fed up with all of the harassment that was still going on at the time as I on March 9, 2001, decided that I better continue to try to build a corporate conspiracy case against all of the parties that were very much involved back. So once I went back home to started to do some brain storming of my very own about just how I was going to at least going to find a way to at least prove in a court of law of me to been agreeably physical and sexual harass by several of my former coworkers. And from there I finally came up with the good enough ideal to hire a private investigator to try to help me to prove a very good court case in the eyes of the law. I taking the liberty of searching through the yellow pages to see if I could find a good enough private investigator who would try to help me to prove my court case of a corporate conspiracy that involved my former employer at The corporate law firm of The O'Conner, Sapp, Dash & Marshall LLP. And when I finally came across of one as when I contacted the man he told me that his name was Wayne Western as I given him a telephone call on his mobile cellular phone service as I spoken with him about how I wanted him to help me to prove a conspiracy conspiracy that involved my former employer at the O'Conner, Sapp, Dash & Marshall LLP corporate law firm.

And from there I told my former private investigator Wayne Western who was also a former New York City police officer that I wanted him to first follow my office building neighbor female mate whose name she told me was Theresa Lasey as I also continued to explained to him just how there was a corporate conspiracy that was still going on at my former employer corporate law firm of The O'Conner, Sapp, Dash & Marshall LLP about how there was a guy who I at one time worked inside the company law firm mailroom center 2nd floor department whose name was Stone Casey and how he was the very one to started a very ridiculous office rumor of just because I taking out our mailroom manager Henry Hernandez secretary whose name was Gloria Knight as I also taking the very sweet liberty to purchase her a big bouquet of red roses as I tried to convince her to start a romantic relationship with me as I started to give him a very hard cold hearted stair of my eyes as I overheard him say to the other mailroom staff members that everyone should take real good and close notice of that guy Romeo Devine as he went on to continue to say that everyone should take notice of my very cold hearted looking stare as he told everyone in the 2nd floor mail center that I looked so very much so made that I looked like I could be a part of a New York City mafia family that might been sent into the company to steal money from the company just like a professional theft would. And from there I told my former private investigator how there was one summer night were I was hanging out with my youngest adult uncle whose name is Salomon Gilbert at the neighborhood of the Astoria, Queens New York corner grocery/delicatessen store who owner was name Troy Munoz as he been such a decent friend to my family members up until one day as several of his customers also been watching a paid preview Heavyweight Championship boxing fight as I sat myself down on a plastic milk crate when incomes a gray headed middle age afro American woman as she herself also gotten herself her very own milk crate for her to sit on and from there as many of the people in the nearby by area been enjoying themselves while watching the heavyweight boxing match as that very same lady begin questioning me about where did I worked? As I gotten rather worrisome of why this lady was asking me just where did I worked at as I had felt that she already realized my employer location as she said that she recognized me from the Midtown Manhattan office in the Time Square Plaza area. And from there I told my private investigator Wayne Western that I knew that the corporate conspiracy that first started at my corporate law firm of O'Conner, Sapp, Dash & Marshall LLP would up in the street of New York City. And from there I also explained to my former private investigator that my employer at the midtown Manhattan corporate law firm even began to spied on my son Romeo Windgate-Devine and his mother whose name is Elite Windgate with a Spanish lady that also worked my job as I figured that she must of been told about my very humorous situation about how my employer wanted to know if I was an associate with a New York City organized crime family.

So from there I explained that I was trying to build myself a court case of either to try to prove of a corporate conspiracy that first started only in my former employer at the corporate midtown law firm of The O'Conner, Sapp, Dash & Marshall LLP of me to be sexually and physically harassed or to having the good possibly to prove that the company spread a very false and slanderous corporate rumors and lies of me to be a part of a New York mafia gangster family that was supposedly sent to my place of employment to try to extort money for employer. And from there I told my Private Investigator who was also a former New York City police officer Wayne Western that I wanted for him to start a private investigation to see just where my two female office building neighboring mate lived at in the Astoria, Queens New York area where I live at where I met the middle aged Afro-American lady who told me that her name was Theresa Lasey and my neither corner delicatessen/grocery owner whose name is Troy Munoz to see if he could get some information from him about what he might of heard about any new lies that were being said about me about me and my job conspiracy situation as well as I also went on to also tell him to also find out just where that other lady who happen to be going off to when she left from our workplace that was of Spanish decent who approached my common law wife whose name I explained to him was Ms. Elite Windgate and our toddler son Romeo Windgate-Devine as I continued to also tell him that very same lady was going around my son's mother neighborhood of the Long Island City New York area as she convince for my child mom to sign her very own name and address on a partition form that also had also saw few other people name on that her form. And from there I informed my private investigator Wayne Western that I was able to snatched that Dam neighborhood partition right out of her hands that my neighbor office mate taken her very own liberty to collect as many of actual signatures as she possibly could at that time as that very same woman went on to tell my common law wife Elite Wingate that my employer at The O'Conner, Sapp, Dash & Marshall LLP who were in the Midtown section of the Time Square Plaza area spread the word at the company and the New York City streets that many New Yorkers should better keep a very close and watchful eye of me because as it often been said at my workplace that my workplace reasons to believe that I could be a part of a New York mafia gangster family who could be working for a criminal family. So from there I told my private investigator Wayne Western that wanted him to follow those two midtown Manhattan females office building mates that were in the Time Square Plaza area from our place of employment to their very own homes where they individually live.

And from there I told my guy private investigator that I also wanted him to snap and take several photographs of those two noisy middle aged ladies and even my very own family household that was located in the Astoria section of the Queens New York area because it was even also said by my employers at the O'Conner, Sapp, Dash & Marshall LLP corporate law firm that even my very own parents whose name I had explained was Mr. & Mrs. Damian Sr. and Jahtayshia Devine also been a part of my job corporate conspiracy situation as it was said by my employer that my very own mother and father were the sneaking behind my back as they began doubt me by calling my place of employment to try to find out what was going with me concerning rather the law firm had any actual proof that youngest son Romeo Devine could possibly be also a part of a New York City mafia gangster family and from there he told me that he wanted me to show and point those two women out to him that were spying on me out to him that I worked with at my employer office at The Time Square Plaza midtown Manhattan area as he also continued to say that he would get right on the case just as soon as he possible could as he also told me that I would hear back from him within a matter of a few days as I said that I would wait until I would hear back from him. And from there I called my common law wife Elite Windgate to tell her about my good news of how I hired a midtown Manhattan private investigator whose name I said was Wayne Western and how I paid him to try to gain some actual proof of my try to help me to try to prove my corporate conspiracy problems that I had with my former employers at the O'Conner, Sapp, Dash & Marshall LLP corporate law firm in the Time Square Plaza section of New York City. And from there my common law wife Elite Windgate began to asked me well isn't that rather expensive to do so? And from there I told her that it cost me exactly $500 in cash for the entire investigation to than take place as I also explained to her that I pay already paid him in advance as I also went on to tell my son mother that I was trying to get some actual evidence of either harassment/sexual harassment or of a corporate conspiracy that originally started with my employers at the O'Conner, Sapp, Dash & Marshall LLP in the Midtown Manhattan area of New York City that my employer were spreading the very false rumor to all New Yorkers that they all better start to keep a very close and watchful eye on me for anyone to see and report any illegal crime activities that I might be doing with any of any New York mafia crime families. And from my common law Elite Windgat wished for me to have the very best of good luck and for me to also be very much so very careful in me proving my employer corporate conspiracy.

on March 14, 2001, as I received a telephone called from my common law wife Elite Windgate as she told me that she miss me a whole lot as she went on to continue to say that our young son Romeo Jr. was going to be spend most of that day with her mother Ms. Wonda Windgate and her younger sister Epiphany Windgate as they told her that they were than going visit a good friend of their very own family. And from there my son Romeo Jr. mother Elite went on to say that she thought that it would be a sweet and thoughtful ideal for just the two of us to spend some romantic quality alone time together with it being just the two of us in my family basement home in The Astoria, Queens New York area. And from there I told my common law wife Elite Windgate that I to go and pay my family doctor whose name was Freddrick Linden a visit to get some nerve medication to try to stop me from being so very stress out at my workplace that was causing me a whole lot of problems back. And Elite still insisted that she still wanted to come over and lay herself down as she said that she would be waiting up for me in my family basement apartment home where I live at. And from there I said that it would be okay for her to do so while I was at my doctor office in the Astoria, Queens New York area and from there I told my mom and dad that I was on my way out to visit my family doctor Freddrick Linden to see if he could prescribe me some nerve medication to help me to relax myself a little bit whenever I was at work. And from there my mother Jahtayshia and Damian Sr. Devine and asked me if I was okay?

And from there I told them both no not really because that I was still feeling rather so much pressured from my employer at the midtown Manhattan corporate law firm of The O'Conner, Sapp, Dash & Marshall LLP about how they were still harassing/ sexual harassment me about how most of coworkers really did believe the very slanderous and false rumor of me to possibly to be a New York mafia gangster that was trying to rob the company blind of its money just like a professional theft for a organize crime family. And from there I told them both that my common law wife Elite was on her way over to pay me a visit while she also even said that if I was still be at my family physician office that she said that she just wanted to come over and wait for me in our family basement while her very own mom and younger sister Wonda & Epiphany where spending the day with our little baby Romeo Jr. And from there my parents told me that would be just fine for Elite to do so as they agreed to do so as they also went on to say that they would agree to let her inside our family home whenever she was to arrive on that day and from there I thank my parents and soon after that I was on my way to than visit my doctor office as I headed out of my family front door way. And from there I called my common law wife Elite Windgate to tell her that it was okay for her to come over and wait for me until I was to come back to my family home and from there she there told me that she would be waiting up for me so that she and I could have some very romantic very private play time of sorts.

Already proof read above story line!

And from there I gotten myself a little sexual excited with me than thinking of Elite as I told her that I couldn't hardly wait to once again have her in my arms and from there I said that I would see her in my bedroom when I gotten myself back to my family house. And when I arrived back into my family home my common law wife Elite Windgate calling be to hurry up and come downstairs so that she may speak to me about something that was very much important to me as I was on my way down to see her. And when I saw her she whispered to me about how she overheard my very own father Damian Devine Sr. come in the house to tell my mother Jahtayshia Devine that the word that was going on in our family neighborhood streets of the Astoria, Queens New York area that their very own son Romeo Devine hired a private investigator to start an investigation that involved our local corner delicatessen/grocery store owner whose name was Troy Munoz. And from there I been in total shock of what I just heard from my son mother Elite as I was also trying to figure out just how my parents found out about me hiring a private investigator to help me to prove my corporate conspiracy situation that first started in the midtown Manhattan employer that was called The O'Conner, Sapp, Dash & Marshall LLP corporate law firm who was the ones who began to spread the very false and slanderous rumors, lies about how my job had some crazy reason to believe that I was a New York mafia gangster that was trying to steal way from my place of employment.

after that I told my common law wife Elite Windgate that I would have to contact my private investigator whose name was Wayne Western who I told her that she should also make a mental note to herself of that man just in case something was to ever terribly happen to he and I and from there she said that she would do so, as she told me that she would also tell me that she would even them inform her very own immediate household family members what was going on with me trying to also desperately to prove my job corporate conspiracy situation. And when I spoke to my private investigator Wayne Western about how my very own common law wife Elite Windgate overheard from my very own father whose name I explained was Damian Devine Sr. as she told me that how he heard a guy in our family neighborhood of The Astoria, Queens New York area whose name was Romeo Devine started a private investigation that involved my employer at a corporate law firm of The O'Conner, Sapp, Dash & Marshall LLP and that delicatessen/grocery store owner whose name was Troy Munoz. from there my private investigator been in totally shock of what he just heard from me. As he said what? And that he also had continued to asked me that just how he wondered just how that information about him to be investigating a case in my neighborhood of the Astoria, Queens New York area gotten the word to the people in the nearby area? And soon after he thought about just how could that could actual happen he told me that oh wow as he realized just how he made the very bad and very costly mistake of going to visit a guy friend of his that also lived just right across the street from Troy Munoz delicatessen/ grocery store that was called Astoria delicatessen and grocery store as he told me that he told his male friend that he was in the neighborhood at that time working on a corporate conspiracy case that also included talks about the word that was going on about a guy who is name Romeo Devine was trying to prove a possible corporate conspiracy case that started from the midtown Manhattan Time Square Plaza area. So from there my former private investigator Wayne Western informed me that he also told his guy friend who he told me should remain nameless must alerted that corner grocery store owner whose name was Troy Munoz that he was being investigated by one of his local customer whose name was Romeo Devine to see if he himself became a coconspirator against one of his customer whose name was me Romeo Devine. And from there I was so very disappointed with my private investigator Wayne Western for him not to kept my corporate conspiracy case totally confidential instead of me to hear about how he then stopped by his male friend apartment house to do some personal socializing while he was to only be working to try and prove a corporate conspiracy for me. And from there he told me that when entered the store than proceeded to place a listening wired device in with some of the store bulk of their grocery inventory but as my private investigator Wayne Western also went on to tell me that the store owner must had saw and known of the private investigation that was going on about him to see if that very same afro American middle aged lady whose name was Theresa Lasey and my neighborhood local corner of The Astoria grocery store owner still been keeping a very close and watchful eye and ear on me as possible numerous verbal communicational reports might been talked about me from my home town of the Astoria, Queens New York area all the way to my employer at the O'Conner, Sapp, Dash & Marshall LLP.

And from there my private investigator Wayne Western also came up with some information about those two neighboring female coworkers whereabouts in where they lived at that particular time as he told me that the Afro-American middle aged lady lived right across the street of the Astoria delicatessen/grocery store that was owned by Troy Munoz and as for that other lady who was of Spanish decent saw that he was following her as she ran herself off away from my private investigator Wayne Western. And from there my private investigator tried to come up with yet another way to prove my corporate conspiracy situation of my former employer of The O'Conner, Sapp, Dash & Marshall LLP midtown corporate law firm as he made the suggestion of that he wanted another chance to come into my workplace to try once again to plant yet another wired listening device to try to listen in any and all harassment/ sexual harassment or corporate conspiracy issues that I may still been facing at that particular time. But from there I told my former private investigator Wayne Western that I thought that he wasted to much of my time as well as my hard earn money by him to been giving out my confidential information to his male friend who he told me that while he was in my neighborhood hometown of the Astoria, Queens New York area he was not supposed to say anything about any corporate conspiracy case or it whereabouts where he was assigned to investigate and from there I told him that he was fired from future investigating my New York City conspiracy case as I just walked myself away from that incompetent private investigator who ruin my private investigation. And from there I went back into my family home in the Astoria, Queens New York area to call up and tell my common law wife Elite Windgate all about that I had to fire my former private investigator Wayne Western. And from there Elite asked me the question of just what I was planning to do about all of my problems that I still at that time? And from there I just told her that I was not quite sure at that time and that I to also think about what my next move was going to be for me.

So on March 21, 2001, as I still been working at my former employer at the corporate law firm of O'Conner, Sapp, Dash & Marshall LLP I heard a big announcement from some of the much nicer female associate secretaries whose name were Shirley Rouse, Margerette Flecture, Tina McGraw as they all said that they all should stop bothering that very nice and handsome man Romeo Devine who just so happen to also be our very good and very hard working mail men clerk whose been with the company for a few years now. And from there I also heard the very same three ladies say that how they heard about all that was going on with me Romeo Devine and his common law wife whose name that they heard from the copy center day time supervisor whose name was Carlton Circuit who was also trying to be all up in his common law wife whose name they discovered was Elite Windgate who as they talked about how we a son together whose name that discovered was Romeo Windgate-Devine as they also said that was a dam shame that my privacy been almost totally invaded straight from the corporate law firm of O'Conner, Sapp, Dash & Marshall LLP. And so from there once that the people who also worked on the forty-second floor of the Telecopy/Fax/Word Processing department been talking about how it was no longer humorous at all just how they also heard about how much that they must my very own parents worrying about me as they continued to say that they know about how my very own mother Mrs. Devine been calling my place of employment just to check up on me as her youngest adult son just to see just how things were going on with my coworkers at The O'Conner, Sapp, Dash & Marshall LLP corporate law firm New York corporate conspiracy situation as my place of my employment was trying to make me a publicized criminal figure of some soughts. so after that I arrived back at my family neighborhood of the Astoria, Queens New York area when I saw that very same middle aged lady who been one of my employer at the O'Conner, Sapp, Dash & Marshall LLP neighboring office mate whose name that she told me was Theresa Lasey saw me coming off of a New York City Transit Authority bus as I also heard her to begin to talked about me to say to a few strangers on the street of 212th Place as she said there goes that New York City wide alleged mafia gangster criminal figure that was coming off from our workplace of the corporate law firm of O'Conner, Sapp, Dash & Marshall.

from there I overheard some people in my former neighborhood of The Astoria, Queens New York area tell my former female coworker neighboring employer office building mate whose name was Thereasa Lasey that she that corporate law firm of The midtown Manhattan corporate law firm that was called The O'Conner, Sapp, Dash & Marshall LLP should have never started spreading around a very rumorous and slanderous lies about how this very honest and very hardworking guy whose name was Romeo Devine who was just a New York mailman who was just trying to do a very good public service to be one of New York finest mailman while he was just trying to make all of his mail deliveries on time in the big apple of the New York City area. And when I overheard the good people from my former neighborhood of the Astoria, Queens New York area as they taken a very firm stand to tell my former office building neighbor female mate whose name she told me was Theresa Lasey to take a hike and back the hell away from that good Romeo Devine and from there I stepped up to her myself as I agreed amongst the people in my former hometown as I told her that she should make herself to be very much so scarced from us all and from there she walked herself away from the small crowd as we began to laughed at her as she went about her very own business at that particular time. And from there I slapped a few high fives to the around the way guys as I also thanked them all for standing up for me concerning my crazy employer office neighboring building mate as I also explained to the people who were standing on the corner that my job stress me out so very much that I said that I was going to get myself something to eat and drink for my dinner and from there I also explained that I was just going to lay myself down to go right asleep. And from there everyone who was actual a total stranger to me told me to go ahead a rest myself quite a bit because they said that they totally understood what I was going through with those disturbing coworkers of mines as I also thanked some of the good people of the Astoria area.

shortly after that on March 29, 2001, which was the job floating holiday of good Friday that year as I still be living in my immediately family home in the Astoria, Queens New York area as my two parents Jahtayshia and Damian Sr. just asked me just how my work day went? And from there I informed them both that my employment at the midtown Manhattan corporate law firm of The O'Conner, Sapp, Dash & Marshall harassment issues was still going on and that I just an unpleasant run in with one of my female coworkers who I previous meet at the Astoria corner Deli/grocery store that was owned by Troy Munoz who she once introduces herself as Therease Lasey. And from there my two parents just said to me well now that now that the three day holiday weekend was among us all how about if I was to asked my son mother Elite if she could bring over there youngest grandson Romeo Windgate-Devine over for a nice family visit? And from there I told the both of them that I would have to check with the mother to see if she could bring our little bundle of joy by our family home. And once I finally giving my common wife Elite Windgate a call to see just how my son mother and our child been doing she herself told me that she at that particular time wasn't feeling very well as she said that she felt rather sickly.

And from I felt rather sorry for my common wife/mother of my child as I also said to her that his other two grandparents been asking about if little toddler Romeo Jr. could come over our family home in Astoria, Queens New York area? From there, she told me that no, she wasn't feeling so very well, and that she was going to be staying at her family townhouse in Long Island City, New York area. And from there I said to her that even though she could not make it over to pay myself and my family a very nice visit that I was still willing so very much so to get on a New York City Transit Authority bus to pick up our son and to also have the two of us to take a taxi cab back to my very own family home while I also recommended that my common law wife Elite Windgate gotten herself plenty of rest and relaxation. But my common law wife Elite told me that she did not really totally trust me and my mother and father Mr. and Mrs. Devine because of all of the dysfunctional things that was going on in my family household that to do with all of my job conspiracy problems as she also continued to say that how I confided in her to tell her that I even believed that my very own mother was calling my employer at that corporate law firm of The O'Conner, Sapp, Dash & Marshall LLP behind my very own back. And from there I been very much so very surprise at what I just her coming from my common law wife/mother of child. And from there I just told her that no matter what stressful pressures that I might go through with on my very stressful job at the corporate firm and even my very own two parents as I said to Elite that I am still a very strong-minded individual who can still independently be a very good and caring father to take care of our son Romeo Windgate-Windgate on a weekend basis. But my common law wife was still not convinced at all of me to take good care of our son with my mother and father Jahtayshia and Damian Devine Sr. and from there I told Elite that I would give our son a call back later that very same evening as I been rather disappointed in her as I just hung up the telephone while she was still taking to me. And from there I went back upstairs to tell my mom and dad what my common law wife Elite and I just discussed with each other. As I to break the very bad news to them both just how my common law wife Elite

Windgate told me that she did not trust me to care for our very own son at our family household. And from there my parents said that they were feeling rather disappointed of my child mother. And from there they asked me well what are you going to do about us all to continue to have little Romeo Jr. visit our side of the family our son? And from there I began to think about it a whole lot as I decided that the only good way to handle a situation such as that was to resolved issue of me to get my legal father visitation right from the Queens Family Courthouse in the Jamaica New York City area in order for me to try to have my son Romeo Windgate-Devine without his mother constant self supervision and my mother Jahtayshia and father Damian Devine Sr. very much so agreed with me.

On April 1, 2001, which so happen to been April Fool's Day as I decided to call into my employer workplace at the corporate law firm of O'Conner, Sapp, Dash & Marshall LLP in the midtown Time Square Plaza of Manhattan to tell them that I need to take a personal day off from my workplace as it soon been accepted by my former 2nd floor mailroom manager whose name was Henry Hernandez. And from there I saw my two parents Jahtayshia and Damian Devine Sr. as I told them both that I been on my very one way to start to head out straight to go to the Queens Family Court House in the Jamaica, New York area, to get my parental rights separate from my son mother. And from there my folks wished me to have a whole lot of good luck in doing so as I given them both a hug as I left out our family doors. And once I arrived there I told one of the family court clerks that I wanted to filed a family court partisan to serve the mother of my child in order for me to try to receive joint custody or visitation of or son Romeo Windgate-Devine. And once I spoken to one of the family court office clerk they given me a family court partisan to have my son Romeo Windgate-Devine mother who is Elite Windgate legal served by a New York City police officer along with me to also be present of that time that she was to be served by law enforcement.

very soon after that I started to head straight to my common law wife Elite Windgate neighborhood police department percent in the Long Island City Queens New York area to have a police officer serve her a family court summons. And once I went inside I showed two male officers my family court summons to have my son Romeo Windgate-Devine mother whose name is Elite Windgate served with a summon of my visitation rights to appear in the family courts of law. So shortly after that the two nice police officers drove me straight to my son Romeo Jr. mother townhouse home in the Long Island City area of Elite Windgate neighborhood where she lived. And once the two police officers and I arrived there as I rang her door bell as she been so very much surprise to see me on my very way to see her right along with two of the New York finest police officer as they both asked her to state her name as she said that she was Elite Windgate and from there as she looked at me with her to been so very much angry with me as she asked the three of us, just what was the very meaning of this visit? And from there the officer step right in front of me to tell her that she was to accept a family court summons of me to file a family court partition for us to make a family court appearance there on June 21, 2001, which so happen to be the day after Father Day and from there Elite female family members gotten themselves so very much upset as they close their very own door as they all started to shout out to say what and that they could not just believe what just happen with me to be serving those dam court papers.

And from there the two Police Officers and I left out from Elite and our little toddler Romeo Jr. hallway area as they asked me if I wanted a short way ride away from the area? In order for me to avoid any conflict between my common wife Elite Windgate and myself. And I said yes and that I would be so very glade to accept there nice offer to secure my very own safety. So from there I taken myself back to my own family neighborhood of the Astoria, Queens New York area to break the good news that I went to their grandson Romeo Jr. neighborhood where he lived with his mother Elite, his grandmother Wonda, his aunt Epiphany and his uncle Epico of the Windgate family. And from there I went back to my own family home in the Astoria, Queens New York area to break the good news that I had went to my son Romeo Jr. mother Elite's townhouse apartment home to serve her a family court summon that was given to me from the courts. And from there my parents said that was a very good thing that I did in order for myself and even my very own side of my very own family to have the official legal rights to my own son Romeo Windgate Devine that should remain separate from his mother Elite Windgate.

on April 16, 2001, my son mother Elite Windgate been rather so very still very much angry with me to the point that she would repeatedly started to call and harass me while I was still very much employed at the corporate law firm of the O'Conner, Sapp, Dash & Marshall LLP in the midtown Manhattan Time Square Plaza area as the company Telecopy/Fax operator night time supervisor whose name was Tearra Simpson started to complained about it to me. And from there the company night time supervisor told me that I better start to do something about my baby mama about her to stop calling the job while I was still on company time as I told her that I most certain will do so. And when I arrived back to my family home in the Astoria, Queens New York area I went right straight downstairs to my family basement apartment where I at that time still lived, as I raced myself to the telephone to call my son Romeo Jr. mother Elite's townhouse home to find out just what was up with her to be constantly calling me while I was still at my workplace? And once I picked up my telephone receiver I began to shout out at my common law wife Elite Windgate as I asked her what the hell was up with her repeatedly calling me while I was at my place of work?

And from there she started to complained about just how she was very much so upset about me for previous bringing the New York City Police department to have serve her those dam family court papers? (As she put it). And from there I explained to her that was my legal right to do so simply because lam our son Romeo Jr. very pride and responsible father. And from there I told her that she should not have told me that she did not trust me with our young son Romeo Jr. And from there Elite said once again the reason why she felt that way was because she explained that she thought that I was under way to much stressful pressure from my job and from my very own two parents. So from there I told my baby mother Elite Windgate that as we were both romantically still in an intimate relationship that she should trusted me more and a little more faith in me. And from there she also complained that she taking real good notice of my very own father Damian Devine Sr. and his very bad drinking habits of his favorite alcoholic bear beverage which is taken close notices that it was mostly Colt 45 malt liquor. And from there I told her that I would always protect our son Romeo Jr., to always make sure that he was always very safe and secure so no physical harm would come his way. And from there, she told me that she still did not trust me or my household immediate family members at all. And from there my son mother Elite gotten so very bold enough to tell me that because she was my baby momma that she felt that she the very right way to call me at any dam time that she dam well please to do so and she also told me that I to just deal with her and her very bad attitude whenever she felt like having one.

And from there I asked her oh yea do you really think so? As Elite told me year that right you betcha man and from there I told her that I wanted her to please put our son Romeo Jr. on the telephone so that he could talk to me as his daddy and from there she agreed to do so. once I spoken to my young son Romeo Windgate-Devine on the telephone as I again spoken with him to hear how he was doing as I had to explained to him that it would be a few months before I was to visit with him again. And from there he asked me why Daddy why? from there I just told him that me and his mommy a little problem that we were going through with as I also told him that I always wanted him to remember that his Daddy will always love him a whole lot no matter what and from there he said to me that he love his good Daddy so very much too. And from there his mother taken the telephone away from him as she told our son to tell me goodbye for now as we hung up our telephones.

the very next evening of April 17, 2001, I decided to filed a telephone harassment charges right against my very own son mother Elite Windgate as I at that time round to explained just why I to bring my complaint to my hometown of Astoria, Queens New York police department as I talked with one of the police detectives. And after the officer allowed me to filed an official complaint of my telephone harassment issues he told me that he would pick my son mother up from her townhouse apartment home to have her official arrested as the police department detective told me that he would very soon have to bring her in the neighborhood of the Astoria, Queens New York police department to have her to be lock up to spend a full night in the percent jail house. And from there I said that would be fine for him to do just that and from there I went back to my own family home that was on 212th place in my own hometown of the Astoria, Queens New York area. about two days later as I gotten off from working so very hard at my employer office that was in the Time Square Plaza section area. I received a telephone call from my common law wife

Elite Windgate as she told me that a police detective called her home and told her that I went down to the police station to previous file some official charges of telephone harassment while I still been at my workplace of my employment of the midtown Manhattan corporate law firm that was called the O'Conner, Sapp, Dash & Marshall LLP. And from there I told her yea you are got dam f***ckin right that I did just that as I future explained to her that one of my employer company department night time managers whose name just so happen to be Terra Simpson asked me just who was the lady that was constantly kept on calling me while I was still on the company time?

And from there she warned me to handle my personal business with those to many constant personal calls that were coming into the office for me. And I explained to her that was the actually reason why I gone to the cops make an official complaint about her in order for her to always realized that at that I was the only actual working parent at that particular time while she been just laying herself around her family town house home just watching the television and caring for our son little son Romeo Jr. As I also went on to explained while she refused to get herself a full-time job as I even future told her that I was the only one parent who was still working at that time. Than from there on April 18, 2001, Elite told me that a detective called her once again to bring my son mother Elite Windgate to be brought up on official police charges of telephone harassment that been filed by her child father Romeo Devine. And from there my child mother Elite claimed that she was feeling like she was going to have a very serious emotional panic attack about those charges that I official brought up against her as she started to beg me to come over so that I may accompany her to have those harassment charges dropped once and for all.

And from there I also asked her does she solemnly swear never to ever telephone harass me at least whenever I was at my workplace? And from there Elite told me yes and that she most certainly does agree to what I was asking of her as I told her that I was on my way to see her and our son little Romeo Jr. And from there when I arrived back to my son Romeo Jr. and his mother Elite Windgate townhouse home the police detective than shortly arrived to pick her up to have her placed underneath arrested at least for one night only. And as the very same detective been rather surprise to also see me at his purps townhouse as I had to explain to him that I was going to be dropping the police charges against the mother of my child. And from there the police detective said that it would be okay for me to do so but as he also explained to us both that he still to have my son mother Ms. Elite Windgate place under a temporary arrest as he read her the right to remain silent as he also slapped the handcuffs right on her two risks.

Than once we both arrived at my very own neighborhood police department in the Astoria New York section of the Queens New York area as my son mother Elite Windgate been taking into police custody as we were inside the police department vehicle just riding in back set as the detective told her that he had to take her to a jail holding cell that was only right downstairs in the police department basement while I was to prepare to have all of the charges dropped against her. about an hour later she was brought up from the police department basement jail cell while she was once again placed back into a set of handcuffs as it been time for her to face the court judge as he asked her just how does she make her plead as also said that she pleaded herself to be guilty as charged your honor and from there I also informed the judge that do to I to mostly to depend on the defendant to care for our child back at her home that I was official going to be dropping the charges that I originally brought against the defendant. And from there the Astoria police department judge dismissed the charges that was brought up against the defendant Ms. Elite Wingate as she been finally official released from police custody. And from there my son motor Elite Windgate thanked me for not to keep her lock up inside of my neighborhood police department in the Astoria, Queens New York area.

And from there I said that she was quit very much so welcome. And soon after I began to say to her that since I avoided her to not to spend the night in the police jail house that I thought that it would be so very fair if she would agree upon me to bring our son Romeo Jr. over some times without her to always to feel that she to always feel like she to always be watching us all while we were to visit our son Romeo Jr. in my own family home instead of her to be always watching over my side of the family shoulders as we all felt that she herself didn't even trusted the our son Devine sided of the family. And still to my very own surprise my son mother Elite Windgate still very much disagreed with my reasoning. And from there we began to start back just arguing with each other and soon after that she walked herself away from me as she said that the next time she was to see me again would be her very guest in the Queens Family court house in the Jamaica, New York area, as she caught the city bus to go right back to her very own family townhouse home Long Island City. And from there I told my parents what I just went through with the grandson Romeo Jr. mother Elite as my very mother Jahtayshia Devine told me that I did the right thing to have those charges dropped because that wouldn't be a very good thing for our little son to miss his own mother Elite as he would always be looking for his mommy to be always close by him inside their very own family townhouse home with their very own family members.

on April 30 of the year of 2001 as I still very much been employed at my former employer at The O'Conner, Sapp, Dash & Marshall LLP of the corporate law firm that was located in the midtown Manhattan Time Square Plaza area as it been time for me to begin to make my daily inter-office mail run deliveries as I hand went back up to the company forty-second floor telecopy/fax department center as I saw three of the mail room center clerks who were still assigned to worked work inside the company forty-second floor telecopy/fax center as I saw two of my mailroom center coworkers whose name were Terry Helwigg and Thomas Browney who also witness with their very own eyes that very same day of how now the former employee whose name is Denise Hailey once upon a time verbally and physical harassed me. So from there I started to think back when I went to try to have some official physical and sexual harassment charges brought up against my former employer at the corporate law firm of The O'Conner, Sapp, Dash & Marshall LLP in the midtown Manhattan section in the New York area as I previously been told by The Department of the Division of Human Rights that in order to try to prove an official sexual and physical harassment case that would possibly be filed against my job at the law firm than I was told by a supervisor who worked there whose name was Sally Kendricks I should think about how I should try to get some my departmental coworkers home telephone numbers just in case that I might be able to try to build a court trail case that would be against my place of employment as I figured that I would try to very soon enough try to leave that employer company of The O'Conner, Sapp, Dash & Marshall LLP and to enter into another job. So from there my departmental mail clerk associated whose name were Terry Helwigg and Thomas Browney indeed exchanged telephone # with one another and shortly after that I told those same two guys that maybe we should called each other up so we may hang out sometimes and from there Terry Helwigg and Thomas Browney said that sounded like a good ideal for us to all to do some time together in the very near future. And from there I said that I would see them both later on doing our work day and from there I said my goodbyes for that particular time as I went back to the company of The O'Conner, Sapp, Dash & Marshall LLP 2nd floor mailroom center to continue to make all of my mailroom mail deliveries.

on May 7 of the year of 2001 which was mother day holiday season that same year as my now former common law wife whose name is Elite Windgate given me a call at my family house in the Astoria New York area to start her complaining of her to asked me just why I didn't taking some time out of my day to pick up the telephone to give her a call so that I may wished for her to have a very wonderful happy mother day that very same year? And from there I just told her that my very reason for me to not to be contacting her by the telephone on that very special particular holiday for all of the mother was because as explained to her that I didn't think that she was being a very good mother at all to our young son because even though I do try my very best to try to provide for our son Romeo Windgate-Windgate financially by me to always pay his child support payment on time on a bi-weekly basis as I also continued to say that from out of the very kindest of my own heart as I even take our son clothes shopping for him to have some decent fashionable clothes to wear. And that I also went on to let her also now that even though I was at that particular underneath a whole lot of emotional pressure at my former place of employment at the midtown Manhattan corporate law firm of O'Conner, Sapp, Dash & Marshall LLP during the five day work week as I further explained to her that she as my son mother who still very much so wanted for the two of us to still have ourselves a continuous intimate and romantic relationship with each other as I also went on to say that she should have a whole lot more faith in me. And from there my former common law Elite Windgate hand told me that she herself still didn't trust my father Damian Devine Sr. because she told me how she taken notice that whenever my dad would began to start to drink that he couldn't hardly even never walk up the family flight of stairs in his very own household.

And from my son mother Elite continued to talk about how she even thought that even my very own mother Mrs. Jahtayshia Devine was even a little crazy in her very own right because she told me about the very time that I confided in her about how my mom two previous nerves emotional breakdowns. And from there I just told her that if she still felt that very same way about me and even my very own family members that I thought that the very best thing for us to do was to remain permanently separated as far as us to no longer to never again to have an intimate relationship with each other. And from there my ex-common law wife Elite Windgate claimed that my decision that I just made as she said that was just find with her and from there she slammed down the telephone as she just hang up on me. So immediately after that I called back to asked to speak to my son Romeo Windgate-Devine and when I finally did he himself been to become so very much happy to speak to me as his Daddy and it was all a very good conversation from there as he and I just been joking around with each other while we were also been making funny noises to each other while we were still on our fifteen-minute telephone conversation.

on May 10 of the year of 2001 I gotten so very much so stress out from all of my employer of The midtown Manhattan corporate law firm of O'Conner, Sapp, Dash & Marshall LLP that I decided that it was time for me to start thinking about to start to leave that job in order to try to find a much more better one that would be possibly much less stressful to me. So I took a personal day off from my workplace at the O'Conner, Sapp, Dash & Marshall LLP corporate law firm as I headed myself straight right back to my former employment job placement agency that was called The Employer Of Institutes. And from there as I once again went back there I was assigned to a new job placement counselor whose he said that his name was Bryce Lancing as he taking a resume from me that I already typed up for myself and from there I also informed him that I indeed wanted him to try his very best to have me placed in yet another mailroom clerk employment position whenever there was one to be available for myself to take. And from there I taking the good liberty to shake my employment placement agency counselor Bryce Lancing two hands as I also thanked him so ever so very kindly and from there I left the Downtown Manhattan building area to start to head my way back to my family home in the Astoria, Queens New York area to tell my two parents what I just did to try to better myself in the professional employment sense. And when I just arrived back at my parents Damian Sr. and Jahtayshia Devine house where I still lived at I informed them both that I was trying to leave that very much so very stressful job that I was still very much so employed at the midtown Manhattan employer that was called The O'Conner, Sapp, Dash & Marshall LLP corporate law firm to try to find a more suitable mailroom clerk employment position to try to better myself career wise.

And from there my mother and father said that sounded such like a very wonderful news for them to both to hear as they wished for me to have the very best of good luck in finding myself a new place of employment and from there I thanked them both ever so very kindly as I embraced the both of them with a huge warm hug. Shortly after that I received a telephone call from my former employment job placement counselor whose name is Bryce Lancing were still be employed at The Employer of Institutes on May 17, 2001, as he indeed founded myself a brand-new employment position for me to become the newest Mailroom/Office Services Clerk to a midtown Manhattan company that was called APL Meadia Management LLC. once I gotten my very good news of myself to finally to be leaving my very troublesome place of employment at the midtown Manhattan corporate law firm that is called The O'Conner, Sapp, Dash & Marshall LLP corporate law firm that was located in the Time Square Plaza Manhattan New York area. And from there I went back to the corporate law firm Department of Human Resources to turn in my letter of resignation to voluntary end my employment position as one of The company of The O'Conner, Sapp, Dash & Marshall LLP corporate law firm at the midtown Manhattan area that was located in the Time Square Plaza New York section.

And on May 30, 2001, my employer placement counselor whose name is Bryce Lancing told me to come into his office in the downtown Manhattan area section in the New York so that he may take me into my brand-new place of my employment at the corporate company that was

called The APL Meadia Management Company and from there I was on
my very way to see him just as soon as I could possibly could do so. And
once I arrived at the office of The Employer Of Institutes employment
placement counselor office to see Bryce Lancing he taking me straight
down to my newest employer office at The APL Meadia Management
LLC. Company and from there we went to my newest employer at The
APL Meadia Management company where I was first introduced to the
company Office Service Manager whose name she told me was Justina
Mainstream as we greeted each other ever so very kindly and shortly after
I also been also introduced to the company Office Service/Mailroom
Supervisor whose name he informed me was Scott Cortez. And from
there I been accepted into my place of employment at The APL Meadia
Management company as I been on my way to begin to start hand sorting
out the company mailroom deliveries after a very successful job interview.

on about June 1, of the year of 2001 as I started to work at my brand-new
place of employment of the APL Meadia Management company as I tried
to my very best of my abilities to try to performed all of my Mailroom/
Office Service Clerk duties. One day on June 8, 2001, my mailroom/
office services supervisor whose name was Scott Cortez saw that I was
having quite of bit of trouble with a few of my job responsibilities while I
still been employed there such as for him to have me to occasional change
several light bulbs while I was giving a very short and unbalanced later to
stand on in order to complete the very small task that was at hand for me
to do at that particular time. And once my former supervisor whose name
is Scott Cortez been so very nice enough to try to help me out whenever
he possibly could do so as he said that he taken very close notice of my
physical handicap with my right leg as he also said that he saw that I
had major problem with me them keeping myself to be steadily balance
and he also told me that he himself would take on the responsibilities
to change all of the company light bulbs. And shortly after that my
employer at the company of The APL Meadia Management LLC other
staff members started to also complained about my work performance a
whole lot as well.

And even though my former Office Service/Mailroom supervisor whose
name is Scott Cortez really tried to cover up several mistakes that I made
while I was still very much employed with the company as he still said

that a lot of the company support staff members hand still started back complaining about my poor non satisfactory job performance was. And from there two of the company receptionist whose name were Shelly Ocean and Nyasia Armstrong try to helped me out with them trying to give me a little extra assistance in learning some office receptionist telephone answering and transferring all of the company calls to the company proper person who were still working at the company of APL Meadia Management LLC and I must say that those two ladies taught me so very well enough. one day on June 8, 2001, my office service supervisor Scott Cortez told me that there was this one lady whose name he informed me was Julie Mosely who been the very one to start all of the complaining about me a whole hell of a lot as he told me to not to worry myself to much about that lady simply because she was known around the company office as a mean moody type person that hardly no one liked to deal with. And shortly after that my supervisor whose name Scott Cortez and I gotten to learn more about each other quite a little bit on a very personal level for the very first two months as we worked right next to each other side by side as some of my other responsibilities were mail sorting and posting of the U.S. stamps on all of the company outgoing mails as well for myself to be responsibilities to make multiple minor repairs on the company multiple copiers who had the occasional paper jam copies that were stuck inside of the company Xerox copier machines. My office service/mailroom supervisor Scott Cortez confided in me about his past criminal history of about how he used to be a big time drug dealer who used to work right alongside of his uncle and many more other drug dealers as well.

on June 10, 2001, my former Office Services/Mailroom Supervisor Scott Cortez told me about how he used to get arrested by the New York Police Department a whole lot to the point that there was a criminal justice honorable judge who giving him his very last option to get out of the drug dealer hustling business or else he continued to tell me that he was warned by the court of the law that if for any reason at all that he ever again ever to enter his own court room for yet another drug possession charge of any kind that he hand told me that he was told that he would to serve 8 years inside of a New York City prison cell simply because he was on his third strike of a unlawful drug dealing. And from there my former Office Service/Mailroom supervisor Scott Cortez told me after dealing with the criminal justice system for so a very long time that he told me that he made the very wise decision to start to work his way up the later in the department of several companies mailroom service centers departments. And he also went on to tell me about how he himself decided that it was time for himself to begin to start to think about how he better began to start to change his own very life around to the point that he informed me that he joined himself in a Treemont South Bronxs New York City neighborhood church where he grown up as a child that was located around the corner from his project housing were he still very much so lived at. And I started back to them remember back when I first heard my former Mailroom/Office Service supervisor Scott Cortez criminal tell his story as I felt finally rather relieved that I finally found a job that didn't harass me in any way to the point that I felt so very good about being still employed at that time.

And from there I also confided with my the Office Service Supervisor Scott Cortiz about how I used to be harassed at my most recent employer at the company of The Midtown Manhattan corporate law firm that was also located in the Time Square Plaza section of the New York New York area and how my previous employer started a very ridiculous rumor that at one time circulated around the entire company of the O'Conner, Sapp, Dash & Marshall LLP with one of my former mailroom coworker whose name was Stone Casey as he told everyone who worked with us all inside the mailroom department that I looked like such a dangerous New York City mafia gangster family member who was trying to steal away there company hard earn money from them at just because he saw me make a very serious angry face at him because I gotten rather up with him talking about me to the rest of the mailroom center staff members about how I must really thought that I was going to going to going to start some sort of romantic relationship with the company mailroom manager Henry Hernandez secretary whose name was Gloria Knight. And when my Mailroom/Office Service Supervisor whose name was Scott Cortez first heard my problems that I had with my previous employer bad situation I was in he told me that the people at my former job must of been very much totally insane to start to spread a stupid office rumor such as that. And as for my work responsibilities were concerned of my employer at the APL Meadia Management was still very much unsatisfied with my work ethic also because there would be sometimes do to there was only two people who worked into the company Office Services/Mailroom department when I would have to also have to work unsupervised without any supervision from my Office Services/Mailroom supervisor whose name was Scott Cortez to instructed me in what to do as I accidently thrown out some of the company very most recent import documentations. But I try to redeem myself by still trying to work so very much hard as I assisted my former Office Service/Mailroom Services Supervisor Scott Cortez by help him to move some of the company heavy furniture around the office as the company decided to downsize the corporate business to only one floor instead of them to have two because a lot of their employees at the APL Meadia Management LLC staff member just recently left there company for good.

on June 15, 2001, my former employer at The company of APL Meadia Management LLC company told my employer Office Services Manager whose name was Justina Mainstream and the company Office Services Supervisor whose name is Scott Cortez taken me out for a very delicious luncheon with them both for the goodness sake that they told me that the company realized that I tried to work my very best to my very own ability as they both also told me that the company of The APL Media Management LLC want to at least show there some appreciation for me to be working above and upon my job description by helping the office to move the company office furniture downstairs to the company next floor down area which was the company 7th floor. But shortly after that I be told that my job experience wasn't quite what the company been looking for as my Office Services Manager whose name is Justina Mainstream told me that she wanted me to start back to contacting the job placement agency where I originally gotten my position of me being one of the company Office Services/Mailroom Clerks. when I did just what my former employer job placement counselor whose name is Bryce Lancing as I informed him that my employment at my very pervious employment at The APL Meadia Management LLC company wasn't quit working out for me very well to the point that I also told him that I needed for him and the employment placement agency of The Employer of Institutes to help me to find a brand-new occupation for myself. And from there my former job placement employment counselor whose name again was Bryce Lancing told me that I been in very good luck as he told me that he just another mailroom clerk position that was just available as he informed me that he thought that would be just so very right for me to be employed at a company that was called The Resolution Outlook Resources LLC and from there I was told by The Employer Of Institutes job placement counselor whose name was Bryce Lancing that I should be in his office the very next following business day.

on June 21, 2001, which was the day after Father Day it been time for my ex-common-law wife/mother of my child Elite Windgate and my family court battle for me to try to get legal joint custody or my visitation rights of our young son whose name is Romeo Windgate-Devine. And as we both entered into the Queens New York Family Court House in the Jamaica New York section as we asked an office clerk who worked there to the pointed us both in the right directing to see the actual Judge (who shall remain nameless) who was handling Elite Windgate and my family court case. And once the office clerk finally did so she first taking my son mother and I to our Judges attorney at the family court law whose name shall remain nameless as well. And from there she taken Elite and I both to a family court office to discuss our parental disputes. And from there I stated my case of just how my child's mother Elite Windgate be totally unreasonable about how she at that particular time did not trust me enough to visit with our child whose name I stated to the family court attorney is Romeo Windgate-Devine as I said that I always wanted to bring him to my parents family home and that I also stated was located in The Astoria, Queens New York without having his mother to always feel that she to always be in my very own family household.

from there the mother of my child Elite Windgate stated that the reason for her to keep our young toddler son always underneath her very own close supervision was because she said that I physically spanked our child with a cotton soft bath robe belt. And from there I tried to plead my court case to say that the reason why I disciplined my young toddler son Romeo Jr. that way was because of whenever it was my intention to discipline our son whenever it was needed that I did not want to spank him with my bear hands or a leather belt because I even realized that form of discipline would be to servear for our son Romeo Windgate-Devine. And from there the Queens family Court Judge attorney told me that according to the family court law rules are concern once a case of child abuse is reported of physically disciplinary action that I used against our son is considered in the eyes of the law once it is officially reported as a case of child abuse. And from there I told the Jamaica, Queens, New York family court judge attorney that I was not aware of that actual fact as I also stated at that particular time I thought of a case of child abuse was only considered putting visual marks and bruises on a child body. And from there I said that I was not aware of the family courts technical child abuse laws. So from there the Judge attorney asked my son Elite Windgat just what did she wanted her to do from here?

And from there the Queens New York Family Court Judge attorney made a suggestion of would it be alright with her to at that very least have for me some professional parental supervision with a child abuse prevention specialist? And from there my son mother Elite Windgate agreed upon that very exact request as we both been told that I was to have a one day a week professional supervised visitation with the a child abuse prevention Supervisor whose name was Theresa Gabriel. And from there shortly afterwards Elite and I left the Jamicia Queens New York Family Court building as I didn't bother to even look back in her very own direction or not to even speak not one single word to her at that particular time and place. And once I gotten myself back to my family Astoria New York I broken the somewhat of the bad news of how my son Romeo Jr. very own mother had reported me for physical abuse to the Jamaica, Queens, New York family court as I also told my parents that the mother of their second grandson Elite Windgate to bring my son little Romeo Jr. all the very way to the Manhattan New York area as it was ordered by the Jamaica, Queens Family Court Judge attorney at law. And from there my mother and father said Oh well son and that they both hope that when I finished my child abuse prevention season just as soon enough as I possibly could so that they could someday soon see their youngest grandson Romeo Windgate-Devine.

So when I my very first professional supervised parental visitation session with my son Romeo Windgate-Devine on the 4th of July of the year of 2001 and the child abuse prevention supervisor whose name was Theresa Gabriel in the Midtown Manhattan New York area as his mother Elite had to leave our child there without me having to see her simply because that was the child prevention abuse center policy of the two parent of the child were not allowed to be in each other present while we a family court case that was still pending. And when I first saw my son Romeo Jr. who was almost of the tender aged of almost two years old as I was so very happy and sad all at the very same time as I try to not even show my very sadness of my emotions around the child prevention service woman whose name was Theresa Gabriel. And as I had a few more child abuse prevention classes I was told by the agency supervisor Theresa Gabriel that my classes were going quite well between my son Romeo Jr. and I and from there I said to her my thank-you's ever so kindly. On the very day of July 18, 2001, when I finished yet another child abuse prevention class with the agency supervisor Theresa Gabriel to my very own surprise as I walked out of the very same building I saw my son mother whose name was Elite Windgate as she was holding our young son Romeo Windgate-Devine in her arms as I asked her just what was she still doing her?

And from there my son mother Elite hand told me that she thought that our son Romeo Jr. and my one hour weekly session that I was attending wasn't enough time for me to be spending with our son Romeo Jr. as she said that she began to realized that my son Romeo Jr. and I need even more time spend together to have any extended quality father and son family time bonding with each other. So from there my son Romeo Jr. mother Elite also complained that she was getting rather very tiresome having to bring in our child one day a week as she also made the suggestion that if I would cancel our Jamacia Queens New York family court case as she claimed that she would voluntary let me see our son Romeo Jr. at my family home in the Astoria, Queens New York area. And from there I agreed with here as I also taking my son Romeo Jr. and his mother Elite Windgate back to their Long Island City townhouse and she along with our baby boy Romeo Jr. and I entered back into their family townhouse as we just sat and talked with each other as I was visiting with our son a little more the actual one hour child prevention abuse supervise visitation visit. And as we still official attended the Midtown child abuse prevention center in the midtown office just until I was able to take off a day of work as Elite and I were told by the child prevention services supervisor whose name was Theresa Gabriel on our very next and last visit of August 18, 2001, that she herself known that my son mother and I were secretly seeing each outside of my child prevention supervise visitation classes as she told us both that the agency always send their very own staff member out to have the parents who have a family court of child abuse just to see where they were to be going and to also to have them all very closely monitor to make sure the parent are not partaking in any criminal activity of any kind and she also sad if we were going to not follow the child abuse prevention rules and regulations that was giving to us both to not have the child parents around each other during the child abuse prevention classes for the reasoning to avoid any physical conflict of any kind and from there it was suggested that we stop wasting the legal system time and handle my son mother and my very own family issues on our very own.

And from there on that very same day as Elite still be waiting outside the child abuse prevention agency as she also told me that we got ourselves caught sneaking around still seeing each other as one family as she giggly laugh. And I told her that on a serious note that as it was agreed upon the very two of us that I would cancel out our family court case only if I could still have my son Romeo Jr. independently on my very own while he was to always be visiting my family home in Astoria New York. And from there my son mother Elite Windgate said that she was agreeing to my request and from there I again taking my son Romeo Jr. and his mother Elite Windgate back to the Long Island City New York townhouse home. And from there after we all arrived back at my son Romeo Windgate-Devine and his mother Elite Windgate townhouse home as I spend a few hours with them and their immediate family members household and shortly after that I giving my toddler son a very huge hug to tell him that I would see him the very next weekend.

on the very next weekend day of August 27, 2001, I called the mother of my child Elite Windgate to see just how she and our little son Romeo Windgate-Devine was doing as I was told that they were both doing quite fine with each other and from there I said that was great news for me to hear. And very shortly after that I asked my son mother Elite Windgate was our baby boy Romeo Jr. ready to pay his other side of the family a good lovable short weekend visit? And from there the mother of my only child Elite Windgate told me well occurse and that I to asked him first of all. And from there I said okay and that sound like good news for me to hear, as I also asked her to please put our son Romeo Jr. on the telephone so I may asked him if in fact he was ready to visit his grand ma Jahtayshia and grandpa Damian Sr.?

And from there my young son Romeo Windgate-Devine told me that yes Daddy and that as he also continued to say that he would be more ready whenever I was to stop by his other family town house home in the Long Island City New York City area and from there I told him that I was on my very own way to see him so that I may pick him up to take him to my very own side of the family home in the Astoria, Queens New York area as I said that I would be there in a little while and from there I was on my way there to pick up my son. And once I arrived back into my son Romeo Jr. and his mother Elite Windgate Long Island City New York townhouse home my little baby boy Romeo Windgate-Devine been so much very happy to see me as he said "hello there Dadeo" as he told me that he miss me so very much so as he also said that he was ready to go over to pay his other side of his family a nice family weekend visit. from there my son mother Elite Windgate sat me down for a few minutes to say that she wanted me to be very much so careful not to let anything happen to our little baby boy Romeo Jr. And from there I told her that she could trust me that our child little baby boy Romeo Jr. would be just fine and from there I also told her that if I needed any assistant with him my mother Jahtayshia Devine was always there to give me a helping hand.

And shortly after that my son Romeo Jr. and I was on our very own way out of his Long Island City New York townhouse home as the two of us as father and son was on our very way for the very first time without me having to have his mother Elite Windgate standing over my very own shoulder just as she used to being way to much over protective and non trusting on me to probably care for our son just as good as she possibly could. when little baby Romeo Jr. and I arrived by a Queens New York taxi cab service as we rang my parents door bell and from there once my parents Damian Sr. and Jahtayshia Devine let myself and there youngest baby grandson Romeo Windgate-Devine in there Astoria New York family household we both been welcomed in with multiple family hugs and kisses as we all did plenty of our close family bonding with each other as my parents also decided to have a nice small family cookout in the backyard of the family household as it been all good from there as it lasted all night long. back in weekend day of September 5, 2001, while I yet another fatherly parental visit with my young son Romeo Windgate-Devine along with the rest of my immediate family members and very shortly after that my son mother Elite Windgate given me a telephone call to see just how things were going on with our son while he been visiting with my side of the family. And from there I told her that things were going quite well as I further explained that our child along with his step-aunts Tameka and Fatima Devine were all bonding so very nicely together as they were just playing with their toys. From there my son's mother Elite said that was great for her to hear that the kids were getting along so very well together. Very soon after that my son's mother Elite Windgate started to verbally sexual flirt with me as she told me that she miss seeing me with our son little baby Romeo Jr. just bonding together just like we used to as a good family. And from there Elite asked me if I miss her very much so?

And from there I told her no absolutely not from there my son mother Elite Windgate verbally began to beg for me to take her back into my life so that she and I right along with our young son Romeo Jr. could once again be a very close family again just as we once were. So from there, I eventually given into her request to once again start back an intimate relationship with each other and from there she been so very happy that I accepted her back into my life that she said that she was on her very way over to my family home in the Astoria, Queens, New York area to see me and our son Romeo Jr. along with the rest of my family members. And shortly after that when my son Romeo Jr. and his mother Elite once again show up back at my family household in the Astoria, Queens New York area as she rang my family doorbell as I myself let her back inside my family home as Elite once again said her hello's to me and all of my immediately household family members as we all sat ourselves down together to once again to start over as a good family toward one another. And soon after the weekend was over with after my son Romeo Windgate-Devine and his mother Elite Windgate left out of my family neighborhood of Astoria, Queens New York to go back to there very own neighborhood in the Long Island City New York City townhouse home as we said our good byes for now to each other.

And shortly after that my two parents of my father whose name is Damian Devine Sr. and my mother Jahtayshia sat me down to asked me just why I allowed my son mother Elite Windgate back into our family household? And from there I explained to them both well the very reason why was as I explained was because my son mother Elite

Windgate verbally began to beg and plead with me to let the two of us get back together with one another as I went on to also to tell them both that I guest that she thought that it would be in the both of our very best interest to stay together in a intimate relationship no matter how dysfunctional she may made it just so we both would not have to be alone. And from there my mom and dad and started to laugh as they said that what ever works for the two of us is okay with the both of them.

said her hello's to me and all of my immediated household family members as we all sat ourselves down together to once again to start over as a good family toward one another. And soon after the weekend was over with after my son Romeo Windgate-Devine and his mother Elite Windgate left out of my family neighborhood of Astoria, Queens New York to go back to there very own neighborhood in the Long Island City New York City townhouse home as we said our good byes for now to each other.

And shortly after that my two parents of my father whose name is Damian Devine Sr. and my mother Jahtayshia sat me down to asked me just why I allowed my son mother Elite Windgate back into our family household? And from there I explained to them both well the very reason why was as I explained was because my son mother Elite Windgate verbally began to beg and plead with me a whole lot to let the two of us to get ourselves back together with one another as I went on to also to tell them both that I guest that she thought that it would be in the both of our very best interest to stay together in a intimate relationship no matter how dysfunctional she may made it just so we both would not have to be alone. And from there my mom and dad and started to laugh as they said that what ever works for the two of us is okay with the both of them. on September 7 of the year of 2001 as I still felt so very good about myself as far professional speaking that I finally gotten myself out of that very crazy conspiracy midtown Manhattan corporate law firm exemployer that was called the O'Conner, Sapp, Dash & Marshall LLP and into another international company that was called the Resolution Outlook Resources as I thought that since the New York City public stopped acknowledging me as I used to also see many people began to bowed there heads to me as a way to let me know that they once feared me of possibly being apart of a New York Mafia family just like my two parents Jahtayshia and Damian Sr. used to do so.

And as my brand-new work environment felt so very so much comfortable for me to work among with my brand-new mailroom management team that consisted of my mailroom lady manager whose name was Stephanie Spreewell along with the department Assistant manager whose name was Maxwell Dabree and the department supervisor whose name was Craig Colon. And from there I also meet my mailroom support staff team former coworkers members whose name were Brassford Devoe, Marlone Evans and Norman Jefferson as the three of the guys accepted me in the department to be just like one of there very own. And from there I was introduced to the ladies of my new employer groups as there name were Kiley Allwood, Bernadette Mc Bean and Sheems Shutts wright along with my favorite two female coworkers whose name were Charmagne Pavlick who told me that she was oldest sister of Charletta Pavlick who was the younger sister of there own family and from there I thought that she was so very much beautiful enough for me to think about me wanting to marry at least the younger sister of the two of them both because she was a nice looking plus size woman that I wished to have the very good chance to become much more better aquated with her if I been given the very good chance to love and even adore her it would make me so very much happy to began a brand-new intimate and romantic relationship instead of me having to still depend on my son mother whose name is Elite Windgate.

And from there as I remembered just how happy I was back as I been thinking that how all of my former employer of corporate law firm that was called the O'Conner, Sapp, Dash & Marshall LLP New York and there New York corporate conspiracy company must of been finally over with as I was thinking as I started to go back to working back into a very peaceful employee environmental surrounding instead of having me to also here of my previous employer of a very false slanderous rumerous lies about me to be very much apart of one of the New York City mafia crime family as I never liked to hearing those very bad things that was said about me to possibly be some kind of professional thief that was just trying to extort money from my former employer as I always thought that maybe some of my former coworker of mine way to much of a vivid of there very own imagination to make up such a non truthful story such as that ludacris one.

So as my latest former employer of The Resolution Qutlook Resources kepted me so very much so very business as my responsibilities were to run all domestic and international mail peaces through there company mail posted machine as I prepared it all to to be shipped out for the United States post office services. once the work week of September through seven through twelve finally ended I was own my very own way to start to enjoy a very nice weekend with my two sided family members. Around the time of December 23, 2001, just a few days before the Christmas Day Holliday Season at it also been time to began to start to prepare for the office party at my former employer office of The Resolution Outlook Resources as I felt so very much comfortable enough to give my son Romeo Windgate-Devine and his very own mother Elite Windgate a telephone call to invited them both up to joined us all and from there my child mother said that they would love to join in on the fun time at my employer office party. And when my family of my son Romeo Windgate-Devine and his mother Elite finally arrived at my corporate employer at the company that was called The Resolution Outlook Resources LLC I welcomed them both with me showing them my very bright a lovable smile as we said our hellos to one another. from there I taking the good liberty to properly introduced my two family members to my favorite female coworkers whose name was Khadine Pavlick and her slightly older sister whose name was Charmagne Pavlick and as the slightly younger sister of the two introduced themselves to my son Romeo Jr. and his mother Elite Windgate as they said there hellos to my child as both of the Pavlick sister felt so very warm a fussy enough to give son there multiple huge hugs of sorts as my son mother whose name is Elite Windgate never any ideal at all that I was attracted to one of my female coworker who just so happen to be Khadine Pavlick way back.

once my former employer at the office Christmas party finally started as the entire employees of The Resolution Outlook Resources support staff members along with my very own family members of my little son Romeo Jr. and his mother Elite Windgate and I walked ourselves right into the company main conference room meeting area. And from there as the office party began as we all a very delicious buffet of a steak, chicken and seafood shrimp, rice, a bake potatoes dinner that my son Romeo Jr. and his mother Elite Windgate and I really enjoyed so very much so. from there all of the merry Christmas Holliday party gotten started as came out good old saint Nick that was other wise known as Santa Clause who happen to actual be my office coworker mail clerk mate whose name was

Brasford Devoe just playing the very good role play. And from there as it been time for my son Romeo Windgate-Devine to step up to sit on good old Santa Claus lap as my coworker professional associate asked my child well there good child just what is your name?

And from there my son Romeo Jr. had been so very much excited as he said that his name was Romeo Jr. And from there the good old jolly Saint Nick of a Saint Clause given my child a very cute little toy pick-up truck for my kid to take his brand-new gift home with him so that he may they start to have a little fun with his brand-new present. And from there I told my little son Romeo Jr. to thank Santa Claus for his very nice and thoughtful gift that he just received from him as they both allowed me to take a picture of them both and from there little Romeo Jr. hand given a great big handsome smile and a huge hug to the Santa Claus as he given him a good old saint Nicholas a gentle handshake. And from there as I remembered, it was all very good times from there as we all just sat around just listening to multiple Christmas songs of sorts as we also enjoyed our selves just sipping from our glasses of pink champagne and egg nook.

And from there as my former employer of The Resolution Qutlook Resources LLC party finally to come to a end as I asked the question of to my assistant mailroom center manager whose name was Maxwell Dabree if he needed my assistance in helping the rest of the office support staff members to help them all to clean up all of the company conference room area? And from there I was told by him that no and that he also said to me that since I brought in my family with me that he also said that it was okay for me to take my son and his mother home as several of he and their other staff members also wished myself and my family to have ourselves a very Merry Christmas and a very Happy New Years together with our family and from there my son Romeo Jr. along with his mother Elite Windgate and I said our very sincere thank you's and good byes as we also wished all of my coworkers to have themselves a very safe and happy holiday season and from there the three of us were on our very own way out from my former employer office building as we headed ourselves straight right back to my son Romeo Jr. and his mother Elite Windgate townhouse home in The Long Island City of the Queens New York area. And from there as we arrived back at my son Romeo Jr. and his mother Elite hometown as we enter back into see my common law family members of the Windgates family as my child grandmother whose name is Wonda Windgate and her youngest daughter whose name is Epiphany Windgate asked us all just how we enjoyed my office Christmas party? And from there my son Romeo Jr., along with his mother Elite and myself as well said that we all had a very good time with our little child having the very good time to have the best chance to finally have the very thoughtful privilege to meet the good old Saint Nicholas or Santa Clause.

And from there my son other grandmother Ms. Wonda along with his oldest aunt Epiphany Windgate giggled and joked around with him as they again called him by there side of there very own family nickname as the always called him cuddles and from there his mother Elite and I just given the family our smiles and laughter's of sorts. shortly that as the Christmas holiday season been upon all of us my son Romeo Windgate-Devine told his mom and I that he was starting to very much miss his other side of our family as he said that he wanted to very so to visit his grandmother Jahtayshia and his grandfather Damian sr. right along with his other two step aunty's whose name is Tameka and Fatima Devine and from there we as both of his parents said that yes that it would be all okay for us to spend some good quality family fun time at his grandparents house in the Astoria, Queens New York area. once myself right along with our son Romeo Jr. and his mother Elite Windgate arrived back at my very own family household as everyone once again been so very much excited to see each other for the entire Merry Christmas holiday and New Years holiday seasons. when the birth of Jesus Christ birthday finally came upon us all we celebrated by having our entire immediate family to just sing out loud to our very hearts contented until whenever felt liked stopping as all of our children awaken up that very same morning to begin to open up there Christmas gifts that we all as there parents told our children that they received those multiple presents from the great saint Nicholas himself that was otherwise known as Santa Clause and our kids plenty of good times just playing around with us all. on December 31, 2001, which so happen to be that year of the New Years Eve Holliday as my mother and father Jahtayshia and Damian Devine Sr. right along with Elite and myself kept our children up for us all to celebrate bringing in the the New Years and when the clock finally strick the hour of 12:00 AM my immediate family and I as my big brother Damian Jr. and his new wife whose name was Tara Devine all began to started to make very happy noises of us all cheering and from there we all began to give each other multiple hugs and kisses on the cheek bones and we once again popped open a very nice chilled bottle of champagne as we said our multiple cheers of joy to one another as we just sat around each other until about 3:00 AM that very same holiday morning of the Happy New Year Day of January 1, 2002.

And once the New Years of January 2 of the year of 2002 finally arrived as I soon return myself right back to my workplace of the Resolution Outlook Resources as I still expected for my work environment to be the very same as I left it as I been making a distribution mailroom clerk run when I saw the company Director of Human Resources whose name is Rita Rite as I greeted her with a friendly hello and a smile as I taking a real good close notice of her very strange behavior of when she taking a very good look at me she all the sudden repeatedly bowed down her head to me and I must say that when I first saw my brand-new employer reaction that very same way as my two parents once did right along with some people from my former home town of the Astoria, Queens New York area I been in totally shock. And as I began to realized that my former employer must gotten a very slanderous words that used to circulate around there very own corporate law firm of O'Conner, Sapp, Dash & Marshall LLP that there was a very slanderous rumor saying they heard about that my former employer were telling all of the New York City public that I could be in fact apart of a New York City organize crime mafia family member that was out to steal away the company money for a criminal profitable gain of sorts right from one of my previous employer job references. I still felt rather troubled that many New Yorkers still known of me as they believed that I was some kind of New York City organize crime mafia gangsters member that was trying to extorted money from my employers at that time as I been very much aware that many people in the big apple been told that they should keep a very close and very watchful eye of me so that anyone who might see me associated with any unlawful criminal as I suspected that several people were probably told if you see something going on with the man Romeo Devine no New Yorker should never even hesitate to say something to there local New York City Police Department, but of course as you might imagined that I was very unpleased with this still disturbing situations.

And once I went back to my family home in the Astoria, Queens New York area as I confided my bad day to my mom and dad that I had at the office of what happen with my employer at The Resolution Qutlook Resources with the company Human Resources director whose name I explained was Rita Rite about how when she said her hello to me as I further explained that the lady bowed down her head to me as a way to acknowledge me about how she must gotten word to her from my other former employer at the corporate law firm that is called the O'Conner, Sapp, Dash & Marshall LLP.

And there my mother Jahtayshia Devine was the one parent who shouted out loud oh no not again Romeo as she asked me just why does this keep on happening to only you? And from there I gotten rather nervous of my mom to be kind of upset with me about my employer corporate conspiracy situation as I told her that the company Human Resources Director whose name I explained was Rita Rite to both of my two parents that the lady must of gotten word to her that she should have my new employer staff members to keep a close and watchful eye on me to see if I am to do any illegal criminal activities of any kind. But I also told my folks that because I raised partially up into the Holly church as I further explained that I was going to start back to going right back to the church in order to pray about all of my devious corporate conspiracy situation of how several employers were spreading the bad slanderous rumerous word around my job that is called The O'Conner, Sapp, Dash & Marshall LLP about how many of my employer were saying that I could very much so be a New York City mafia organize crime gangster member out who was out to steal the company money for a financial criminal gain. And from there both of my parents said son that sounds like a very good ideal for me to do so as they said to me that I should defidently sart to search for a good spiritual church congregation.

And as I returned myself back to my former employer at the corporate place of my employment of The Resolution Outlook Resources as I still founded myself to still be really admiring my former female coworker whose name is Khadine Pavlick as I founded myself to be much more to be attracted to her her older sister whose name is Charmagne Pavlick as the younger sister of the two was more of my type because of her to be the one of the two of them who was the larger and sexy looking body shape figure. And as I than taking the liberty to become much more better aquated with them both as in the Pavlick sisters informed me that they were both faith worshipers of the good almighty God himself. So from there even though I was previous devilious acknowledge by our employer at the company of The Resolution Outlook Resources by the Human Resources Director whose name was Rita Rite I still felt comfortable enough to still accept a church invitation that I received from my two former female coworkers Charmagne and Khadine Pavlick who told me that they were sisters who also lived together as they also informed me that they were very so spiritual worshipers of the good God almighty himself as they seemed to be so very sweet and friendly toward me way back. The older sister who was Charmagne Pavlick mostly greeted me with a very warm and cuddly huge of a lengthy embrace of sorts more her younger sister Khadine Pavlick who I founded myself to be more attracted to her as I felt like she was the prettiest of the two Pavlick sisters.

So from there the older Pavlick sister whose name is Charmagne and I exchanged our home telephone # with each other as she also giving me there church address that she said was located in the Kew Garden Queens New York area and from there I told her that was a great and very thoughtful ideal for her to being giving me such a nice and wonderful invitation to there church as I said my thank you's to her. And from there I even told both of my female former coworkers Charmagne & Khadine Pavlick that I was going to be bringing along my young son Romeo Jr. who they previously meet at the company of our employers of The Resolution Outlook Resources Christmas party right along with my two younger stepsisters whose name I explained was Tameka and Fatima Devine. And from there my now former female workers who were also sisters at birth whose name was Charmagne And Khadine Pavlick told me that sounded all so very much so good to them as they also told me they would see me on January 16, 2002, of there Sunday morning spiritual worship church service. when my young son Romeo Jr. and my two younger adopted stepsisters whose name were name are Tameka and Fatima Devine finally arrived at my former female coworkers of Charmagne and Khadine Pavlick church congregation that was located in there neighborhood of Kew Garden Queens New York section they greeted my family and I with a very warm and friendly embraced as we all sat ourselves down right next to one another as we been listening to our good almighty Godly spiritual word to to be preached among us all.

And shortly after the Kew Garden church worship service was over with as I asked my former female coworker who was still employed right along with me at our worked place of The Resolution Qutlook Resources as I decided to ask Charmagne and Khadine Pavlick if they would like to join my family and I for some delicious lunch? And from there my to female coworkers told me no as they also had continued to explained to me that they both had some after church service business that they to attend to as the Pavlick sister of Khadine Pavlick informed me that the reason why she could not join us all was because she was the church pastor secretary which so happen to be both of her and her older sister Charmagne father. And from there I been a little disappointed that we could not have any good chance to closely bonding time together to see if that Khadine Pavlick and I could possibly have a close intimate love connection of some kind to the point that I was hoping that she and I could one day be able to be possibly to one day to to being getting marriage to one another. And very shortly after that I told my former coworkers of the Resolution Outlook Resources that I totally understood what they just told me as I also said from there that I would see them both in our office workplace the very day of January 17, 2002.

And when I returned back to my former midtown Manhattan workplace on January 18, 2002, of my former employer at the company of The Resolution Outlook Resources as I saw and spoken to Khadine and Charmagne Pavlick as I first talked about just how very much so that me and my family really did in fact really did enjoyed my former female coworkers Holly Worship Christian Praise church service and from there the two sisters thanked me for attending in The Kingdom house of the Lord. And from there it was Charmagne Pavlick who stood herself up to give me a big warm embrace of a huge hug while Khadine just sat herself there in her desk chair as she also said her hello to me. And I must say that I was rather disappointed that I did not received any kind of a affectionate embrace from Khadine Pavlick instead of her slightly older sister who was Charmagne Pavlick and soon after that I told the two beautiful women as I continued on to do my distribution mail clerk run around the office that I would see them both later doing our work day. So when I returned back to the company 9 th mail room center my former coworkers Braseford William and Norman Jefferson asked me well there Romeo just how was your weekend? And from there I told them both that I had a very bless weekend with the two of our fe-male coworkers who just so happen to be Khadine and Charmagne Pavlick.

And from there my two former mail center coworkers mailroom clerks Brasford and Norman began to start to laugh and teas about how I was becoming rather very much to sweetly attractive to start to admire my female coworkers Khadine Pavlick. So after I laugh right along with those two guys I admitted to them both that I was very much attracted to one of the Pavlick sisters as I explained that it was Khadine Pavlick who I had a romantic interest in and from there my two mail center coworkers began to laugh at me as they said that man I just don't know about you Romeo. Shortly after that I taken very close notice just how my new latest employer coworkers attitude toward me suddenly started to change toward me as the three guys whose name were Norman Jefferson, Brassford Devoe and Marlone Evans as they began to all of a sudden some what of a bad tempered attitude toward me with out me to not even give them any reason at all to do so and from there I tried to figure out just why. So on about January 24 of the year of 2002 as I felt that I still needed to be prayed for as I asked my two stepsisters Tameka and Fatima if they in facted wanted to accompany me right back to my female coworkers church of Charmagne and Khadine Pavlick church service?

And from there my youngest stepsister whose name is Fatima Devine said that no and as she also went on to say that was enough religious holly worship service for her for now and my other sweet younger older stepsister whose name is Tameka Devine also told me no as she told me that she would also would not be attending my lady coworker friend Charmagne and Khadine Pavlick christen Christian Worship of Parayers church service in the Kew Garden section of the Queens New York area. from there I also called my son Romeo Jr., back at his and his mother town house home to hear if he wanted to spend yet another weekend with his Daddy and as I spoken to him he told me no Daddy and as he also went on to explained that he felt like he was much so to very too tired to come along with me as he also told me while I was to still be going there as he asked me to please very much so pray for him and from there I told him indeed I most certainly will do so my son and from there I told him that I love him with all of my heart and soul my son and he told me that he would always love me to as he called me by the nickname that he giving me which is Dadeo and I told him that I would soon speak to him later on during that very same day and from there I so after left out the door as I was on my very way out to yet another Christian Worship of Parayers church service. And from when I arrived back at my former female coworkers of The Population Qutlook Resources whose name were Charmagne and Khadine Pavlick church service as I once again greeted them both at the church congregation that was called The Holly Worship of Praise in the Kew Garden New York section of Queens New York as I sat ourselves right down right next to the both of them as they asked me just wear were my son Romeo Jr. and my two little stepsister Tameka and Fatima that day? And from there I told them both that they all had decided to not to attend that particular weekend as I said that it was just me this time around that would be joining them all.

And after the church service was very so much over with there was a man who repeatedly kept on asking me the question of just how did I enjoy there Holly church congregation service? And from there I told the man that I thought that the spiritual preaching service going so very well that very blessed day. And from there that same very strangely religious man also kept on repeatedly asking me if I well kept on kept on coming back to there church of Holly worship? And from there I suspected that something was up with that man very strange attitude as he repeatedly kept right on repeating himself to me and from I answer to him to say yes and that I told him that I love there Holly Worship Of Praise that I indeed was planning to also planning to pay them all yet another visit for yet another church service and from there I told my coworkers Charmagne and Khadine Pavlick that I would see them both in our employer office at The Resolution Outlook Resources on the very next business work day of January 25, 2002, and from there they they waved there hands to me as they said to me okay there Romeo as they also went on to say that would see me there in the office and from there I left out there holly place of there worship.

once I returned back to my former place of my employment of The Population Qutlook Resources as I been making yet another distribution mailroom service mail clerk run as I taking my mail cart around the company tenth floor as I saw my two female coworkers who were Khadine and Charmagne Pavlick as I said my hello's to them both as this time they seemed to very much annoyed with me that as there was a Spanish guy who was also apart of the company support staff team whose name was was Pedro Artez as the three of them all were in a very deep conversation of I overheard the younger Pavlick sister tell him that she was getting rather very sick and tired of me to kept on showing up attending at there family church holly worship service because she also said that the only reason why I kept on showing up at there family church service was because she went on to continue to tell her coworker male friend that she was very well much aware that the guy Romeo Devine was very much attracted to her as she also said that she discovered that actual fact from the two of the company of The Resolution Outlook Resources two mailroom clerks were name Brasford Devoe and Norman Jefferson and from there she went on to even say out loud that she wanted nothing to do with me ever again outside of the workplace. soon after that my male coworker whose name was Pedro Artez called me over to his desk side to talked to me about how our female coworker who was Khadine Pavlick told him to tell me that I better back myself off from visiting her and her sister Charmagne church service every again before she and her family members would fine someway to try to somehow want to have me arrested possible someway. And from there I told my coworker Pedro Artez that it was okay by me to keep it all on a very professional level with the two Pavlick sisters of Charmagne and Khadine. from there I once again heard about my old corporate conspiracy problematic situation how all of my employer at The Population Qutlook Resources heard about just how everyone in the New York City area knew about how the word was out that all of of the big apple should keep a close and watchful eye to see if I was unlawfully involved with any New York City organized crime family activities of any kind to do some sort of criminal racketeering unlawfulness that might could be brought up against me to possibly have me place in a New York City prison.

So from there on January 25, 2002, I realized that even though my former female coworkers who was Charmagne and Khadine Pavlick were than claiming to be real true Christians of our almighty God and savior I really felt that the two of them were all a bunch of fakes and fony type of people right along with there unholy church congregation as they never accepted me as the very fact was that I was trying to desperately trying to fine a good Holy christen church to try to join as I only saw them all as a bunch of fake a fony worshiper of a Christian belief if they could not see and believe just how much of a loving and caring type person that lam toward all good people. So from there I just focus on just doing my mailman clerk center responsibilities of making my multiple hand deliveries as I would be sending out all company of The Resolution Outlook Resources mailings of sorts in order to properly provide for myself as we as my young son Romeo Windgate-Devine (other wise known as to my very own immediate family members as little Romeo Jr.) Although my former female coworkers of Khadine and Charmagne Pavlick never did finally accepted me into there immediate family the slightly older sister wanted to remain to still be rather friendly toward me with her to still having herself to embrace me with a warm huge and a sweet smile of her very own. on about January 27, 2002, I started to develop some romantic feelings toward the company older sister whose name is Charmagne Pavlick instead of her younger sister Khadine the oldest sister seemed to be the kindness of the two with a much more sweeter personality.

One day of January 28, 2002, my former female coworker who used to work with me at the corporate non profitable organization of The Resolution Outlook Resources whose name was Charmagne Pavlick once tried to convince me of how a much smaller woman is so much better than a bigger one as she placed my two hands on her abdomen so that I may feel and see the difference as she proceeded to display to me her firm stomach muscles. And from there she tried to also convince me that I should stop focusing on me always wanting to be intimately involved with the much larger type of a women and she also said that I should learn just how to appreciate a woman with a smaller sexier size such as herself. And about two days later of January 30, 2013, of my former female coworker who been of our former employer of The Resolution Outlook Resources as she was apart of the company Information Technology Department as it was her sole responsibility to maintain the maintenance of our employer telecommunication department telephones services. And it would be sometimes whenever she was to to see me began to to start sweating a whole lot she herself who make a small workplace display to take it upon very own herself to wiped down my face and forehead with some soft perfume scented tissues as she take it upon her very own self to even tuck in my shirt right into my pants trousers sometimes when it would need to be done. And very shortly after that my former female coworker whose name is Charmagne Pavlick kept on being a little bit to much overly concern about me as the rest of the company staff members began to verbally harass the both of she and I as the other employees who was annoying us both because as I heard some of the other employees staff members talking about how they did approve of the ideal for the two us to be thinking about becoming intimately involved with each other in some kind of romantic office romance of any kind because it was also talked amongst my former employer at The Resolution Outlook Resources that how they heard all about what was supossitely going on at my previous employer at the corporate law firm of The O'Conner, Sapp, Dash & Marshall LLP of just how the word was going around the office and The entire New York area of just how I might be apart of a major New York mafia organize crime family.

soon after that as I was still very much so still trying to still to to the very best of my own capability to performing my duties as one of the company of The Resolution Outlook Resources inter-office mailman as I was really trying not to show any of my office mate any of my emotional feeling as I found myself to need to take a immediate bathroom break as I would find myself to having myself to start to began to crying multiple tears of sadness because I was starting to develop some intimate feeling toward my former female coworker who was Charmagne Pavlick and this time around I didn't even feel as if I was intentally being infatuation to have my coworker to try to keep me in a calm behavioral manner but I eventually pulled myself together as I gotten myself back to the company business as usually as one of the company New York inter-office mailman. on January 30, 2002, as it been a very busy day in the non profitable office of my former employer of the company that is called The Resolution Outlook Resources as I been taking on the 9th floor mailroom responsibilities of just trying to hand sort out and make my hand deliveries that was supposed to been shared by my other mailroom clerk whose name was Bradsford Williams as he was usually the lazy type of a guy that I considered to be a slacker that was mostly off the job on while as he wouldn't always take on his very fair share of the mailroom center work load. And as there would be multiple times when the mailroom center assistance manager whose name was Maxwell Dabree would began to start to complain about why the company mailroom center work load was becoming overloaded with piles of mail pieces that was spread out around all over our workplace area? And from there I explained to my mailroom center assistant manager that even though it was rather much so very busy at that particular time in our department as I complained that my other departmental mailroom center coworker who was Brasford William was being totally a lazy employee that left me must of the heavy work load to do for sometime 1/4 of our job work day load. And from there my former mailroom center assistant manager whose name is Maxwell Dabree told me that he would try to get me some assistance because he told me that he had my departmental 9th floor mailroom center coworker who was actual Brasford Devoe run out to have him to do something that was very personal for him and from there I said to him please be sure that he defiantly was to send someone else to help me with the mailroom center much heavy work load responsibilities and from there I was told that yes and that someone would be in to help me just as soon as soon as someone was available for me. And very shortly after that my former mailroom assistance manager Maxwell Dabree left out of the 9 th floor mailroom center area as I continued on to sort and send out my employer company United States and International mailings of The Resolution Outlook Resources non profitable organization but no one still never even show up to give me a much need helping hand. And as the very same thing just kept on happening with my departmental 9 th floor mailroom center coworker whose name was Brasford Devoe with him still not to constantly being there to help me out to carry on both of our mailroom center responsibilities there were many of the other support staff members who came into my workstation area as they than began to start complaining to me just why I didn't have my mail clerk coworkers to come and help me with some of the company mailroom work? And from there I just told a few of the staff members who were two ladies whose name were Hedi Dean and Harriette Tates that my 9 th mailroom center partner who was Brasford Devoe was running some kind of a very personal errand for our company mailroom center assistant manager who was Maxwell Dabree. And from there the two ladies told me as they said in said in a professional and personal speaking of the matter that was at hand was that the only reason why my mailroom center coworker whose name was Brasford Devoe was getting away with him to avoid his job responsibilities was because it was explained to me that the assistant mailroom manager whose name was Maxwell Dabree and my 9th floor mailroom center mail clerk whose name is Brasford Devoe grown up as childhood friends together and from there as the two ladies and also went on to say that the entire office of The Resolution Outlook Resources non profitable organization been taking a real good close notice of the one sidedness favoritism that was going on between the two of those two guys.

And from there the two ladies Hedi Dean and Harriette Tates along with a few more other support staff members told me that they were going to make a verbal complaint about me to constantly needing some help with the company mailroom center responsibilities situation. on February 1, 2002, my mother Jahtayshia and Damian Devine Sr. asked me just how things were going on at my latest employers job at The Resolution Outlook Resources non profitable organization? And so from there I told them both that things were not going so very well as I would have normal expected it to be with them all. As I further also explained to my folks that how I was showed some tender loving care by one of my employer at The Resolution Outlook Resources staff members whose name I explained was Charmagne Pavlick as In when there would be sometimes when that particular woman who who would take it upon her very own self to began to wipe down the wet right off of my face with a perfume scented tissue as well as to take the very liberty to even tucked in my shirt right into my pants.

And from there my father Damian Devine Sr. began to start to laugh at what I just told him. And from there I I further also told him to wait a minute as I continued on to tell him the rest of the story about how that there was more to the story for me to tell them both about after that happen between the both of my female coworker whose name I once again explained wa Charmagne Pavlick as I further told them that there was some of the company who did not aprove of that very same woman and I having to be much to close in a friendship with one another simply because it was talked about among the other employer support members about how they learned about just what one of my previous employer at the corporate midtown Manhattan law firm that is called The O'Conner,

Sapp, Dash & Marshall LLP about how all of the New Yorkers should start to keep a very close and watchful eye on me to see if I would be up to no good at all while it was said that I could have been associate with a New York City mafia crime gangster family of some very find. And from there my two parents Jahtayshia and Damian Sr. Devine turned around and said that after hearing me tell all of the job drama that I was going through as they felt rather threaten by me going through all of that as they called it that unnecessary problem as they both began to threaten me about if there was any even the slightness truth of what my employer was saying about me of me to possibly be apart of a New York City mafia gangster family of any dam kind as he also said that I might have to put a folding bed in our family garage for me to sleep into there just until I was very shortly after that find myself a brand-new apartment place to live in as it was insanely warned that if any thing was to ever happen to there two young daughters who are Tameka and Fatima Devine as threaten me that they would also hurt me in some bad way. And from there I began to beg my mother and father Jahtayshia and Damian Sr. Devine to not to throw me out in the the family back yard into the garage area or to even think about hurting me in anyway possible as I began to start to weeping of tears as I said please believe me mom and dad lam not a New York City mafia gangster of any kind at all as I further also explained to the both of them again that it was a very insane and ridiculous of a slanderous rumor that was started by one of my former mailman center coworker who actual name just so happen to be lack Casey who

And from there my folks said to me okay and that they both also went on to tell me that I better not because they also said that they did not want any kind of trouble from any of my employer mentally disturbing situation, and from there I just told them both okay and as I also thanked them both for them to continuously allowing me to current living situation to remain the very exact same way as it always been at that particular time and place of my residence in my parents home in the Astoria, Queens New York area and from there I given my folks a very warm embrace of a huge hug as I also taken it upon myself to kiss my mother Jahtayshia Devine on her right sided facial cheek area? And from there I said that since I had another much stressful work related day at my place of employment that was called The Resolution Outlook Resources as I continued to also say to them that I was going to called my little son Romeo Jr. and his mother whose name is Elite Windagate just to see just how they were both actually doing with each other at that particular time. And from there my two parents and I said our goodnites to one another as we all taken our very own selves to bed to get a very good night rest until the very next early morning time. on February 8, 2002, my grandmother whose name is Alicia Gilbert paid my immediate family a nice family visit right along with her youngest son whose name is Solomon Gilbert for about two weeks time.

And as I sat down with my grandmother Alicia Gilbert I began to start to complain about how my very own mom and dad Jahtayshia and Damian Sr. Devine been so very much non trusting of me as I also explained to her that I was being very emotionally stress out at my place of my employment that was called the Resolution Outlook Resources about how there was a very slanderes much insane rumor that was going on at my job with many other former coworker people who worked there was saying that I could possibly be a New York City mafia gangster who was sent in by a New York City organize mafia criminal family. And from there I sat there with her as I began to wonder as I also asked my grand ma Alicia Gilbert the question of just why do you think my two parents could even have any doubts about me and not to being very understanding of me to think of me to be a New York City mafia criminal gangster instead of them to always think of me as there very own lovable youngest son? And from there my grandmother Alicia Gilbert just told me that maybe it was my father fault after all who been trying to turn my very own family against me to attempt to make the family believe in such of a foolish slanderous rumor was because as she explained that he himself used to be a type of a young man who used to hang out in the New York City street as she said that she hand used to see him as a little boy just hanging out with several street hustlers himself that was something like a hoodlum. And from there I very sadly complained to my grandmother Alicia Gilbert that why my very own two parents miss treated in a very poor and unlovable manner such like our family outcast of my very own family.

So from there she just told me that maybe my mother and father was just very much confuse and some what very much ashamed of themselves to them admit that they actual believed of all of my employer job situation as my grand ma Alicia Gilbert told me that I should just have a very nice sit down talk with my mom and dad to try to make them understand that you (as in my very self) am definitely not a New York City mafia gangster of any kind and as she also continued to say to me that I should just tell both that I will always love them both very much with all of my heart and soul. And from there I told my grandmother Alicia Gilbert that sounded like a very good ideal for me to do just as she instructed me to do so and from there I kiss her on both sides of her facial cheeks as I also thanked her from the very bottom of my heart and soul for the very wise words of wisdom that she giving onto me. And from there I just did just what my grandmother Alicia Gilbert suggested for me to do as I sat both down of my mother and father Jahtayshia and Damian Devine Sr. to have a good nice long talk about my employer problems that I was having with my former place of employments. So from there I told them both that it seemed as if they both for sometime now started to think about me as if I was a actual possibly New York City mafia criminal gangster who they started to also become very much fearful and paranoid by acknowledging me by bowing there heads and turning there very own bodies to the household wall all because I on several occasions confided with them both as I told them both about how there was a very slanderously and very insane rummerous lies that was started by one of my former company mailroom center coworker whose name I explained was Stone Casey.

And once I explained to them both that under no circumstances at all lam I any kind of actual New York City mafia gangster at all. My parents told me that they were very much already aware of that fact as they further went on to tell me that that will always love me no matter what and from there I thanked them both for being so very much loving and understanding toward me. And from there my two parents of my father Damian Sr. and my mother Jahtayshia Devine along with her very own mother whose name is Alicia Gilbert (AKA) my dear sweet grand mama as I giving her that very nickname my very own self as we all a big family warm family embrace of a family circular hugs as we also said that we love each other all so very much so and from there we shared yet another delicious family lunch and later on that very same evening we also enjoyed a nice family dinner as we even said a good family holly spiritual prayer at our family table and very soon after that we all began to start our very close family feasting of sorts.

on Valentine Day of February 14 of the year of 2002 which was once again my young son Romeo Windagate-Devine 2 year old birthday as his mother whose name is Elite Windgate giving me a telephone call to ask me just how should we celebrate another of our little baby boy big day? And from there I asked my mother and father Jahtayshia and Damian Devine Sr. if we could throw a little party for there little grandson Romeo Jr? And from there my two parents said that yes and that it would be just fine and dandy to do so just as long as my son mother Elite and I were to keep a very close and watchful eye on all of there grandson Romeo Jr. guest that were going to be attending. from there my son Romeo Jr. mother whose name is Elite Windgate started to make a small guest list of my family good neighboring friends who our son been friends with that consisted of Jerry Ramous who again been accompanied by his two parents who were Willimeana and Alfonso Ramous along with some other friend of our family who were Louie and his wife Aretha Nicholas as when they all arrived for our back to back yearly birthday party for our adorable birthday boy. And from there we yet another birthday very special surprise 2 guests for the little kiddy's of ours as it was yet another surprise knock on our family household door and from there everyone there I said well there I wonder just who could it be knocking on the door at this time of the evening?

And from there to the childrens very surprise it was two Morphine Power Rangers who appeared in our family living room and from there they put on such a great and fantastic lazor sword show for us all to to enjoy as it turned out to be so very much exciting for all of our kids and even the rest of us parents to the very point that non of us didn't even seemed to even want the exciting show to never end as all of the kids right along with all of us parents cheer the Morphine Power Ranger lazer show on by just cheering and clapping of our hands together to show our entertainment just how much we appreciate them both so very much so for gracing our family presents. And shortly after that our entertainment guest began to pass out some of there surprise gifts of some plastic multi colored lazer lights and it seemed like all of the kids there liked the show so very much so that they decided to call on the Mighty Morphine Power Rangers to give them both a warm and friendly hugs and shortly after that our mighty heroes where on there very way out of our family door way to save the world from unwanted evil doer danger. (laugh out loud).

soon after that we also sang the tradition happy birthday song to our guest of honor which was Elite Windgate and my very own son Romeo Windgate-Devine as we very shortly after that we all brought out a Mexican Pinyata that was of course very much so filled up with multiple favorable candies for our children to start to enjoy as our child very own mother and I lifted him up from our family living floor so that he may cracked open the horse shape artificial pony sugary tasteful treats. And from there shortly after that we thanked all of our neighborhood friends of the Astoria, Queens New York area and very soon after that our guest left our family home to tend to there very own families of sorts as we all said our good byes and good nites to each other. And soon as our guest left for that very same lovely and exciting evening I had yet another special romantic surprise just waiting for my once again common law wife Ms Elite Windgate as we said our I hope that we all have a good and very restful good night wishes to each other as we all left off of out of our family living and dinning room area to start to began to head to our very own bedrooms.

And from there I taking my son little Romeo Jr. and his mother whose name is Elite Windgate right straight back downstairs to my family basement apartment were I once lived in to began to start our small but very romantic celebration on the most romantic day of the year which is February 14, 2002, by presenting my again common law wife Elite Windgate with some long steamed red roses, a red hearted shaped box of assorted cadies along with me to also bring out a chilled pink bottle of non alcoholic champagne for just the two of us to to enjoy as our young son little Romeo Jr. hand even gotten himself some good and tasty chocolate treats that we both shared with him and very shortly after that we gotten ourselves ready for our bed time as we also wished each other to have ourselves a very good nights restful sleep time until the very next morning time was to arrive the next following day. And about 2 days later my common law wife whose name is Elite Windgate and I right along with our 2 year old whose name is Romeo Windgate-Devine gotten our very selves up on the very next morning time of February 15, 2002, to once again joined my immediate family for some little small talk very private time as we also enjoyed yet another delicious breakfast time for us all back. very much soon after that my common law wife/mother of my child Elite Windagate told me that she was going to be starting to working at her brand-new employer place of employment that was called The Gentleman Fashionable Tuxcedos Warehouse. So very soon after we told my two parents Jahtayshia and Damian Sr. Devine that we both to be on our very way back to my common law wife Elite and son Romeo Jr. townhouse home back in the Long Island City New York area.

And from there my common law wife Elite Windgate also informed me that she to get herself up the very next morning time as said to me that her very own mother who was Ms. Wonda Windgate had a very busy day that she previous planned for her own very self and from there my son Romeo Jr. mother Elite Windgate asked me if I could come over to her family townhouse home that was located in the Long Island City section of the Queens New York City section to baby sit our young son? And from there I agreed that I would stay over for a short period of time as we informed my immediate family members that my son Romeo Jr. and his mother whose name is Elite Windgate right along with my very own self that we were on our way out of our family home in the Astoria, Queens New York area as I also told them all that we were headed back to my common law family townhouse household which was the Windgate family of the Long Island City New York area. And as we once again said our goodbyes for now to one another as we were on our very way out of my family doorway area. once we all gotten ourselves there as we hand said our very hello's to my son Romeo Jr. and his mother Elite Windgate family back into the Long Island City area as we all greeted each other with a warm and friendly huge and hello's as I was to spend a few nights with my common law family of the Windgate family.

on February 16, 2002, as I was just visiting for a very short length of time as I been baby sitting my young son Romeo Windgate-Devine for only a few days when I began to notice that my common law wife Elite Windgate much younger sister whose name is Epiphany Windgate began to start to sexual teasing me whenever her much older sister who is also the mother on my son Elite Windgate wasn't looking around in the family living room area by shaking her own buttocks body parts right in front of there family television area while been watching one of my very entertaining action pack shows as she was performing a booty clap dance as she also taking the sweet and sexy looking liberty to sStoneed that fat round rump shaker of hers just right in front of me as I began to also start to get a very firm sexual arousal of her all of her sexual tease of a show that she was putting on for me as her nephew father which is me Romeo Devine. And from after seeing my common law sister in-law Epiphany Windgate act in such a very sexual manner such as she used to I must admit that at that particular time and place I been in totally shock of what just happen right in front of me as I must say that situation also kind of made me a little nervous just with me knowing that my son Romeo Jr. was just in the very next room with his grandma Ms. Wonda Windgate as well as my son mother Elite Windgate been in her very own family kitchen area while she been preparing our family hearty dinner meal of chicken breast with pasta shells with Parmesan Alfredo sauces and a small seafood delicious serving of Octupuss along with some sweet and sour sauces. very soon after our family dinner was over with my son mother Elite Windgate prepare herself for her work evening shift as she left out her family Long Island City town house home as she given me and our baby boy Romeo Jr. and quick kiss a huge goodbye for until she was to be leaving out to head to her employer workplace which was called The Gentleman Fashionable Tuxedo Warehouse in The Rockaway Park Queens New York section as her mother also driven her oldest Elite Windgate daughter to her workplace.

from there as I been taking so much very good care of my son Romeo Windgate-Devine as we been just sitting up on his family sofa fold out bed area as we been watching a very humorous comedy show as we been both laughing a hole lot. And very shorty after that it been time for me as my son very proud father to put my very own son Romeo Jr. to sleepy time in his very own bed as we slepted right in his family living room area. on that very same exact evening as my son mother Elite Windgate younger sister whose name is Epiphany Windgate been coming out of her family bathroom shower as I also been at that particular time on my very way to her family kitchen area to get myself a tall glass of ice cold water to cool myself off with a cold drink as I saw my common law sister in-law come right out from the bathroom doorway as when she saw me she herself said to me as she been just standing there in a white wet bathroom large towel that she thinks that she and I should give my and her big sister Elite Windgate and our very own son Romeo Windgate-Devine and half baby sibling/baby cousin to bring into this very big beautiful world of our because she told me that she thought that I myself was so very much sexy and handsome enough looking for me to also want her to also be my baby momma just like her much older sister and soon after that she made that very lovely confession to me about just how she was feeling about me to also to want me to also be her very own baby daddy as she blew me a very sweet and sexy kiss as she just walked herself away as I n't even didn't even giving her any kind of a answers right and there simply because the two women who are my son Romeo Jr. mother Elite and oldest aunt Epiphany Windgate are sisters who were very much so still living together as I been trying to avoid any kind of civil female family possible rivalry between to the two of them. And for the rest of that very same evening as I been watching my son Romeo Jr. just sleeping himself away so very peacefully like as I lay myself down for that very same evening as I tried to figured out just how was I going to be handling my brand-new much to difficult situation of just how I was going to be dealing with the two sisters who are apart of my son Romeo Jr. female family who were my son mother Elite Windgate and his oldest aunt whose name is Epiphany Windgate with them both finding themselves so much very so attracted to me way back in the days.

February 17, 2002, when my common law wife whose name is Elite Windgate returned herself back to her very own family townhouse home in The Long Island City New York as she once again said her hello's to myself and my son Romeo Jr. and the rest of there family members that very same morning. as my now former common law sister in-law whose name is Epiphany Windgate entered there family living room area as she also saw myself sitting right there beside her older sister Elite Windgate and our son Romeo Jr. which is also her only nephew as she seemed at that time to develop a very upset and jealous attitude of sorts to see the three of us all sitting there together as a close nit type family and from there I was rather a little surprise at her slightly mad reaction as she said her hello as she also rolled her eyes at me in a very disappointing manner as I must say that at that exact time I felt so very bad for her as I could show her any kind of affected love at all. So on February 19, 2002, as my common law wife Elite Windgate and I was just sitting ourselves around on the couch area as her much younger now adult sister who was nineteen years of age who was Epiphany just been passing by there family living room area as she was just been entering her family kitchen area as I was told by Romeo Jr. very own mother to take a very good look at Epiphany

Windgate just walking by all three of us all. And from there I said to her yes and that I do definitely do see her as I also asked her just what about her are you asking me about her?

And from there my common law wife Elite Windagate told me to take a real good look at her younger sister Epiphany Windgate very much enormous breast size. And from there that was another very shocking moment to her the mother of my son ask me such a very sexual questions such as that particular one. So from there I asked her just why did she wanted me to take a good enough visual notice of her younger sister Epiphany Windgate? as my common law/mother of child Elite Windgate asked me just which sister did I actual think had the biggest breast bra size? I had a question of my very own to asked her as it was my very own dear common law wife Elite Windgate who is the mother of our child Romeo Jr. just why are you trying to have me to be very much sexual arouse by your much younger sister Epiphany Windgate large frame sexual body shape? And from there Elite said no that not it at all. And from there I said to her that I felt that she was trying to starting to sexual teas me about her much younger adult sister Epiphany Windgate? And from there she answer no as she been claiming that is defiantly wasn't even thought me personally speaking I thought that is actual was sexually teasing about her younger sister Epiphany Windgate. As I also asked her the question of would she herself be very much so willing to ask her youngest sibling sister Epiphany Windgate if the three of us could have a intimate sexual three way relationship with each other where I also said that I would defiantly accept her as my lawful wedded wife right along with her younger sister Epiphany Windgate to be my live in lady friend as I further explained that the two of them could share me in our hopeful family bedroom together every single night of the rest of our lives? And to my very on surprise she once again denied me of yet another of my three way sexual intimate close relationship request as she called me a very overly sexual nasty pig type of a man as she immated the very sounds of a porky pig noise as she said ook ook hell no you may certain not underneath any kind of dam circumstance at all will I ever have any kind of nasty sexual freaky threesome of any type of relationship with herself and her younger sister whose name is Epiphany Windgate, and from there I gotten rather so very much upset with her as I began to shout out at my common law wife about how that she better not never again verbally sexual tease me about her younger sister Epiphany Windgate and from there she said nothing else that was concerning the issue that was discussed back.

on February 25, 2002, I felt that it was time for me to think about going back to my very on family household in the Astoria, Queens New York area as I said my goodbyes for now back as I once again embraced my son Romeo Windgate-Devine and his mom Elite Windgate and even my common-law mother in-law who is Wonda Windgate with another warm family kiss of the facial cheek area and a big family group hug. once I gotten myself back to my family home in the Astoria, Queens New York area as it been about 11:00 PM that very same evening as when I walked myself inside I saw my two parents Jahtayshia and Damian Devine Sr. having a very big verbal argument as my dad who been underneath the very bad influence of a multi liquor alcoholic bear beverage as he went into the family downstairs closet area to get that very same lead pipe that he once struck my older brother Damian Devine Jr. right on top of his head area back in the day. And from there he gotten himself very much close to my mom as her back was turned as he also grab her two hands as he also held up his pipe weapon as he attempted to try to strike her right in her head area, but before he landed his very damaging heavy blow to my mother I myself snuck up right behind him as I snatched his lead pipe out of his hands as I pushed him back away from me as he also proceeded to take out a steak knife to try his best to cut me in my stomach muscle area as I myself felt that I had no other choice but to defend myself and just as well as my mother Jahtayshia Devine as I strucked my very own father Damian Devine Sr. in his very own head area as he begin to bleed from his forehead area he had dropped his kitchen utensil weapon. very shortly after that as the blood started to bleed from his head area as from there as he began to wash out his head injury area of all of the blood that was leaking from his for head area as he demanded me to assistant him in giving him some paper towels so that he may proceed to wipe his head down to stop the bleeding.

And after all of that very violet commotion was finally over with my mother Jahtayshia Devine told my father Damian Sr. to go some where and sit himself down to rest his knotted head injury as I taken it upon myself to get my dad some ice in a bag so that he may start to place it on the very top of his forehead area to to start to heal his head wounded area. very shortly father that he said that he was going to his bedroom area to lay hisself down so that he may began to try to fall himself to sleep so he may rest his head. And from there my mother Jahtayshia Devine said to my dad Damian Sr. Devine just you wait a dam minute there Mr. want to be head buster man as she continued to say to him that since he insisted on being a abusive violet alcoholic drunkin type of a violet type of a man as she also continued on to further say to him that he wasn't going to be sleeping with her in there usually husband and wife bedroom area as she left him yet another alternative to sleep upstairs in our family arctic bedroom area just until he was to learn how not to become a violet drunkin husband of a man. And from there my father develop a little slight of a attitude to say that he didn't dam care about her at that very particular moment as he from there taken out the family folding bed that was located in our family attic area.

of March 6, of the year of 2002 it been time for my youngest stepsister whose name is Fatima Devine 5th grade Elementary graduation ceremony as it all normally seemed to be all so very well up until after it was finally all over with when all of the very sudden as my two parents of Damian Devine Sr. and my mother Jahtayshia Devine somehow someway my youngest sibling sister bow down her very of little head toward the grown as she pause her very own self as I asked our family if they wanting to take a family photograph with us all to to be together? And from there my parents very much quick response was to tell me no thank you and from there as I remembered that very much special day that I felt a little shock to still see my two parents some kind of way to have there very own daughter Fatima Devine to start to acknowledge me in such a very mental way as I remembered way back just with me feeling so very much sad of my mom and dad made me feel back to still be so very much paranoid enough to even have there very own step child daughter to start to act that very strange way toward me in a very paranoid state of mine as back I really love my little stepsister whose name is Fatima Devine so very much just well as my oldest younger stepsister Tameka Devine as my heart very much sadden. soon after that we called ourselves a taxi cab car service as we been on hour very own way back to our family home in the Astoria, Queens New York area. about March 20 of the year of 2002 as my dad Damian Sr. started back with his bad smelly constant alcoholic drinking habit as he once again started to began to start back arguing and also wanting to once again began starting to want to become so very physical as in a attempted fist fight with my mom Jahtayshia as that exact time around there was no lead pipe involved for him to try and do any more violet physical harm to anyone as he gotten himself so very much upset that he said that he was on his very own way to start to head out of our family doorway to start to go right straight to our cousin Pedro Hillman apartment housing that is located in the Brooklyn New York section.

And from there I myself begin to start begging him to please calm himself down so that he may just go right up our family stairwell to head himself back to his bed that was in the upper floor attic area. And from there he started to agree with me as he said okay there son as he also said that he would try to sleep his favor malt liquor beverage off until the very next waking morning time arrived. And from there I said to my father Damian Sr. that sounded like such a very great ideal for him just to sleep it all off. But right to my very own disappointment my father Damian Devine Sr. came right back down our family stairwell to once again start right to began to once again start to back only verbal arguing this time around as he said to my mother Jahtayshia Devine that he was going to start to physical hurt her in a very much painful way. And from there I beg him once again to just please take his self back to his upstair bedding area as he just kept on with his very angry argument with him also saying that he was never in his lifetime a got dam f***ckin alcoholic of any kind at all. And from there my father Damian Sr. begin to start to run toward my mother Jahtayshia as he made a attempt to try to grab at my mother house rob collar garment as I ha stepped in between the both of them to have them both separated from one another as my dad had enough of all of his vicery as he said once again that he was leaving out to good to his other woman house in the Brooklyn New York area as he began to start laughing and very soon after that he once again left out to go wherever he was really headed to that was somewhere in the New York capital of the Brooklyn New York area.

on March 15, 2002, my mother Jahtayshia Devine younger sister who was also my youngest aunt whose name is Shellby Ruckust came up from Knoxville Tennessee with her three children that consisted of her only son whose name is Gunnar Ruckust Jr. as he had taken some time off from the United States of the National Guards as his two younger sisters who are Eva and Kharma Ruckust. And from there my mother Jahtayshia Devine told her much younger adult sister Shellby Ruckust that her current marriage situation as she continued to talk about just how she and my father Damian Sr. were have there big problem of them to be getting right into to many very physical violet situation of him to been been drinking a whole hell of a lot. And from there my aunt Shellby Ruckust told me the story of how she remembered the very exact time when she herself was riding right along with her big sister which is my mother Jahtayshia Devine as they both been riding in back of my other uncle Darren Welsh by his marriage to my biological aunt on my father side of his family as her name is Kiley Welsh in there car as I was told from my mother much younger sister that she remembered one that particular day when my mom been trying to get her very own self out of my dad family vehicle as he been so very much of a drunkin man as he very badly kicked push his wife right out of his sister car ride as my mother also been pregnant with me as she fell straight down to the ground right on her stomach. And from there I said to my mother Jahtayshia and her sister Shellby Ruckust that must be the very exact reason why I develop my very serious current medical condition of as I was born with water on my brain. And from there I asked my mom was that the actual truth that I was just told by my aunt Shellby?

And from there my mother broken her secret silence truth of the matter as she said yes and that was the actual truth of what really really happen with the two of us when she was pregnant with me as she continued to say that she thought that my dad at least to make a very sincere apology whenever he was to to bring his self back to our home to his very own family and from there I told my mother that I would discuss it with him. on March 13, 2002, as my father arrived as he hand given my mother a very sincere emotional apology as she accepted his sorryness as she told him that she was feeling much better to have him come back into our family home. And once my aunt overheard her big sister Jahtayshia telephone conversation of that at that particular time that her brother in-law Damian Sr. was on his very way back to our family home to her sister family she said to us both after spending a week time with our family as she continued to say that she to start to get herself prepare to head her and her very own family right back to her very own Knoxville Tennessee family household to get her very own children back to prepare themselves all for there back to school Spring Break recess period. And from there we said our goodbyes for now to each other as we all said that we would speak to each other by way of the telephone the very next evening and from there my aunt Shellby and my three first cousins that consisted of Gunnar Ruckust Jr. Eva and my youngest cousin Kharma Ruckust left out of my family home with a full size plate of my mother delicious plate of food to go.

when my father Damian Devine Sr. finally did arrived back at our family Astoria, Queens New York family household I told him just how I heard about just how I really gotten my head medical condition of me to currently have water on my brain as I told him that my aunt/his sister in-law whose name is Shellby Ruckust told me that he was the very one who cause my very own mother to have a very costly bad fall to the ground area as she been kick pushed to the ground by him as he was trying to help her to get our of his sister Kiley and her husband Darren Walsh family car. And from there my father given me his very sorrowful apology as he asked me to please forgive him of his very bad mistake of him to been not thinking straight with him to been drinking just a little bit to much of his small bottle of his favorite alcoholic beer beverage and from there I told my dad that yes I did in deed now accepted his apology of him and even my very own mother as we just giving each other a very firm family very big huge hug.

on March 23 of the year of 2002 as I been in our family basement apartment area as my very own father Damian Devine Sr. called me to speak with him about my youngest stepsister who is Fatima Devine and my nephew Rashad Devine as he asked me the very question of just what happen between the very three of us? And from there I said to my dad that my nephew Rashad Devine been making verbal threats of him to say to me that he is now big enough to beat me up and strong enough to through me down on the floor all by his very own self as I also explained to my dad Damian Devine Sr. that my youngest stepsister whose name is Fatima Devine also joined right in with the non sensible behavior of her to say to me that they both didn't even trust me any longer because as the very two of them asked me just why my employer right along with the rest of all of the people who lived in the New York City area been keeping a close and watchful eye on me and my family? And from there I explained to my father Damian Devine Sr. that I told both my youngest stepsister who was Fatima Devine and my nephew Rashad Devine that it was a very unfortunate and uncomfortable corporate very slanderous conspiracy situate about me how there was a office slanderous rumor that started about me with many of my office coworkers saying that the word that was going on the job was that I my very own self could be apart of one of the New York City organize crime family that was to do the company some very serious financial damage. And from there as I also explained to my dad that my youngest stepsister who was Fatima Devine also said that she did not no longer didn't even trust me anymore as she raise up her two handed in a fisticuffs style to me as she to told me that she was also going to beat me up and down on the floor something badly. And from there I also explained that I told my stepsister Fatima Devine if she was to ever step to me to threaten me ever again as I said to her that I would have her be placed in hand cuffs by the Astoria New York City police department if she did not shut up her very disrespectful got dam f**ckin mouth up as I also reminded her for her to not to forget just who also assisted in helping our very own mother and father raise you little girl and as I further explained that she herself bowed down her very own head in a very paranoid state of mine as she ran herself away from me in the family basement area.

But for some odd reason my father Damian Devine Sr. told me that he didn't even believe me about what I just been telling him about his as he called my younger stepsister Fatima his little precious girl and he also ordered me to get the hell up out of his and my mother Astoria, Queens New York area household before as he said that he was to be going the neighborhood police department to force me out of there household. And very soon after hearing that from my very own father Damian Devine Sr. say that to me as I rush myself straight right downstairs to start to pack my all of my clothes as I put them all in a bag as I just headed myself right out of my family household where I once grown up as a child. And from there I also known just where I was going to be going to as I went to a Rockaway Park Rooming Boarding House that was called The Rockaway Park Parkaway in Home Beach House where I gotten myself a small hotel room that I located on the internet as I paid my two week rent of the very amount of $300 which also included with the electric billing rental payment. On March 29, 2002, as I once again received yet another telephone call from the mother of my child who is Elite Windgate as she told me that she once again needed me to come right over to baby sit our young son Romeo Jr. as she also explained to me that she gotten herself in a very big argument with her much younger sister who is Epiphany Windgate as she also went on to further explained to me that just how it been all about when her youngest sibling decided to bring in her boyfriend who I also had previous meet him myself as his very own name was Mathew Mathers as I also told that my common sister in-law and her boyfriend spented the night together inside the family one bedroom townhouse home as there mother Ms. Wonda Windgate was been away on her employer business trip for a company that was called The Metropolitan Care Center of the Tri State, as the mother of my son also explained to me that she felt rather very uncomfortable having that same guy around without her to having me to also be around to look out for her just in case something was to happen to her and our baby boy Romeo Jr. aka as his nickname to be Cuddles as she also told me that she and her sister were not even speaking to each other at that particular time. And as I been very much aware of that my common law wife been the nervous type of a woman when it came to being around men as she even said to me that she thought that I myself might someday somehow might very well do some kind of harm to her and from there I tried once again tried to reassure her that I would never physical do her any harm whatsoever. So from there I asked my son Romeo Jr. mother Elite if she wanted me to come over that very same evening as I also said to her that I would be there in the next morning time and from there my son mother told me that yes and that I better make dam sure that I was to be right on time at 8:00 PM and from there I had said that I would be there right on time enough to keep a very watchful eye on our young son to have me to baby sit him as she also continued to say that she may take her very own self to her workplace in The Rockaway Park Queens New York section so from there she said that she would see me in the very next morning time. on the very next morning time of March 24, 2002, as I arrived I my very own self mistakenly overslepted that very same morning as I jumped myself up into the shower to try to rush my very self right over to my son Romeo Jr. and his mother Elite Windgate townhouse home as

I also tried to called them both as I gotten no answer at all from them both and from there I went to see if some how they might possibly still be there.

And one I gotten myself there in my son Romeo Windgate-Devine and his mother Elite Windgate family townhouse home which was in The Long Island City of the Queens New York area as I first knocked my fist on there family doorway to see if they both already left out there place as of yet. And as I gotten absolutely no answer at all from anyone in there very own family to give me any kind of a response as I had taken a very good look around outside there townhouse building to see if I saw any kind of sign of my son Romeo Jr. or any other of his family members as I taken a very good notice that my son oldest aunt who is Epiphany Windgate car was still very much outside where the family live at. And from there I became kind of puzzled of just why my common-law sister did not even have the common decency to at the very least to answer my knock at her family door way back. And as I further thought about just how I forgotten my mobile cellular phone right inside of my common law family town house home as I giving my common law sister in-law Epiphany Windgate a very loud shout out to please help me by opening the door to pass me my cellur phone as I gotten absolutely no answer back from her as I figured out that she must of a made and jealously attitude with me to not even assist me back. So from there I left out away from my son Romeo Jr. and his mother Elite Windgate family town house home area to try to call my child mother and when I finally did I kept on getting a telephone busy signal.

So from there I decided to go right straight to my common law wife Elite Windgate place of her employment which was called The Gentlemens Fashionable Tuxecedo Warehouse in the Rockaway Park Queens New York section to try to pick up our young son Romeo Windgate Devine from his mommy workplace. And as I only two 25 ct quarters left of my left over spare change to make a attempt to try to make a called to my son mother cellur phone and to my very much very disappointed the called did not go thru at that particular time as I ran right out of my extra change. And from there I had yet another ideal of that how I was going to make a small attempt to try to get the attention of my son Romeo Jr. or even his very own mother Elite by throwing little tiny rock pebbles at her employer window area, but apparently she did not in fact notice it and from there I even given her a verbal shout out of her very own name which I began to say Elite, Elite it me Romeo and that I was also standing myself outside to come and pick our son little Romeo Jr. and to my once again very own disappointment she still did not in fact still hear me as I was very desperately trying to still get her full attention back as I failed to also do so. as I been trying to figure out just what I was going to possible do next to try to to alert my son Romeo Jr. and his mother Elite I taken very close visual notice of a young man who was of a Puerto Rican Spanish decent as he was just standing there while he was holding right in his very own right hand a .38 caliber hand gun pistol as he at that time looked right straight in my very own direction as I gotten so very surprise to see a shocking situation such as that one that I was currently in as I put up both of my hands as I also given that very strange guy the two figure piece sign as I beg him not to please hurt me as I also told him that I was a very hard working proud father who was just trying to get to see about my young son whose name I just referred to as Jr. And from there to my very spiritual blessing from the all might God which is our heavenly father himself the young Puerto Rican young man gotten himself into a car that was park in the street as he enter on the passenger side of the vehicle as he was driven away with a young male associate of his.

And soon after that very shocking moment that happen to me back I began to wonder if my son Romeo Jr. mother Elite Windgate gotten herself so very much so upset with me about the very fact that I was so very much late to getting to her family townhome in the Long Island City New York area as I began to wonder if she sent that young man who was of a Puerto Rican Spanish decent who displayed his .38 caliber pistol to trying to at least give me some kind of mental very disturbing warning about how made she was that she had to bring in our child right into her place of her employment of The Gentlemen Fashionable Tuxedo Warehouse in the Rockaway Park section of the Queens New York as I began to start to wonder about that entire frightening incident about if my son my Elite Windgate somehow gave a good enough description of me to that very same guy to to try to try to scare me about she must of felt that she could possibly lost her job because she wasn't really allowed to take any day off of work as she no other choice but to bring our young son Romeo Jr. in at her workplace of her employer office and from there

I just left the area as I taken my very own self back to my hotel boarding rooming house which was located in Rockaway Park New York area. So after a few days pass on by as it been the day of March 27, 2002, as I received a quick telephone call from my son Romeo Jr. mother Elite Windgate as she began to scream and shout out loud to ask me just where the hell was I and why didn't I get there to her family townhouse home in The Long Island City of The Queens New York area? And from there I started to argue the very fact was that I made the very mistake of leaving my mobile cellar phone right inside her family household as I went on to even further explain to my common law wife Elite Windgate that when I arrived at her family residence just how when I saw her younger sister Epiphany Windgate car park right outside of there building where they live at as I been very much well aware that my common law sister in-law was at that exact time was still very much inside of there family townhouse home as she refuse to even answer me at there family door. And from there my common law wife Elite Windgate explain to me just how so very much upset I made her that as she made a emotional threat that she really wanting to put a real bad very physical hurting on me in some kind of unpleasant way and very soon after that she demanded me to bring myself back to her Long Island City townhouse home so that I could visit both she and our son Romeo Jr.

And when I finally arrived back at Elite's and Romeo Jr. and there family place where they live at as I entered to see about my son Romeo Windgate-Devine and his mother Elite Windgate as she her very own self started to shouted out at me to say right in from of her very own mother who is Wonda Windgate oh no Romeo might really might want to really want to really want to hurt us all in a very bad and harmful way. And from there I just stood right there just thinking that in fact maybe it was my very on got dam mother of my child Elite Windgate who sent out that same young Puerto Rican was of Spanish decent of a guy who was holding a .38 caliber handgun pistol in his right hand as the guy hand looked right into my very own direction as I also remembered just how very scared I was at that particular day and time as I also began to think back when we were both in my very own family house of the basement area as I been just preparing my common-law wife Elite Windgate and I both another very delicious dinner meal as she made the very verbal threat of that if I in fact was to ever made her to ever become so very

229

angry at me that as she told me back in the day that she would send out one of her drug dealer associates to do me some very real serious bodily harm. And from there I just pretended like nothing ever even was said as I just taking the very liberty to huge and kiss my common law wife Elite Windgate and my very own son Romeo Windgate-Devine as I just amazing just sat my very own self down with the Windgate family just as if nothing ever even previous happen as I asked the mother of my child which was isn't parenthood of a good dedicated father just grand? And as I just began to start to laugh at my very own question as I once again just started back very closely bonding with my son Romeo Windgate Devine. And soon after that I told my son Romeo Jr. and his mother side of the family that I was very much exhorted as I also explained that I was on my very own way right back to my Rockaway Park New York City rooming boarding beach house as I also given my son Romeo Jr. and big firm huge hug as I also told him that if the good almighty God is very much so willing that I would see him again so very soon enough so that he would not start to miss his Daddy so very much.

Then on March 30 of the very year of 2002 as I was still working right inside of my former employer office that is called The Resolution Outlook Resources as I overheard a conversation about me just about how the entire company known about that very same young Puerto Rican guy that been standing right there just a very few feet away from me while he was facing my very own direction as it was said that the young man recognize me as two out of the three of my employers some how made me a very visual famous so that all of the New York City public would know just who I was just in case as my place of my employment multiple coworkers to also one day to have me to be placed into the New York City police custody and from there there was even also talks about how that I was even made to been so very famous all over the Inter-Continental of the United States of America. So from there I thought it was time for me to put in for some vacation time with me to temporary get out of the state of the New York area and head myself right straight on the other side of the country which is the sunshine state of California and after my time off from my employer was approved of I went straight home to start to pack my bags to see if what my coworker where saying about me to possibly be well known enough of a New York City mafia criminal gangster as I was going over there to see if anyone recognize me of to be falsely accused to be just like a unlawful person of interest. once I gotten myself back to my parents house I told them both that I decide to take off some time off of my workplace that was called The Resolution Outlook Resources LLC to head myself to the state of California as I lied as I just told my folks that the very reason that I was going over there was to to see just how the other side of the country of the United States lived when actually I was checking to see about my former employer corporate slanderous conspiracy situation. And from there both of my parents of my mother Jahtayshia right along with my father Damian Devine Sr. asked me why was I so very much interested in going all the very way across the country? And from there I also explained that I just also wanting to see what it was like over there and that maybe I would see a live taping of some kind of show that was already on the television.

as I still been there at my very own family household in the Astoria, Queens New York I informed my son Romeo Jr. and his mother Elite Windgate that I was about to take a week long vacation in the state of California as she herself told me that she was not going to allow me to leave out of New York City area without me to also be taking her right along with me because she also complained that she was so very stress out from working so very hard just to try to make ends meet as she also told me that we were not going to be also bringing our young son Romeo Windgate-Devine right along with the both of us because she said that she need herself some stress free time off away from just having the very responsibility of being such a good mommy to our son as she referred her very own self as to be. So from there on March 31, 2002, my son mother Elite told me to start to began packing up my duffle bag and head myself right back to her townhouse home in the Long Island City New York area so that I may see our son Romeo Jr. just before she and I were to going to be leaving out to head our very ourselves right straight to the United States of America West side of the country side and from there I told her that I would be right there just as soon as I could possibly could be right there with the both of them. And from there as I arrived at my son Romeo Jr. and his mother Elite Wingate family townhouse home my son Romeo Jr. told me that he was becoming so very excited about the California trip that I along with his mother was beginning to head out there to see the very sights of the area as he also asked us both the very question of could he go come right along with us both?

And it was his very own son mother Elite who was the very one to turn our son Romeo Jr. down as she broke her very disappointing news of that no she did want him to come along with us as she further explained to him that she needed a very restful break for her ever day routine and from there our son became a little sad that his mother was the one who wouldn't even let our child go go right along with his two parents but he eventually got over his mom disappointment as I myself did not really didn't even mine if the three of us were to all go together as a family. after my son mother Elite Windgate and I left out of her Long Island City New York townhouse home we both headed ourselves straight to the Los Angles California area as I was still thinking to my very own self about my two out of three former employers of The New York City conspiracy situation of how there be talks about just how I been broadcasting on a New York City television so that everyone would recognized me to see whenever they were to see me in the New York City streets area as the very bad word was put out by my previous employers of the company that is name The O'Conner, Sapp, Dash & Marshall LLP corporate law firm right along with the non profitable organization that is also called The Resolution Outlook Resources job were I my very own self was once employed at as one of the company mailman clerks as I looked around to see if anyone in the Los Angeles area recognize me from two of my now former New York employer mailman that was also said to be a New York City mafia gangster associate who was sent out to steal away my employer money away for some sort of criminal gain of sorts. But as Elite and I been to several California city of Santa Monica and even the Beaverly right along with us to have our very own selves to lay ourselves out in the sand and sun of the Venus Beach California area as it turn out to be all so very much good as no one seemed to recognized me or even the mother of my child Elite Windgate like back in the New York City area. And from there the mother of my child and I very much so also enjoyed a few tapping seen of several television shows that turned out to be so very much entertaining to the both of us as we both also enjoyed several nights as we been dinning out way back.

And shortly after that as we had such a very good time of being on the country westside it was time for us to start to head ourselves back to our home state of the New York City area as we left from the great sunshine state of the California West Side area as I also remembered thinking about just how glad I was that my two out of three former employers that goes by the name of The O'Conner, Sapp, Dash & Marshall LLP corporate midtown Manhattan law firm right along with the other employer of the non profitable organization which is called The Resolution Outlook Resources LLC lied to me only to trying to fool with me as they led me to wasted a trip to to believe that they had me broadcasted on television that they said was supposed to be also noticeable all across the United States of America.

after my very own son mother Elite Windgate and I brought ourselves right back so very safely and soundly from our west side of the United States of America of the state of California as I was asked to spend a few more nights with her and my son Romeo Jr. in there own family Long Island City town house home as I very so much agreed to do so to began to continue to do some more good family bonding of course. And very soon after that it been the actual time for the mother on my son Elite to leave out her family townhouse home as she given our son Romeo Jr. and I a big quick hug goodbye just for a little while until she finished her evening work shift at her employer at the company that went by the name of The Tuxedo Gentlemen Warehouse in the Rockaway Park section of the Queens New York area and from there she left out to be on her very own way to her place of employment. that very same exact night of April 8 of the year of 2002 as I been playing right along with my very own son who is Romeo Jr. as I heard my child oldest aunt whose name is Epiphany Windgate started to shout out loud that she was on the very top of her family buck bed area just in case that as she said that I was to try to come after her as she also shouted out at me by her calling me a man beast of a could be very dangerous of a man. And from there I shouted out back at her to say to her oh dear sweet heart of a common law sister in-law Epiphany that I would never want to hurt the pretty little hairs on your pretty head and from there she said nothing else to shout out to me about just how scared she felt as I figured out that she to must also been very physical abused by her eldest brother whose name is Mason Windgate as he been a violet drug addict abuser who always tried to scare his own female part of his very own family members in order to get some money from them so that he may had enough money for his costly drug habit as well as he said that he also needed some extra money so that he may purchase for food.

the very next night of April 9 of 2002 as I been asked of my son mother Elite Windgate to spend yet another night with our son Romeo Jr. just until the very next day with our son as she hand told me that her very own mother who is Wonda Windgate had her very own self a prior engagement of April 10, 2002, as I said that it would be okay for me to do so and soon after she made the three of us yet another tasteful family dinner meals as she very soon enough left out for her nightly work shift. And when my common law wife Elite Windgate much younger sister who is Epiphany Windgate entered back into her family Long Island City of New York townhouse home as she saw me just sitting there all by myself while my son Romeo Windgate-Devine been right inside there family upstair bedroom just playing with his grandmother Wonda Windgate as my common law sister in-law told me that she brought her very own self a .45 caliber pistol hand gun to protect herself from me just in case that I was to try to do any physical harm to her very own personal self and from there she left out from her family downstair living room area as I been very much frighten for my very own life. And soon after that my little son Romeo Jr. came back from the family one bedroom town house room as he spended little more time with his grandmother Wonda Windgate to spend some quality time with his dear young dadeo which is me Romeo Devine as he used to sometime refer to me as. And again very shortly after the very second time where I felt so very much so threaten by my common law wife Elite Windagte much younger sister whose name is Epiphany Windgate as they both made me feel sometime very uncomfortable by there very emotional disturbing family behaviors as I decided that I was no longer going to be doing any more of our family bonding with my son other side of his family of the Windgates all because I felt that there family angry emotional problems issues were to much for me to ever bear any longer and from there I told my son Romeo Jr. that I would be only seeing him at his and my side of the Devine family for now on in.

And from there I given my son Romeo Jr. a big high five sorts of a hand lap of the right hand as I told him that I would see him real soon enough and from there I was out of the Windgate townhouse family home for good as I headed myself right straight back to the Rockaway Park section of the Queens New York area to just sit on the beach side until I been ready to go inside of the hotel boarding rooming house where I once live in for the rest of the evening. And the the very next day of April 11, 2002, as I been riding on the New York City Transit Authority A train as I been just sitting right there when all of the very sudden appeared my favorite female coworker who was Khadine Pavlick and to my very own surprise she her very self just pass me right on by as if she did not even see me just sitting right there as she just went on to the very next train car. on the very next day of April 16, 2002, when I went back into my workplace where I still worked at in the corporate non profitable organization which is called The Resolution Outlook Resources LLC as I been running the company inter-national and Domestic letter mailings to go out in distribution transit for it to been delivery to it's proper destination as I heard two of my mailroom center male coworkers say that as our female coworker who was Khadine Pavlick also entered into the room as they been talking about how she seen me on the A train just recently as the two guy that were Brasford Devoe who told our other mailroom center coworker who was Norman Jefferson told her that she should just sat herself right down next to him to started to talk to her guy Mr. Romeo Devine as those same two guys began to start to laugh at the both of us and from there she herself took the liberty to start to grabbed a hold of my two hands as she said that she was in need of a very good husband of a man as she very shortly after that left out of the 9th floor company mailroom center of The Resolution Outlook Resources as she been just teasing me by grabbing my hands as I began to start to wonder why. And I then began to wonder if my immediate family used to been looking in the basement area where I once live at as I began to suspect someone in my very own family must of saw my manuscript of my autobiography to my latest then employer as far as I could figure out that the only reason why my former female coworker whose name is Khadine Pavlick all of a very sudden wanted to go ahead and go get her very own self married to me was because as I suspected that some one from my family house hold of the Astoria, Queens New York area must told that same woman on the job that I wrote myself a book for a financial gain of sorts. And as back in the company mailroom center as Khadine Pavlick didn't even say a single word and if I must do say so myself I thought that type of behavior coming from my favorite female coworker was rather strangely odd for the very simply fact she previous turned me down to for us to have a intimate passionate relationship with each other.

when I only visited my very own parents Jahtayshia and Damian Devine Sr. house that is still located in the Astoria, Queens New York area as I also came up with the ideal of that I was going to try to go down to the main New York Police Department where I could get myself registered for me to to have a license pistol to protect myself from any unwanted harm that might come my very own way in the streets of New York City. So as I started right back with me to began to start back dating on a telephone chate line service as I connected my very own self to a sexy sounding afro American woman whose name is Vanity Devinley as we planned to meet up with me in the Bronx New York City East side where we very much enjoyed a very entertaining Caribbean Festival as it turned out to be pretty normal up until I was once again acknowledge by the New York City people in the public eye as they all said to me that we see you there Mr. Romeo Devine of a New York City mailman. As they asked me the very question did you heard me? As I waved my hand right to the people as I said oh yea my good New York people as I said to the public that I heard you loud and clear as I said let us all have our very selves a mighty good time of a very entertaining day and from there it all turn out to be one blessette day of a very nice enough of event as I was even more surprise that my former employer really did have me over publicize by way of a video camera that once been held by a very strange small camera crew but I tried to turned my bad situation into a very position one as whenever some was to acknowledge me a New York mailman from my two of three of my employers I would just try my very best to try to so them all just how much love that I would always have for the New York City area. And once it was all over with as I told my newly then lady friend who was still Vanity Devinley that I hand a application from the New York City Police for me to get a license pistol permitted as I further explained that I needed a about three signatures in order for me to get myself my very on hand gun for the sole reason of that my neighborhood of the Rockaway Park Queens New York section was full of lots of violet crimes as I also told her that I would only use my firearm in a self defense of any dangerous of any unwanted situation.

And so from there after my lady friend who was at that particular time was still Vanity Devinley agreed to sign on the dotted line of my pistol hand gun permitted application as I thanked her with a big fat wet and juicy kiss and a big huge hug as I said that I was so very much glad that she cared enough about my very own safety to help me to the have some self protection for my very own self so that I could still be around in life itself for her just as well as my son whose name I explained to her was Romeo Windgate-Devine and my lady friend said to me that I was very much so very welcome to have her to been looking out for my very own personal well being in the rough streets of New York City area. one day of April 20, 2002, as I been only visiting my parents Jahtayshia and Damian Devine Sr. as I said my hello's to them both just as well as my two much younger stepsister whose name are Tameka and Fatima Devine and I went downstairs to my family basement area to start to clean up some mess that I might of previous left unclean or unorganized as I laid my hand gun of my pistol permit of my application right there down on my old kitchen glass table when all of the very sudden to my very own surprise in entered my family basement area my youngest uncle whose name is Solomon Gilbert as he and I began to laugh and talk with other another and just as soon as I turned my back side to take my very own self to the family basement bathroom area as I returned back from there when all of the very sudden my application for me to go down to the main office of The New York Police Department to hand in my papers work to be filed right into there data system data base when all of the very sudden my legal form all of the very sudden just disappeared from the family downstairs basement table area as right along with my mother Jahtayshia Devine youngest brother whose name is Solomon Gilbert also stepped himself away from the family basement area as I very strongly suspected that it was him who removed my paper work as I remembered just how I was upset about the whole thing. later that very same evening as my uncle Solomon Gilbert made himself repair as he brought him self a hand gun of his very own as he walked around our family home in the Astoria, Queens New York h as he soon once again left out the family home when all of the very sudden I heard a gun shoot go off in the airway as I remembered that wasn't very fair as I figured out that it must of been him who had the dam very nerve to very previous steel away my handgun New York City pistol permit paper work and very soon after that I left out of my family home as I went right straight back to the Rockaway Park Boarding Rooming House as I was remember just how very unfair my family used to treat me with them not wanting me to began to protect my very own self in the very dangerous streets of the New York City area. very soon after that I soon been terminated from my place of my employment that I was once employed at the non profitable organization that was called The Resolution Outlook Resources of nearly of 3 1/2 years of service for not quickly learning the company brand-new high tech of there new mailroom machinery operations. So after I go out of my job in the mailroom services I decide that I was going to apply for my very own self to receive some Social Security Disability Benefits for my very own self after working for more fifteen years of service do to my very serious medical condition that develop from my some what sometime abusive alcoholic father Damian Devine Sr. as I was told by my mother Jahtayshia Devine much younger sister whose name is Shellby Ruckust as she was the very one who have previous told me that my very own father physical abuse my very own mom when she been pregnant with me as she said that she was kick pushed right out of his side of his very own side of the Devine family car.

And on August the fourth of the year of 2002, which happen to be my actual birthday as I received my approval letter that my father Damian Devine Sr. called me and tell me that he was in fact holding it for me until I was to to then come by the family house to pick it up. And as I received my letter of my absence letter of the department of Social Security Administration Benefits as I thanked my dad Damian Devine Sr. for assisting me with properly filling out of my application as he said that I was quit very much welcome son to have him do so very well by me back. Then all of the very sudden as I been just right downstairs in the family basement when I overheard my very own family members of my my parents of Jahtayshia and Damian Devine Sr. and even my much older brother whose name is Damian Devine Jr. who now resides some where in the state of Washington, Georgia area as he been talking about just how I been put on my Social Security Disability Benefits monthly payment plan from the state of New York as the question been asked by my oldest sibling yea but did anyone ever find out if his younger brother Romeo Devine Sr. was ever associated with a New York City mafia organize crime family of any got dam kind? And from there I made my appearce right in front of the three of them all to say to m all hell no lam not no kind of criminal of and f**ckin kind as I continued to also say that if they all ever wanted me to ever again to very considered for all of my immediate family to make me just to love them all like apart of my family just as always without them all to not have any doubts in there very own sane mines to wonder if I was to be any kind of apart of a New York City mafia gangster as I continued to also say that I must find myself a nice enough holly Christian church going woman who also should also come from a good rounded good Christian family of her very own that is more willing to help me to maintain a very normal family life style that I would be maybe to marry myself into as Iam in search of a very special enough lady to wed me as my lawful wedded wife and I also went on to also say that I do love my family so very much with all of my heart and soul but after all of the problems that been so very much apart of with them all to at that particular stressful that I was be harassed by my previous employer as I said that I felt like my family that I was born into which are the Devine right along with my common law family members which were the Windgate family all the very while as I been dealing with a very stressful corporate conspiracy situation that spreaded all of the city of the New York city as they they had very foolish suspected at least of my very Devine side of my very own family that I could in fact could very much actual be apart of a New York City mafia gangster of the New York City area trying to extort money from out of the companies that I once worked at for just as I said to my very own family that ideal that came up with my now former employer is now all behind me as I would never have to worry my very own self with another ridiculous slanderous rumor of any dam kind at all simply because I would be now collecting a United States of America Social Security Disability Benefit monthly check.

As I also said to the three of my immediate family members that they all been putting me through a lot of unwanted stress at that particular time as I also had reminded them all that my two out of three then employers then situation of the company of The O'Conner, Sapp, Dash & Marshall LLC and the other corporate non profitable organize that was then called The Resolution Outlook Resources LLC was now completely over with. And as I then also continued to then say that I wasn't then going to then be accepting them all right back into my very own life until they would then once again then start right back to then treating me just like a normal family member should then always be treated. And from there I then said to my very own immediate family that Iam out of here until further notice as I then threw up my then two handed two fingered then place signs and from there I then left out of my then family Astoria Queens Meadows Queens New York as I then went right back to my very own room that I then still been living in the Rockaway Park Queens New York section. And then soon after that on August 31 of the year of 2002 as I then broken of my previous relationship that I then had with my then lady friend who was then Vanity Devinley for the very reason she then told me that she then never wanted to then live with me as a romantic couple while we then been underneath one roof as she then also then informed me that she didn't never wanted to then even have any children with any man for the reason of she then said that she did not ever want to then take a very risky chance to then having a man child to then have him just walk out off on her to then leave her and there child to then depend on only herself as she then also went on to then say that she then worried that she would then mostly have to then raise up the child on her very own. And even though I then tried to then convince her otherwise that I would then never then treat her and our then possible future child in very same way as it then turned out that she still did not believe in me so from there since I then still wanting very so much to then still then have even more children I then decided that I was then going to then break up with my then lady friend who was then Vanity Devinley as I then just walked myself very sadly away from her as we then both then said our then goodbyes to one another. Then as I began to then be very much tiresome of then still living in that Rockaway Park hotel room house I then found myself a nice co op apartment house in the Crown Heights Brooklyn New York City area where I still await to find a one real true very dedicated love someday. And even though that I could then never find any actual witness of any of my now former coworker of the corporate midtown Manhattan law firm of the company that is called The O'Conner, Sapp, Dash & Marshall LLP and of my then other very last employer of the non profitable organization that is called The Resolution Outlook Resources LLC to then try to prove a then corporate conspiracy that was then about me to then be slandered for me to possibly have a criminal connection to a New York City organize crime mafia family. And as from I am just living myself a good holy Christian life. (And that concludes my Romeo Devine biography of (a New York Mailman Corporate Conspiracy Story.)